LIFELONG LEARNING

Also available from Cassell:

Susan Askew and Eileen Carnell: *Transforming Learning: Individual and Global Change*

Judith Chapman and David Aspin: *The School, the Community and Lifelong Learning*

David Johnstone: *Further Opportunities: Learning Difficulties and Disabilities in Further Education*

Katherine Lea: *Careers Encyclopedia, 14th Edition*

Lovemore Nyatanga, Dawn Forman and Jane Fox: *Good Practice in the Accreditation of Prior Learning*

Stewart Ranson (ed.): *Inside the Learning Society*

Michael D. Stephens: *Adult Education*

Richard Teare, David Davies and Eric Sandelands: *The Virtual University*

Diana Thomas (ed.): *Flexible Learning Strategies in Higher and Further Education*

John White: *Education and the End of Work: A New Philosophy of Work and Learning*

Sheila Wolfendale and Jenny Corbett (eds): *Opening Doors: Learning Support in Higher Education*

Lifelong Learning

Riding the Tiger

Jim Smith and Andrea Spurling

CASSELL
London and New York

Cassell

Wellington House   370 Lexington Avenue
125 Strand   New York
London WC2R 0BB   NY 10017-6550

www.cassell.co.uk

First published 1999

British Library Cataloguing-in-Publication Data
A catalogue record for this book is available from the British Library.

ISBN 0–304–70587–X (paperback)

Typeset by Kenneth Burnley, Wirral, Cheshire
Printed and bound in Great Britain by Redwood Books, Trowbridge, Wiltshire

Contents

For

Jade, Freya, Rowan and Nona:

lifelong learners

Foreword

The challenge of sparking and sustaining individuals' motivation to learn is at the centre of the Foundation's research agenda. We are committed to realizing the concept of learning as a lifelong activity, not restricted to the first stage of a human being's existence nor limited to a particular set or sequence of learning experiences or techniques. Funding original, leading-edge thinking is one of the ways in which we seek to generate the new ideas and perspectives that will shape and drive the fundamental changes needed to achieve our objective.

Bringing these new insights and options into the public arena in an accessible, stimulating form is a crucial part of our creed. The works we support must meet the challenge of originality, intellectual rigour, and the potential for application. Beyond ensuring that these conditions are met, our motive is solely to contribute an independent, informed and coherent voice to the public debate and the on-going policy development process that lies beyond it.

Lifelong Learning: Riding the Tiger represents one of the Foundation's first commissions and we have been delighted to support its preparation and publication. The time is right for the holistic perspective it offers. Consultation documents were published in 1998 in England, Scotland and Wales. Though each presents a distinctive set of priorities and a particular route-map, they share the common belief that lifelong learning must be a critical element in establishing the UK as a competitive force in global markets and as an inclusive learning society. One of the major challenges in building a learning society is the sheer scale and complexity of the intellectual and practical transformation it requires. This book presents the case for fundamental changes to our existing education system and an alternative model embracing learning in all forms at all ages. It is argued both as a polemic and a change manual. In commending it to all stakeholders in the education and business communities, we believe it offers the potent combination of vision and guidance that is needed to realize a fundamental lasting change in the fabric of UK society.

COLIN GEORGE
Chairman, The Lifelong Learning Foundation

The Lifelong Learning Foundation

The Lifelong Learning Foundation is an independent, non-political organization based in Manchester, England. It exists to promote the values and goals of lifelong learning through funding innovative research and development activity and disseminating its outcomes.

The Foundation lays particular store by the following:

- Originality of approach.
- Quality of ideas and project leadership.
- Potential for application.
- Well-considered arrangements for disseminating and sharing outcomes.
- Funding projects, not organizations.

Further information about The Foundation and its work can be obtained from the Director at:

The Lifelong Learning Foundation
PO Box 98
Sale
Manchester
M33 2UJ
United Kingdom
Tel./Fax (44) 0161 976 4664.

Preface and Acknowledgements

Within a generation the notion of the perpetual student as wastrel has given way to talk of 'lifelong learning for all'. The implications of this shift in attitude are profound, yet most people – including educational professionals – have still to come to terms with what it means.

Our aim in this book has been to define the reach and potential of real lifelong learning, in a way that helps the general reader to develop the debate about what should be done. We have drawn widely on educational, economic and cultural themes in assembling an overall picture of what lifelong learning involves, and the changes needed to put resources of time, space and money into place to sustain it. The book concentrates for the most part on the situation in England, but it is nonetheless relevant to other parts of the UK, and to places further afield.

We have aimed to give an overall picture without exhaustive attention to detail, nevertheless we hope that there is plenty in the book for readers who have thought deeply about the issues. We are interested to know how far the analysis and vision presented here coincide with the thinking of other commentators.

Our sincere thanks are due to the Chairman and Trustees of the Lifelong Learning Foundation, who commissioned the writing of this book, and in particular to Dr Christopher Brookes, the Foundation's Director, for his imaginative and encouraging support.

We are also grateful to Giles and Janet Pepler, our colleagues at Bamford Taggs, whose work made the task possible in the available time. Janet contacted 80 people in more than 70 organizations in the public, private and voluntary sectors. Giles shared the interviewing with us, as well as contributing his own insights from his experience as college principal in the further education sector.

There is unfortunately not room to mention individually the large number of people who helped with our research. Those listed below made particular contributions, in terms of their time or material provided. To everybody who contributed to the research we offer our warmest thanks. The book itself, of course, remains our responsibility alone.

John Allred, Information for Learning; Meg Bond, Warwick University; Fiona Blacke, Scottish Campaign for Learning; David Bradshaw; Alan Clarke, NIACE;

Bert Clough, TUC; Sally Dench, Institute of Employment Research; Geoff Ford, NICEC; Fiona Frank, Lancaster Employee Development Consortium; Frank Coffield, University of Newcastle; Ken Franklin; Bob Gibbs, University of Nottingham; Toby Greany, Campaign for Learning; Lucy Hodges, Lancaster Employee Development Consortium; Ian Johnston, Sheffield Hallam University; Bill Lucas, Campaign for Learning; Geoff Lucas, QCA; Stephen McNair, NIACE; Alan Rogers, Reading University; The Scottish Office; Jim Soulsby, NIACE; Brian Stevens, Finance and Education Services; Mike Thorne, Napier University; Patrick Vaughan, DfEE; Tony Watts, NICEC; Chris Wood, QCA.

JIM SMITH AND ANDREA SPURLING
bamfordtaggs@msn.com
June 1998

Part I

Chapter 1

Starting Points

Three things prompted us to write this book: the injustice of the nation's unequal learning record; the calamity of the UK economy, trapped in a pit of low skill and poor application of knowledge; and the conviction that a way towards a more humane and civilized society can be found through lifelong learning, centred on ethical and democratic principles.

The failure of the education system for the majority of the population reinforces low self-esteem for large numbers of people and widens existing rifts in society. As competitive pressures intensify on a global scale, the low-skill trap becomes increasingly dangerous both for social structure and for the economy. It is profoundly worrying to see so many people in full flight from realizing their capabilities. Britain's general culture of learning has evolved over generations, and is now seriously out of joint with the times.

Many people over the years have tried to make improvements within the established format of the culture; but, just as with old software, there comes a time when patch-and-mend becomes counter-productive. That time has come for learning. Britain needs a new general culture for lifelong learning, in tune with the needs of multiculturalism and the demands of the twenty-first century. It is no longer enough to tune up the old structures to squeeze out just a modicum of extra performance. A complete change of direction in learning is now imperative, and that means fundamental change to the general culture of learning itself.

This book aims to establish what this new culture of lifelong learning is; to see why it must be introduced; to explore what the new learning culture will entail; and to present the resourcing systems needed to carry it through.

THE SEARCH FOR MEANINGS

The central theme of the book is 'the culture of lifelong learning'. Although the phrase has been much used in the last few years it is seldom defined, and its meaning is contested. Many take it to be the rhetoric of political spin doctors, and a passing fad. On the contrary, this book seeks to show how it can become the central operational concept in the management of radical change in the UK learning system.

As our aim is to be of practical help, we must define our terms clearly. As lifelong learning is itself a topic for learning and debate, fixed and immutable definitions cannot be laid down for all time. The definitions we offer below provide tools for change and reflect and interpret the flavour of the feeling of the unfolding discourse as it is now. But because the task is about lifelong learning, there is always the possibility that today's focus will resolve into something different with the passage of time.

To construct robust meanings for the key elements of a lifelong learning culture, we must unfold a series of notions. First there is a need for clarity about *learning* itself, about who *the learners* are, about the *stock of knowledge*, and about *teaching* and *education*. Only then can the composite notion of lifelong learning be stated and its hidden assumptions be made explicit.

Learning

Learning is a *process* carried out by individuals and groups. What is learnt, i.e. the output, counts as knowledge or skill. This can take the form of the ability to do something which could not be done before; or a new understanding about the world or about something of spiritual, emotional or aesthetic significance. It is not necessary for the process to be understood as learning while it is actually taking place. The significance of a learning experience may only dawn later, in the light of subsequent events or reflection. What is learnt may be retained in the learner's mind for years, below the threshold of introspection.

Throughout this book we use wide definitions of learning process, intention, and provision, except where they are restricted by the context. There are different modes and categories of learning, some relating to the *type of process* and others to the *type of output* from the process. The process items are listed for convenience in Box 1.1 and the output elements are covered in Box 1.2. Later chapters will make widespread reference to these.

Process
There is a useful but slippery distinction which applies across the modes of process shown in Box 1.1. It separates *formal* (literally 'shaped') learning processes from *informal* ones. Signs of formal learning include: going to a special place for the learning; finding a teacher; finding time to engage in learning; paying a fee; buying materials; seeking a qualification; and having a learning schedule which is not primarily intended to be fun (although it may be incidentally enjoyable). In contrast to this is informal learning. This tends to be unplanned, even opportunistic, such as reading before sleep; watching an interesting programme on the television; looking over someone's shoulder at work; or dropping into a museum. Such learning can be anything but casual, and its impact is much understated. It can be the predominant element in learning lives.

The learning process can also be described in terms of the intentions of the learner. It may be *intentional,* in the simple sense that a person is purposefully pursuing it, by some recognized process. It includes both formal and informal learning; but it may also be *unintentional,* where there is no overt process and purpose. Infants learn on a massive scale by 'just picking things up', without any conscious intention of learning.

Modes of delivering learning include:

- learning with or without a teacher;

- learning solo or in groups;

- learning face-to-face with/at a distance from a teacher;

- learning in a specialized learning environment, such as a classroom or training workshop; or in a non-specialized environment, such as the home, library, workplace;

- learning as a discrete activity; or as part of another activity, e.g. on-the-job learning.

Box 1.1 Modes of learning delivery.

- vocational/non-vocational learning

- training/vocational education

- academic/non-academic knowledge

- general knowledge or skill/specific knowledge or skill

- transferable/non-transferable knowledge or skill

- key or core skills/other knowledge or skill outputs

- critical learning/functional knowledge and skill

- implicit/overt knowledge and skill

- research and development/stored knowledge

Box 1.2 Learning outputs: important distinctions.

For adults, much that is learnt through experience is achieved in the same way. The problem is that the learning outputs may be invisible and hence undervalued.

Learning providers are all those given responsibility to manage the intentional learning process. This terminology is still frequently taken to refer to educational institutions only – schools, colleges, training establishments and universities. But in the lifelong learning context, households, communities, employers, all kinds of associations, and even individuals are also learning providers. They are at least as important as the institutions, in terms of influence on motivation and opportunity.

Outputs
Learning can also be defined in terms of learning outputs and their characteristics (see Box 1.2). Many of the notions are hard to pin down.

Vocational knowledge/skill is specifically intended to be of value in the world of work. All other kinds of knowledge are *non-vocational*, according to official usage. Policy-makers, and particularly those in the Treasury, have invested much in this distinction. There are tax incentives and loans for designated *vocational learning* which are not available for other kinds of learning. But the truth is that separating the vocational from the non-vocational is like trying to cut through water. Any prior intentions of the learner or the educator may not be enough to make the labels stick, for one person's leisure course may be another's vocational objective. Similarly, a learning experience undertaken for vocational purposes may have, or come to have, value in contexts other than work. The persistence of the distinction in the face of these common difficulties is a litmus test for the prejudices of the current learning culture.

Training is a special case of vocational learning. It is vocational learning which has an emphasis on practical competences and experience as outputs. It is hard to separate from vocational education.

Academic knowledge is difficult to define closely. In this book we use a view of human talent or capacity akin to Howard Gardner's multiple intelligences.[1] One of those is linguistic or literate intelligence, which refers to a particular ability to learn through language and written texts. The current culture of learning stresses this capacity; and the curricula in schools, in the past and still commonly today, have been based on 'grammatical' themes and subjects which favour these particular learning capacities and styles. Academic knowledge is used here to refer to the output of any subject taught in this particular way.

General knowledge/skill is knowledge or skill which is useful across a wide variety of contexts, both in the world of work and also in social and domestic life. In the economic sphere it is largely synonymous with *transferable knowledge/skill*, which refers to knowledge or skill which is developed in one context but which also has value when applied in other contexts. *Non-transferable knowledge/skill* is only of use or application in a specific context, and not elsewhere. A particular firm, for example, may have a unique filing system. Being able to use it may be of no interest at all to any other employer, so this knowledge and skill has no value in any other firm. In practice, the generality and transferability of learning outputs are properties which are clear at the extremes, but not at all clear in the middle ground.

Key/core skills are an important sub-type of general knowledge/skill, where the applications are so general that they are essential for effective roles in society. These include, for example, the ability to read; to communicate; to calculate; to find things out; to use information and communications technology (ICT); to work in teams; to network; to cope with change; to manage time, and so on. There are different levels ranging from the basic or foundation level which is relevant to everyone in society, to the higher-level skills needed to lead major enterprises.

Critical learning is the ability to penetrate superficial meaning in order to expose underlying significance. It is distinct from *functional learning*, which involves the unquestioning learning of facts, issues or procedures. Critical learning is a key concept for educationists, and the source of much suspicion among politicians subjected to the critical enquiry that promotes it. This is crucial to the process of advancing knowledge, and to promoting wider understanding and assent. Acquiring this skill can be transformative – for learners and for society. The skill can be lost through neglect and be dulled by the exercise of power.

Implicit knowledge or skill arises where neither the person concerned nor anyone else can identify what is known, or can talk about it, or value it off-the-cuff for what it is. Such knowledge or skill is often the product of unintended learning. It may remain below the threshold of perception until it is discovered by intention or crisis.

Research and development are special forms of intended learning undertaken expressly to find out things which have not been known before, and which are intended to be newly stored as knowledge assets. Learning which is not of this special kind normally involves accessing established knowledge and skill already held in store.

These various notions of learning will become relevant in later chapters. The current culture throws so much light onto the vocational learning concept and onto academic prowess that the other dimensions of output are often lost from view.

The learner and the learning organization

Our second step is to look more closely at the learner and the learning organization. The learner is the individual who gains the knowledge or skill. That is straightforward. But in what sense can an organization, as opposed to an individual, be a learner?

Some would say that treating an organization as a sort of person writ large – an autonomous organism having its own knowledge and skill, over and above the knowledge and skills of the people who constitute it – is a dubious and dangerous notion. It attributes personality to a body which has no claim to be human.

On the other hand, teamwork and collaboration may help an organization to develop its ability to marshal and apply the knowledge and skills held by its workers, or maintained by the organization in 'knowledge banks' such as libraries, databases or files. In such cases, the value of the knowledge and skill made available *collectively* is more than the sum of its constituent parts. It is perfectly sensible therefore to talk about an organization learning, when it improves its ability to manage knowledge and skill in this way. Indeed it can learn even if the individuals in the organization are themselves learning nothing new, just so long as the organization's ability to access its knowledge is enhanced.

Learning organizations can therefore be seen as organizations which are particularly good at this collective learning, and at improving the collective application of what has been learned at the individual level. They have understood the value to learning of good working relationships and good networks.

Similarly, a locality where a number of learning organizations have learnt how to share knowledge and skill, by establishing and maintaining effective communication networks, may become a 'learning city', a 'learning estate', a 'learning valley', and so on. Groups and communities of all kinds can learn in this collective sense, whether they are families, firms, associations, local communities – or even the country as a whole. There is hardly a corner of today's society where collective learning by groups is not an issue.

The stock of knowledge

At any given moment, there is a stock of knowledge and skill stored by each individual and, by extension, by each learning organization. Not all such knowledge and skill remains at the conscious level, and some of it is essentially unique and private to individual learners. But the vast bulk of a person's knowledge and skill can be shared with, and learnt by, others. Where it can be passed on it becomes *intellectual property*, and may pick up a market value.

Looming far above the immediate knowledge of individuals and organizations therefore is the vastly greater pile of storable and transmittable knowledge. It has been laid down over the years, safe from the failing memories of the individuals who first generated and owned it. Whether it be in the form of books, archives, databases or specimen collections, this stored knowledge and know-how is essential to the survival of the planet and its life forms.

Stored knowledge can decay, and it can be destroyed. Sometimes loss is dramatic and wilful, like Hitler's burning of books. Sometimes it is gradual and the result of neglect. Knowledge decay happens at the individual level too – skills and knowledge once possessed can become rusty as the memory fades, unless constantly reactivated through use. *Un*learning of this kind is often insidious. It advances like dry rot, the effects only exposed at a critical moment. In the world of business, accountants have ways to write off the value of lost assets and to charge for depreciation. But they have failed to establish any way to account for knowledge-capital and its accumulation and decay.

Teachers and education

The third step in clarifying terms is to look at teaching and education. In everyday usage, learning is equated with education, and all learning is treated as taught learning. Teaching and education are of central importance, but these limited interpretations prevent us from seeing the full ramifications of the lifelong learning concept. Working for *lifelong education* is very different from working for *lifelong learning*.

Teachers draw on their own or other people's stock of knowledge in order to help others to learn. The techniques they use range along a spectrum, from prescriptive and didactic at one end, to facilitative and supportive at the other. In practice, the former is more commonly used in teaching young children, and the teaching of adults tends towards the latter. The case for having teachers is that good teaching can help learners to learn better – and sometimes more cost-effectively – than they can on their own. Poor teaching, on the other hand, is more than a failure to teach well: it can do long-term damage by undermining learners' confidence in their own capabilities.

In some cases people can only learn if teachers are on hand to dispel the difficulties. In other cases, self-instruction may be more of an option. But even among skilled learners, self-instruction is seldom enough in itself. It is a well-established tradition in the performing arts, for example, that even the most expert and experienced performers continue to receive tuition.

From the teacher's point of view, good teaching goes hand-in-hand with good learning. The best teachers are also experienced learners, constantly challenging themselves in new areas – not only as a way to gather new knowledge and skill, but specifically as a way of keeping close to the discomforts and rewards of the learning experience. Good teaching is the most effective of all instruments for building and changing the learning culture of the country.

Education is learning which involves qualified or unqualified teachers. It refers to teacher-led learning processes at an individual or group level. Education in its basic sense usually relates to a curriculum of a particular content or kind, and is provided in institutions according to specific timetables and policies for quality, achievement and coverage. It commonly also denotes the management and governance of these matters in society.

But education is not just institutional. It is at its most effective and informal where it bears on children and young people in the home. Intentionally or otherwise, ordinary adults are teachers too. They decide by agreement or assent, and according to informal domestic policies, what the younger members of the household need to learn (the informal curriculum) and how they will be taught it (in this case, teaching as an aspect of parenting). These arrangements need constant renegotiation: as parents learn about parenting, and delegate some of their responsibility to the formal educational system; and as the young learners themselves develop their own skills and styles of learning, and grow to take on full responsibility for their own learning.

The final distinction, used in many places in this book, depends in part on institutionalized education. *Initial learning* covers people who are in compulsory education in school (up to age 16); or who are attending a course of further education or higher education up to degree level, following on from statutory education without a break. *Post-initial learning* covers any formal learning, whether education or not, beyond that point. Postgraduate education is part of the latter category. This distinction is defined by the learner's experience. This means that the same course may be taken by younger people as part of their initial learning, and by older people as part of their post-initial learning. It is central to all discussion of lifelong learning that both elements make up the field of debate.

Lifelong learning

The ground-clearing work on definitions having been done, the holistic notion of lifelong learning can now be identified. Our concept consists of a two-part framework:

1. an empirical element, reflecting the *factual nature of the learning* which counts;
2. a moral element, reflecting *four principles of conduct.*

Each of these elements is indispensable, and the two are interdependent. Lifelong learners behave in accordance with the first, while acting in accordance with the second. This definition is fundamental to the whole argument.

At the *empirical level* – lifelong learning is intended and planned learning, which goes on more or less continuously over the lifespan. Box 1.3 sets out the features. Together these criteria leave some room for informal learning within the idea of lifelong learning, but the latter must be built on a good solid backbone of *intentional and planned learning* if an individual or organization is to claim to be a lifelong learner.

At the *moral level* – lifelong learners will additionally live by four basic moral principles: personal commitment to learning; social commitment to learning; respect for others' learning; and respect for truth (see Box 1.4). Observance of the four principles is not as easy to verify as the empirical criteria, and may be contested ground; but the principles have a degree of internal consistency.

Taken together, the different elements of the definition interpret what most people now active in the current debate on lifelong learning seem to have in mind. At the core is the idea of the person who practises learning consistently and persistently, and who so values the learning activity as to be passionate in its favour. Such learners will show personal and social commitment to learning. It would be unthinkable that they would either deny to others freedom of thought, or personally disregard logical argument or demonstrable fact.

- Lifelong learning relates to learning *throughout the lifespan* – covering all life from cradle to grave, and starting at any age.

- *Learning* has the widest possible boundaries. It includes all the main types and classes of learning: vocational, critical, formal, and the opposites of all these. It includes formal and informal education, and self-directed learning.

- *Continuity* is not of the very strictest kind. It allows for some gaps and delays, so long as a broad momentum is maintained.

- *Intention and planning* on the part of the individual or organization is seen as an ongoing intent to learn. It is expressed through some form of personal/organizational plan or strategy for ongoing learning which is maintained and acted upon over time. The plan might be written down as an unfolding concept, subject to reappraisal over time; or it might be held in the mind, more informally.

Box 1.3 Features of lifelong learning.

- *Personal commitment* means individuals take a personal interest in their learning programme, and take a large measure of personal responsibility for carrying it through successfully.

- *Social commitment* means that learners share their learning with others, and encourage others with their learning, and in their successful application of learning in daily living.

- *Respect for others' learning* means that the learner recognizes the rights of all individuals and organizations to be lifelong learners, and to be able to express their points of view freely.

- *Respect for truth* means the learner is prepared to change any opinion – even those long and dearly held – in the face of evidence and rational argument.

Box 1.4 Moral aspects of lifelong learning.

This two-faceted definition of lifelong learning has some notable implications:

- The definition clarifies the distinction between *learning* and *the learned*. A part-time student may pass the test with flying colours, while a poor professional may find it difficult to qualify as a lifelong learner.
- Scenarios where much learning is being done (high volume), but where it is fragmented and aimless (shows low commitment), or is unintended (even casual perhaps), cannot be lifelong learning. This sets aside the trivializing definition asserting that all of us are lifelong learners simply because we all learn from day-to-day experience, whether or not we are conscious of it.
- Learning which is enforced in a context where learners' free speech and discussion are denied cannot be lifelong learning. In China during the Cultural Revolution, for example, daily incantation of Chairman Mao's Little Red Book was required. But the oppressive context in which it took place puts the exercise outside our definition of lifelong learning, with its reliance on individual commitment and respect for truth.

- High participation in learning across a social group cannot be assumed to indicate high participation in lifelong learning by that group. The learning may be strongly clustered into certain sub-groups, or it may lack continuity or any of the other essential elements.

- The suggested criteria exclude a number of other specific restricted usages. One is the use of 'lifelong learning' to cover activities which may involve learning, but which are pursued primarily as personal leisure activities. This usage is common in the United States. Also excluded is what – as long ago as 1976 – the OECD dubbed 'recurrent education', and what is often called 'adult education' or 'continuing education' today. These terms are ways of bundling together education and training which is available to adults outside formal provision for initial education (including initial higher education). At the time of writing, this is the default definition often used by the UK government.

A GENERAL CULTURE OF LIFELONG LEARNING

Countries and international bodies across the globe have recognized the urgent need for lifelong learning on something like the wide-ranging and radical definitions which are set out here. The European Union, the OECD, UNESCO, and the Nordic countries have all made major policy statements in recent times to this effect.[2] One thing they all stress is the need for a *general culture* of lifelong learning. Everything which follows in this book will swing on what a 'general lifelong learning culture' means.

First it is necessary to be clear what culture itself is. Culture is a characteristic of people in groups. These may be whole nations, or groups within nations. Each will have a set of identifying values, behaviours, attitudes, beliefs, symbols, rituals, dress and regalia, which underpin a sense of personal and group identity for members of the group. These components fit together as a set of complementary and mutually reinforcing elements. Together they form a recognizable syndrome typical of the group, to which individual members are encouraged to conform by the rewards and sanctions of the group's traditions and laws. These cultural components are very important for personal and group motivation.

A few group members may possess all the characteristic cultural features – like people who can wear an 'average-sized' shoe. But there will be many who approximate to the archetype (for whom the shoe rubs or pinches at certain points), and others who recognize that the archetype is typical for the group to which they belong, even though it is not strongly descriptive of themselves.

A learning culture brings together the attitudes and expectations which a group has about learning – as expressed through the values, motivations and behaviour of its institutions and individual members – and the learning that individuals undertake as typical members of the group. A learning culture can be fully understood only against the wider cultural frame within which it is set. Learning culture is not much debated. People who say that 'The UK has no learning culture' generally mean that it has no homogenous learning culture. For them, the many distinctive learning cultures currently expressed in various groups in Britain are invisible and simply do not register on the popular scales of social comment.

We take a very different view. The next chapter will examine learning culture as it is in the UK today. Despite much differentiation by group at the general level, learning in twentieth-century Britain has been shaped by the inheritance of a dominant learning culture which is competitive in its style and elitist in its aims, and which supports and is supported by traditional academic values and power structures. Despite repeated attempts to introduce different values and behaviours, and despite the development of divergent values and practices in Scotland, Wales and Northern Ireland, the strength of this cultural tradition has constantly renewed and reasserted itself – in England, in particular.

A general lifelong learning culture would have the characteristics set out in Box 1.5. How the new culture of lifelong learning would relate to the different social, ethnic and religious groups in Britain is crucial. Some advocates of lifelong learning culture seem to see the culture change as one which would replace the different learning cultures of the various separate groupings with a single, common, undifferentiated lifelong learning culture. They argue for this as a means to meld the population together in a 'melting pot' of social structure.

A general lifelong learning culture would:

- meet the *wide definition* of lifelong learning set out above;
- be *open to all*, regardless of personal wealth or means;
- be *general*, in the sense that lifelong learning would become the norm for a substantial majority of the population.

A general lifelong learning culture would not be a mass culture in the sense of imposing uniformity and homogeneity in learning culture across the many groupings which contribute to a multicultural Britain.

Box 1.5 Characteristics of a general lifelong learning culture.

Others consider that there is room for a considerable display of 'cultural biodiversity' within the latitude of the lifelong learning definitions. On this model, strongly advocated in the following chapters, each cultural group may adapt the application of lifelong learning culture to its own cultural setting. This will allow self-defined groups to feel they can adopt cultures of lifelong learning without destabilizing the core features of their own culture and traditions. At the same time it will develop enough common feeling about lifelong learning between the groups to contribute strongly to mutual understanding and co-operation between different communities.

SOME IMPLICATIONS OF THE GENERAL LIFELONG LEARNING CULTURE

The aim of a general lifelong learning culture raises inconvenient and uncomfortable issues. Some people will have deep concerns about any talk of 'building a new culture'. It could easily be seen as a totalitarian enterprise, where self-selected architects of a new social order step forward to set their mark upon history. This is why the proposal for a new culture needs to be taken forward as a voluntary enterprise – one which is as much a learning experience in itself as an exercise in the management of change. Any group which comes to feel that its core values are threatened is likely to adopt a stance of resistance.

It is vital therefore to encourage a voluntary assimilation of the lifelong learning concept, so that it may be readily and smoothly incorporated within the culture of various groups. Here the lifelong learning principles are fundamental. They mark the boundary between lifelong learning and other cultures – which may be rich in some kinds of learning, but in kinds which may not be made accessible to all.

Many will feel that it will take too long to change. A new culture will not be achieved overnight, nor can its development be steered by one party in government alone. It is realistic to assume that it may take 20 to 25 years to reach a point where the various change elements have become mutually reinforcing; where the general culture is self-replicating; and where a critical mass of lifelong learners has developed. Success will require long-term policies, trust and real commitments (psychological contracts) between national bodies and successive governments, across all political parties. It cannot be a 'top down' exercise – ownership must be grounded in participation at local and community level.

Lifelong learning will advance more surely if it runs with the main currents in social development. At the very least, establishing a lifelong learning culture requires society to come to terms with the wider processes of culture change, such as postmodernity and globalization. It would be foolish to think that there can be great cultural progress in a hermetically sealed context. Such wider changes and their influences need to be closely understood. Lifelong learners will be very concerned to establish a proper link between their own culture of learning and the surrounding cultural flux.

The new culture must also be clearly distinguished from the concept of self-seeking individualists pursuing economically useful learning in order to maximize their private advantage. The difference lies in the emphasis on the requirement for individuals to show social commitment, and in a wide definition of things to be learnt, including the capacity for critical thought and action.

This point relates to the economic notion of *externalities*. Learning can be treated as an activity which has benefits and costs only for the learner – whether as a private and individual investment, or as an act of consumption. But treating it like this ignores the fact that learning has the capacity to generate large-scale external benefits. These can be seen in the way that one person's learning can motivate another; one person's learning can be passed on to another by example; an extra episode of learning may make costs of further learning cheaper at the margin, both for the learner and for other potential learners; and the more learning people do, the more ways they can find to apply it. On the back of externalities like this, learning can spread like wildfire through families, firms and whole communities. Social commitment means fanning these flames.

A lifelong learning culture expressing personal and social commitment could generate massive beneficial externalities, given the right policies. But the cast of the currently dominant learning culture tells a different story. It is used to sift and grade people to fit the class-defined and unequal opportunities which are available to the population at large. Instead of people catching the 'benevolent virus' of learning from their neighbours or friends, large numbers are positively deterred from learning – switched off despite their many, underdeveloped and neglected capabilities.

Finally, there seems to be no essential difference between the general culture of lifelong learning and what has been called the 'learning society'. Advocates of the latter tend to promote a society where there is something other than just more learning. They want to see learning spread across the population, and they want to see it expressing itself in all its economic and cultural forms. The notion of a general culture has the advantage that it keeps the spotlight on the central issue: the current damping of the natural motivation to learn by the weight of a deeply regressive learning culture.

POSSIBILITY OF CHANGING LEARNING CULTURE

Some commentators, not surprisingly, will say that the aim of establishing a new general culture is unrealistic and that the most that can be achieved is to adapt what we have. Among these are those who have been well served by the current culture and its supporting system, who have a strong grip on the main learning institutions of the country. Learning practices and institutions tend to be conservative, because each generation tries to bring up the next in ways based on its own experience. In Britain this is reinforced by a culture which draws authority from the past. The paternalism which is the occupational hazard of teaching also leaves its cultural imprint.

Nonetheless, examples of major changes in other fields offer encouragement. These include the environmental lobbies, and the movements which have challenged the sexism and gender-based oppression in much of our social and economic life. These have steadily won ground. They provide a model for driving forward a major project for social change. Such examples show that persistence, collaboration and learning itself can open the pathways to change. Introducing a new culture of lifelong learning is a similar task.

The question is how to go about it. Industrial leaders who have embarked on culture change within their organizations have learnt something useful: that it is imperative to avoid the systemic fallacy. Focusing on changes to the system is no substitute for changing the culture.

Governments, civil servants, institutional administrators, auditors and inspectors are all prey to this reductionist stance. Culture and systems intertwine, but they are not the same. Later chapters will argue that systems have a nasty habit of reflecting and reinforcing old cultures. And old cultures have a habit of undermining the shiny new system put forward as the harbinger of change. So we believe that the nation's learning achievements cannot be improved without replacing the old culture and the systems which both support and feed upon it.

NOTES AND REFERENCES

1. Gardner (1993).
2. See Chapman and Aspin (1997).

Chapter 2

The Learning Scene

This chapter explores key features of the general learning scene in the UK today against the backcloth of the notion of a general culture of learning. Our aim is to see how far the current situation approaches the idea of lifelong learning and its supporting principles. Using statistics, we shall examine the stock of knowledge and skill; consider the volume and pattern of learning; and examine the underlying attitudes and motivation which inform the learning record. Then, in less statistical vein, we shall consider some of the main interactions between the learning scene, and the systems and stakeholders which support it.

CURRENT STOCK OF KNOWLEDGE

Just how much does the UK population know? And how is it distributed – both by level of skill and knowledge, and across the population? There are three key features of the contemporary record: the population contains a large minority of people who are illiterate and innumerate, comparing badly with other major countries; the bulk of the population has a poor qualification record; and there is a poor general level of basic skills.

Illiteracy and innumeracy
Figures 2.1a and 2.1b record the UK results of a major international survey, conducted for the OECD.[1] The study examines at different levels people's ability to understand written text, to locate and use information in charts and timetables, and to handle basic arithmetic. The results for the UK show a hard core of very basic illiteracy and innumeracy (Level 1) comprising one-fifth of men and about one-quarter of women. These figures are a disaster.

The OECD has also defined in its survey a minimum level of numeracy and literacy 'required for modern life and work' (Level 3). Figures 2.1a and 2.1b reveal that half of adults between the ages of 16 and 65 in the UK are below that standard. About one-quarter lie between the OECD standard and those with the most severe problems. These represent talents wasted on a massive scale. This state of affairs is culturally

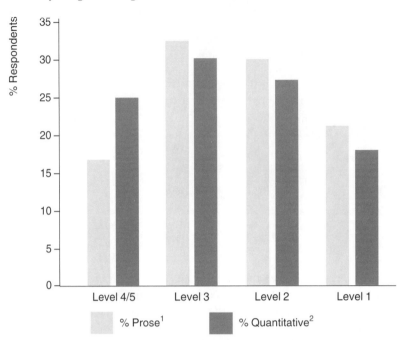

Figure 2.1a Literacy levels of adult males, 1996. Source: Adult Literacy Survey in *Social Trends 28* (Office for National Statistics, 1998).

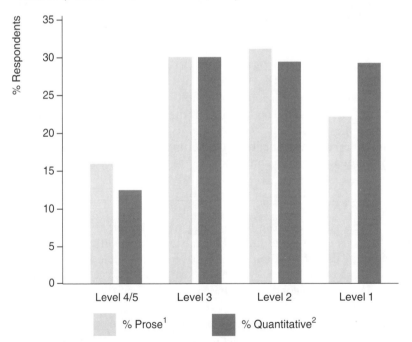

Figure 2.1b Literacy levels of adult females, 1996. Source: Adult Literacy Survey in *Social Trends 28* (Office for National Statistics, 1998).

Notes: 1. The ability to understand text.
         2. The ability to perform basic arithmetic on numbers in text.

tolerated, year in and year out. Other major countries do better, including Sweden, Germany, Australia, Canada, and the USA.

The Basic Skills Agency has shown how damaging to people poor literacy and numeracy can be over time.[2] In 1995 adults in the National Child Development Cohort[3] were tested for literacy and numeracy at age 37, and the association between their scores and past labour market experience was analysed. Those with poor literacy and numeracy had received significantly less work-based training, they had a notably poorer record of promotion, and their income levels at age 37 were much lower. Over two-fifths of men with competent numeracy and literacy had been promoted twice or more between age 23 and 37. This compared with one in five of those with competent numeracy but poor literacy, and one in four of those with competent literacy but poor numeracy.

Poor qualification profile

Figure 2.2 presents the basic facts: overall some 25% of the population aged 25 to 69, not in full-time education, have no qualifications at all; just about the same percentage have a degree or other higher qualifications; and the rest are strung in between. Moreover, a failure to gain qualifications in initial education is particularly damaging to learning at later stages of life. The 1997 National Adult Learning Survey (NALS'97) shows – in line with earlier studies – that the longer people delay the time of leaving initial education, and the higher the qualifications they have when they leave, the more learning they will do subsequently. This is a key point for lifelong learning policy.

On a closer analysis the qualifications profile confirms the deep divisions in the population: among professionals, two-thirds have degrees; among unskilled manual workers, two-thirds of the whole are without any qualifications at all.

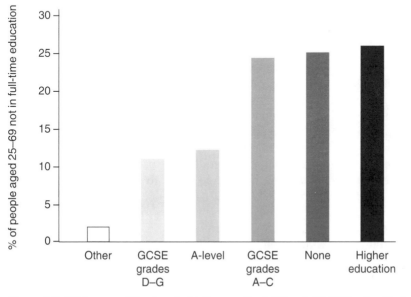

Figure 2.2　Highest qualifications held. Source: *Social Trends 28* (Office for National Statistics, 1998).

National skills profile

The government's 1996 Skills Audit[4] shows that the UK lags behind other major countries in the proportion of the working population qualified at Level 2 (good basic skills level) and Level 3 – that is, skilled craft or A-level academic standard (see Figure 2.3). The numbers fall well short of the National Targets laid down by the National Advisory Council for Education and Training Targets.

In summary, the UK has a well-educated elite whose members enjoy an educational standing on a par with the best world standards. But in terms of the distribution of knowledge and skills across the population, a mass of illiteracy and innumeracy supports a profile which is narrow, thin-waisted and rising to a sharp peak. Britain's skills rest on a crumbling base of under-achievement. A major reason why our present learning culture is so downbeat is the simple mediocrity of this mis-shapen profile. In a culture of lifelong learning there would be more skills and knowledge overall; much stronger basic skills; and much greater volumes of skills and knowledge in the middle ground.

PATTERNS OF CONTEMPORARY LEARNING

Patterns of participation in learning have much to tell about the current learning scene. A number of major surveys in recent years have thrown light on these. The problem of defining learning clearly in survey terms makes assessing the overall size of the learning effort, and trends associated with it, difficult. Nevertheless, the very similar *patterns* of participation shown by the different surveys provide an insight into the present learning culture.

Number of lifelong learners

Statistics permitting, it would be helpful to know how many lifelong learners there already are. This means identifying how many have *lifelong involvement in broadly continuous, planned learning.*

A great deal of learning is going on in the initial education system: the whole age cohort from 5 to 16; some two-thirds of all 16–19-year-olds; and about one-third in higher education, between the ages of 18 and the early twenties (see Figure 2.4). Yet, despite the rapid growth in initial further and higher education in recent years, people in the UK typically drop out of initial education at an earlier age than in many other advanced countries.

In the post-initial category, the majority of adults take part in significant episodes of learning at least on an occasional basis. According to NALS'97, about three-quarters of the adult population had at least one significant episode of learning in the previous three years (see Figure 2.5). But by the same token the survey shows that one-quarter had done nothing in the previous three years. So, *even if the net is cast over a three-year span,* full-scale participation amongst the adult population surveyed (up to age 69) is far from complete.

Other surveys, using different definitions of learning, underwrite the picture of a large non-learning minority. The 1996 Gallup Survey for the National Institute for Adult Continuing Education (NIACE)[5] found that 41% of men and 31% of women

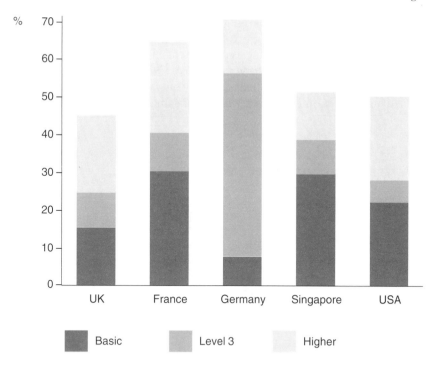

Figure 2.3 The percentage of working population qualified to given level, shown additively. Source: *Skills Audit* (DfEE, 1996).

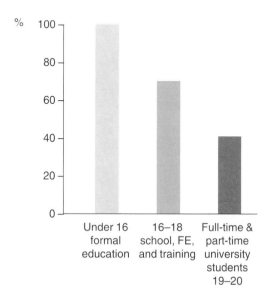

Figure 2.4 Percentage of particular age groups in initial education. Source: *Education Statistics* (DfEE, 1996).

claim not to have done any significant learning at all since leaving full-time education. The title used by NIACE for its survey report – *The Learning Divide* – vividly captures the rift in society between the learning 'haves' and the 'have-nots'. Allowing for major differences in definitions between this survey and NALS'97, these figures imply that most of those who have not learned in the last three years according to NALS'97 will not have learned anything significant since leaving full-time education.

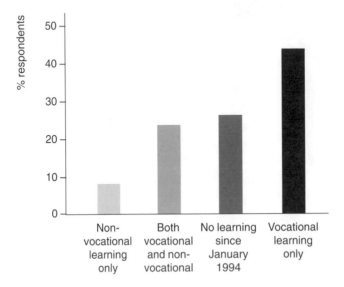

Figure 2.5 Percentage of population in England and Wales, aged 16–69, learning in previous three years. Source: *National Adult Learning Survey* (Beinart and Smith, 1997).

Figure 2.6 Percentages of learners in England and Wales, aged 16–69, in socio-economic groups. Source: *National Adult Learning Survey* (Beinart and Smith, 1997).

There appears to be no direct survey evidence to show the number of participants who keep up their learning in a more or less continuous stream (a lack of evidence which is a cultural indicator in itself). NIACE found in 1996 that 25% of adults are learning at any one slice of time. The number of *broadly continuous learners* must be very much less than this – possibly 15% or so. At best the large numbers of continuing learners fall far short of those a culture of lifelong learning would need, to be worthy of the name.

The available evidence also provides little help on assessing how far the learning done outside initial education is *planned* by the learner in any sense. The NALS'97 showed that over the three-year span nearly a quarter of respondents had received 'any guidance from any source'; for learners the figure was one-third; for non-learners (in the previous three years) the figure was just 6%. It seems possible that the 'planners' are likely to number much less than one-third of learners. Most of the continuous learners are likely to be numbered among them.

Two points emerge from this: the number of lifelong learners actively learning today is likely to be small, perhaps very small; and there is a sizeable body of non-learners who are doing very little learning after initial education, if any at all. These people have in effect switched off from learning – or they have been switched off.

Distribution of learning

The statistics are more helpful in showing how learning is distributed across the population. A general lifelong learning culture would show learning to be evenly spread across the social classes, across the age bands, and across genders and ethnic groups. That is specifically not the case in the present learning scene.

Socio-economic pattern
The NALS'97 (see Figure 2.6) shows that the distribution of adult learning is spread very unevenly against the different socio-economic groups. Among people from an unskilled manual background, the proportion who have done at least some learning within a recent three-year period is about 50%, compared to 90% of managers and professionals in the top jobs. The ratio for vocational learning is broadly similar.

This biased socio-economic patterning persists right across the statistics on learning. Not only is it pervasive in post-initial vocational learning, it appears in initial education also for all ages beyond the age of statutory school attendance. Figures for the whole of further education are difficult to find, and in higher education the statistics are scarcely more visible. The Family and Working Lives Survey[6] shows that of all the people who hold a first degree as their higher qualification, the proportions from socio-economic groups A and B compared with groups D and E are in a ratio of broadly 4.5:1. By comparison, for general learning outside initial education, NALS'97 puts the ratio between the same groups at about 6:1.

The pattern has persisted largely unchanged for many years. In higher education, for example, the 1997 Dearing Committee Report No. 6[7] sums up a wide range of evidence. Paragraph 1.10 says that 'under-representation among lower socio-economic groups has not materially improved over time'. In the wider world of vocational learning, the 1987 Training in Britain Survey[8] showed that 48% of socio-economic groups A and B had experience of adult vocational learning in the previous three years, compared to 22% for Group E. This compares with 85% and 44% respectively in NALS'97. Differences of definition affect these comparisons, but the ratio in each case is roughly 2:1.

This long-term consistency is notable – particularly in the light of improvements in absolute living standards for most citizens over the years, reflected in the large growth and spread of car ownership, and the rise in owner-occupied houses. It reflects very deep forces at work in society and the economy, and calls for close study.

Age pattern
Another major feature of the record is the decline of participation in learning across the (ascending) age groups. Figure 2.7, taken from NALS'97, shows the pattern of declining learning in this model, particularly in the years leading up to and following retirement.

This reflects the old, predominantly male stereotype, where learning was front-loaded into the years of compulsory schooling. But there is more to it than that. Looking behind these figures reveals that the falling-off is principally a feature of vocational learning. There is no doubt that the main reason is economic – that not enough 'working lifetime' is thought to remain for the full value of work-related learning to be reaped. To a lesser extent the decline may also reflect a loss of confidence among some older people in their ability to keep up with younger learners. This flies in the face of psychological evidence, which clearly shows that older people can more than make up for any loss of speed of thought and action by using more effective learning strategies and experience.[9]

Levels of *non*-vocational learning hold up quite well over the age groups, but this too falls off markedly in later retirement. There are still strong myths and social norms which tend to stifle the will to learn later in life. The large success of institutions like the Open University and the University of the Third Age shows what can be achieved

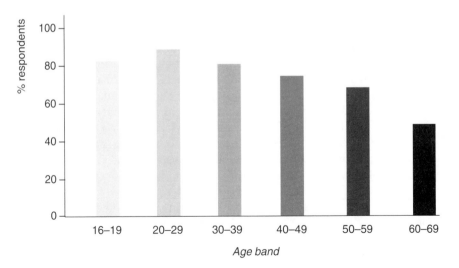

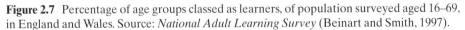

Figure 2.7 Percentage of age groups classed as learners, of population surveyed aged 16–69, in England and Wales. Source: *National Adult Learning Survey* (Beinart and Smith, 1997).

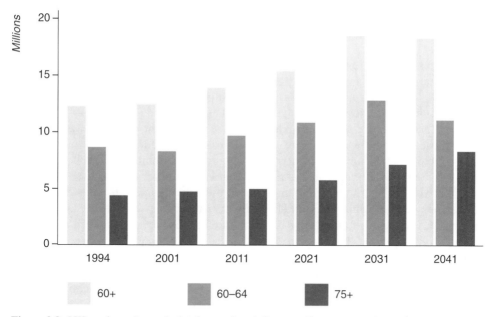

Figure 2.8 UK projected population by age band. Source: Government Actuaries Department.

with these age groups if the myths are challenged. Figure 2.8 shows how urgent that challenge will have to be, because a strong rise in the numbers of older people in the UK is certain to take place in the early decades of the new millennium. More than ever, older people need to use learning to keep fit and active, and to feed their knowledge and skills back into the community.

Gender patterns
The role of gender in the learning process is very influential, and the statistical picture on participation is complex.

Young learners at school need to be stimulated and challenged appropriately by the curriculum and learning environments, but gender differences – reflected in preferences and in rate of maturation – complicate what 'appropriate' means. The kind of competition which can stimulate boys' interest may well discourage girls, for example, and the role of aggression in motivation makes the picture even more complicated. As generations of researchers have explored these complexities, educational theory and the institutions have responded to a greater or lesser extent.

Research during the last twenty years or so has exposed the masculine bias and discrimination in formal education and assessment, and in employment. Adjustments in the initial educational system – such as a reduction in competitive classroom practice, and the use of numbers instead of names on public examination scripts – have gone some way to improving the learning and assessment environment for females.

This may however have reduced the stimulus of the learning environment critically for some males. Under age 16 the participation and educational performance of young white males from poor households currently give particular cause for concern. Many boys become alienated from learning activities in their early teens, and constitute the bulk of the fast-growing statistics on school exclusion. More than two million school days are lost each year through exclusions, predominantly boys – a rise of *450% in the past seven years.*

At ages 16–19, the gender pattern shows divergence again. Overall at age 16, more males than females are outside learning or training. By age 18 the genders have changed places, although the differences are slight. At age 16 more young men than women opt for practical initial training outside full-time education, but more young women than men stay in full-time education. The women who stay in education divide into those who do well and are destined for higher education – the numbers outstripping men at university entry – and the rest. The main problem lies with 'the rest'. While significant numbers of non-academic young men remain in some kind of vocational learning, the learning undertaken by young women in this second group tends to have lower objectives, and they slip out of learning at an earlier age than the young men. In performance terms therefore, except for the academic high-flyers, the gender advantage which shows up clearly in girls' early and mid-school performance falters in the years 16–19.

Despite far-reaching changes in the workplace in recent decades, the nearer that women draw to the world of work the more of a masculine bias they encounter. In the current culture, those who aim for and enter higher education tend to maintain their performance levels for longer than those women who opt for further education and training. Worse problems lie with those who fall away from the academic stream. Disaffected teenage boys receive growing media attention, but added to these are young women who cannot identify with the current routes to success, and who opt instead to follow influential role models into dead-end jobs and early motherhood. This move places serious constraints on their ability to participate in learning later. These are the processes which serve to divide the population, as if it consisted of so many sheep and goats.

In initial higher education, rather more women than men from the age cohort now enrol for first degrees. The proportion has doubled in the last 30 years. Changes in school policy and teaching practice, as well as in the wider society, have contributed strongly to this change. More able young women now come through the full initial education system, so that the educated elite has a better gender balance. But the evidence is that the faltering of academic women's achievement relative to their capacities eventually strikes home during the course of higher education. More men than women get first-class degrees, and later on women have lower graduate earnings in the labour market.

In post-initial learning, see Figure 2.9, figures taken from NALS'97 on participation in the previous three years show that men have the edge over women in vocational learning, but that women have the edge on men in non-vocational learning. These overall differences are not great; but the general picture hides a wealth of difference in the particular. For example, on taught learning connected to current job, 46% of women have experienced at least one episode in the previous three years, compared to 54% of men. This is a large gap. On the other hand the proportions are exactly reversed for learning which is undertaken with a future job in mind.

Women may participate in ways very different from men. In the vocational sphere women experience more very short episodes of learning than men (on how to use an electronic till, for example) although on average the duration may be similar to men's.

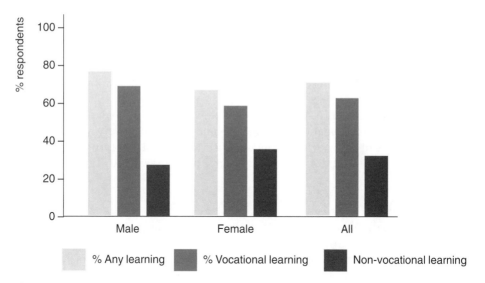

Figure 2.9 Percentage of males and females, in England and Wales aged 16–69, who have done some recent learning. Source: *National Adult Learning Survey* (Beinart and Smith,

They have more on-the-job training than men, much of it based on ICT. On the other hand access to vocational qualifications appears to be broadly equal between the genders overall. Particular groups of women are seriously constrained in their learning chances. These include lone parents with children, and those with heavy domestic and caring roles.

These statistics do not mean that there is no gender problem. They mean that cultural factors, combining with economic factors and constraints on access to learning, chop up the gender statistics into a large array of sub-groups, many of which have very severe, but highly particular, learning difficulties.

Ethnicity patterns
As with gender, the position of ethnic minority groups in learning is complex, and its implications are mixed. The interaction of gender and ethnic issues adds a further dimension of complexity.

In initial education, evidence from the Youth Cohort Study[10] suggests that – other things being equal – being a member of an ethnic minority generally increases the staying-on rate at age 16. Overall the further education colleges have proportionately large ethnic representation, particularly of learners originating in the Indian subcontinent. These students tend to be concentrated in these institutions rather than in the school sixth forms and the sixth-form colleges. They have a relatively good record at completing their studies.

In higher education, ethnic minority groups tend to be statistically over-represented in overall terms, except for Afro-Caribbeans, who are slightly under-represented. Again, ethnic groups from the Indian subcontinent feature strongly. As in further education however, members of ethnic minorities who get to higher education tend to be very unevenly spread. They cluster strongly in a small number of post-1992 universities – former polytechnics which still have a vocational emphasis in their courses. However good these universities may actually be – and they are shaming the rest in imaginative developments in flexible learning – cultural bias in favour of academicism means that their reputation among employers is generally lower than other universities. Moreover, Report No. 5 from the Dearing Enquiry[11] noted widespread worries about discrimination and feelings of isolation amongst ethnic minority students.

For post-initial learning, NALS'97 shows that whites and non-whites have nearly the same three-year participation rates, at 74% and 72% respectively. We can find no particular evidence of any wide-based inequality in this part of the learning scene, once the other factors like income, social class, etc. have been allowed for. That is not to say that it is not there.

Patterns of vocational learning
There are some notable imbalances in the vocational sphere. Firstly, part-time and self-employed workers carry out less vocational learning than full-time workers (see Figure 2.10). For part-time workers, this seems to indicate that employers judge there to be insufficient time in the 'working lifetime' for the full value of work-related learning to be reaped. There is some affinity here with the motivation underlying the reduction of vocational learning among older workers. For some self-employed people it may reflect the acquisition of a particular skill as the basis for becoming self-employed in the first place.

These differences are growing in significance because the labour market is expected to continue turning full-time jobs into part-time jobs, and firms to lay out many more routine tasks to external firms or agencies. The Confederation of British Industry (CBI) has drawn attention[12] to the prospect that the so-called 'flexible workers' – part-timers; temporary workers; contract workers; seasonal and casual workers – may well number ten million by the beginning of the new millennium. Also, that the willingness of employers to pay towards the training of these workers is lower than for full-time workers. Thus millions more flexible workers will be slipping into the learning shadows, increasingly remote from employers' willingness to invest in their learning.

Secondly, vocational learning dominates the total participation in learning in the years after initial education. NALS'97 shows that 44% of people not in full-time education have done only vocational learning in the last three years. This compares with 7% who have done only non-vocational learning, and 23% who have done both. This overwhelming preponderance is an imbalance. For many adults, particularly men, general education takes a back seat when put alongside the economic motive. Yet the economy is changing so fast that general education has become the main ground for continuing employability. The figures also reflect an inclination towards instrumental learning, which is consistent with a view that social commitment to learning is rather low.

Thirdly, there is the bias against lower socio-economic groups. This shows up in the vocational category of learning, as it does elsewhere. It speaks as much of the inclinations of the employer as it does of the worker. Figure 2.11 shows the proportion of employers in a recent survey who offered (any) training to different types of workers. The lower the status of a worker compared with management level, the less the chances of being offered job-specific training by the employer. Even less are their

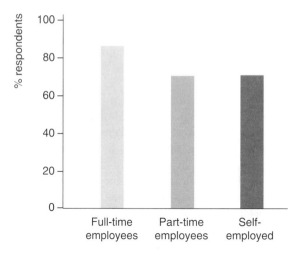

Figure 2.10 Percentage of those aged 16–69 in England and Wales in activity groups with recent vocational learning. Source: *National Adult Learning Survey* (Beinart and Smith, 1997).

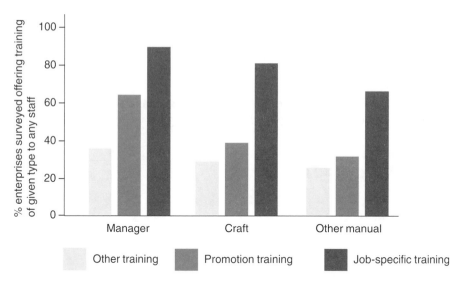

Figure 2.11 Type of training by selected occupation groups. Source: *Employers' Attitudes*, Research Series No. 40, Metcalf *et al.* (1994).

chances of promotional training – and lower still are the chances of support for general education.

A host of assumptions lie behind this picture. They include the view among employers that workers who are encouraged to think about their personal development will demand more remuneration; and also the fear that such workers will be tempted to leave for better jobs elsewhere. UK studies show that these prejudices are largely groundless, and that the true picture may be quite the reverse. As the 14th British Social Attitudes Survey[13] indicates, if employers want access to the services of good workers, they must invest in them. But the old myths still hold sway, especially among small and medium-sized firms. These are all part of a general anti-skills investment culture, which the national Investors in People programme is designed to address.

Overall picture

All this shows that learning is far from evenly spread. The initial education system opens out into a pattern of learning where the age, social class and employment status of the learner matter greatly. An educated elite emerges and draws away from the rest of the population in terms of its ongoing learning – leaving the rest of the population strung between occasional learning or outright non-learning. In the latter camp are around a quarter of the population who are in very severe difficulties with their ability to function effectively in the modern world. These features are inter-related, and the pattern will replicate endlessly if it is left to itself. A shift towards a culture of lifelong learning means taking specific action to pull this cat's cradle of grading and sifting phenomena into a very different shape.

ATTITUDES

Changing the culture means understanding the attitudes and beliefs underpinning the generally dismal picture of participation.

Learning is a 'good thing'

Nearly everyone says that more learning is a good thing, when they are asked (see Figure 2.12). In a recent MORI survey for the Campaign for Learning, 63% of the

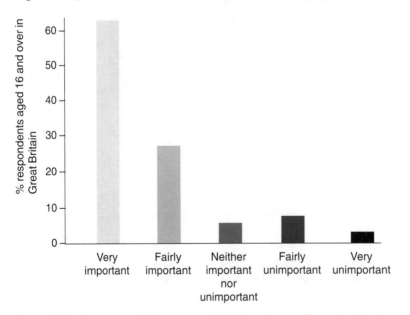

Figure 2.12 The personal importance of learning. Source: Campaign for Learning (MORI, 1996).

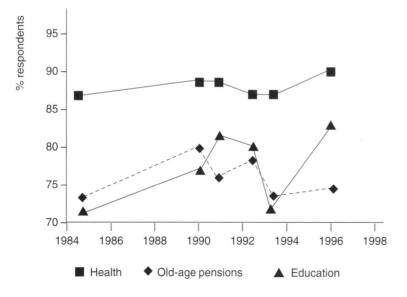

Figure 2.13 Areas of government spending (per cent saying 'Spend more' or 'Much more'). Source: *British Social Attitudes* survey, 14th Report (Social and Community Planning Research, 1997).

sample of adults said that learning was 'very important' to them personally, and another 27% said that it was 'fairly important'. This is nothing new. High ratings of this kind have been found in many surveys over the years. Evidence from the 14th British Social Attitudes Survey supports the general attitude. Figure 2.13 shows the high and rising importance which respondents gave to education as a priority for public expenditure. Public support for education has now overtaken the support for the old-age pension as a spending priority.

There were also good indications in the early 1990s of a rising interest in learning among workers.[14] The reputation of 'good training' had risen so far in the estimation of workers, as a feature of a 'good job', that it was on a par with 'good pay'. This interest applied consistently across the labour force whatever the qualification background of the worker responding. The question left by all these expressions of general support is whether or not people can translate the general attitude into a specific personal commitment. According to the test of actual involvement, a large minority still thinks that 'learning is for other people'.

Employers also profess strongly supportive general attitudes. Figure 2.14, taken from an official 1994 survey of employers,[15] shows strong support for lifelong learning in principle – right across the size spectrum of employers – and for the role of employers in encouraging workers towards ongoing training. Moreover, over 90% of employers saw advantages to their organization in 'lifetime' learning, compared to only 30% who saw any disadvantages. Again a large gap can be seen between general attitude and actual support for learning, particularly if it is general rather than job-specific learning.

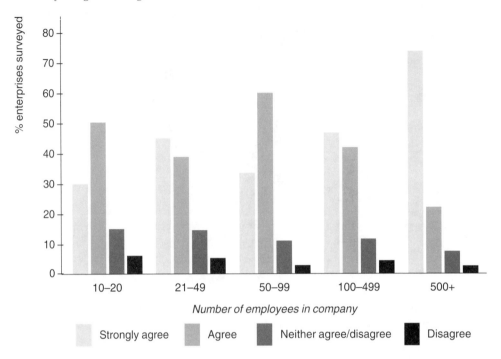

Figure 2.14 Employers' views on lifelong learning ('People should be encouraged to participate in training throughout their adult lives'). Source: *Employers' Attitudes*, Research Series No. 40, Metcalf *et al.* (1994).

Expectations of future learning

A sharper test of commitment to learning is asking how likely it is that a person will do any learning in the next 2–3 years. NALS'97 pressed this question, with the results as shown in Figures 2.15 and 2.16. One-fifth of learners and one-half of non-learners say they are not at all likely to undertake non-job-related learning. The comparable figures for job-related learning are 17% and 57% respectively. These figures show the fruits of the learning divide: those with a history of learning have stronger expectations to go on learning, and vice versa. The non-learning quarter of the population simply projects its non-learning into the future, helping to replicate the cultural problem.

NALS'97 explored this slough of low expectations closely. About one-fifth of adults had done no learning since leaving education, or in the previous ten years. On average, one in two of these say that nothing would encourage them to learn. The proportion increases as it spreads across the age groups: it is 20% for adults under the age of 30; and 70% for 60–69-year-olds. Overall there is a hard core of around 10% of the total population who appear to have abandoned learning altogether. Studies done for the DfEE show that the mind-set of this hard core is extremely resistant to influence. Like a hedgehog, the more it is prodded, the more tightly it curls up into a ball. Group theory holds that members of groups, if put under challenge, tend to root even more firmly into the cultural narratives which give a sense of identity to the group. So people who end up in the motivational black hole may well say that learning is a good thing . . . but find every reason why it is not for them.

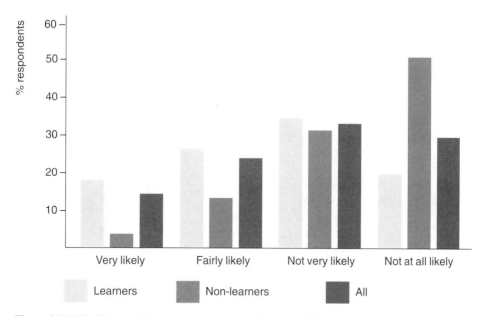

Figure 2.15 Likelihood of future non-job-related learning ('How likely is it that you will do any non-job-related learning in the next two to three years?'). Population surveyed is aged 16–69, in England and Wales. Source: *National Adult Learning Survey* (Beinart and Smith, 1997).

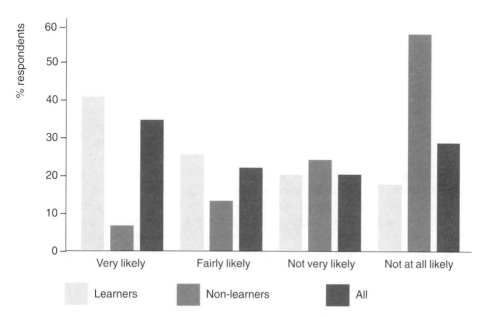

Figure 2.16 Likelihood of future job-related learning ('How likely is it that you will do any job-related learning in the next two to three years?'). Population surveyed is aged 16–69, in England and Wales. Source: *National Adult Learning Survey* (Beinart and Smith, 1997).

Access constraints

Table 2.1 shows what non-learners in general feel about particular obstacles to learning. The distraction of other claims on personal time – particularly family ties and time constraints at work – emerge very clearly. Although greater availability of time would shift only a small proportion of hardcore non-learners back into learning, these factors would appear to pull significant weight among half-involved learners.

Table 2.1 Selected obstacles to learning: non-learners' views.
Source: *National Adult Learning Survey* (Beinart and Smith, 1997).

Obstacle	%
Prefer other things	47
Not interested	32
Too busy with work	24
No time because of family	32
Hard to pay fees	19
Know too little about opportunities	22
Don't have the necessary qualifications	21
Too old	26

Figure 2.17 shows vividly how time in the middle years of life is squeezed by family constraints, corresponding to the main phase of child-rearing. If there is to be continuity of learning across the ages, this is one of the major hurdles to overcome, for even when the time constraints ease in the older age groups, the propensity to learn is not rebuilt. Figure 2.18 shows how people increasingly fall prey to the fallacy that they are too old to learn, as they move into older age groups. Financial problems are also important, although probably not quite so strong as the general shortage of time. Notably, the money factor does not seem to rise in importance as an obstacle for older age groups.

The educational media are still full of 'If only' analyses of non-participation in learning, framed almost entirely in terms of non-motivational barriers to access. The statistics simply do not bear out the overwhelming weight given to this. Reducing access constraints is very important, but motivation remains the fundamental influence behind non-learners. Even if a wand could be waved to cancel *all* the constraints, it would only bring into learning people in two categories: those who want to learn but who are prevented by specific constraints; and those who want to learn but whose sense of general difficulty paralyses their active search for learning. These are not the same as people who just choose to do other things with their time and money.

According to the NALS'97 evidence, and taking motivation for what it is, resolving all access problems might raise participation among the non-learners (defined on the NALS'97 three-year measure) by about one-third – that is, by about 7.5% of the population as a whole. By contrast, a fundamental expansion of motivation could shift the volume and pattern of learning radically. This is where cultural policies and policies for general economic incentives come to the fore. *The battle against non-participation will never be won simply by measures such as flexible opening times, convenient learning centres, or more effective brokerage in the learning market, and the like.*

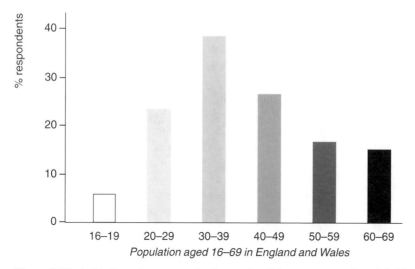

Figure 2.17 Attitude to time constraint by age band (per cent agreeing with 'No time to learn because of family'). Source: *National Adult Learning Survey* (Beinart and Smith, 1997).

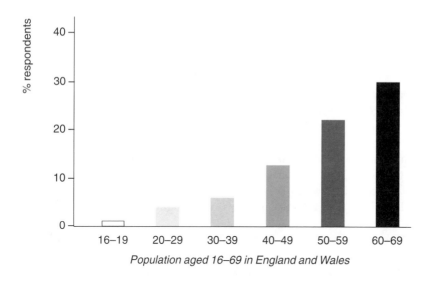

Figure 2.18 Attitude age and learning by age band (per cent agreeing with 'Too old to learn'). Source: *National Adult Learning Survey* (Beinart and Smith, 1997).

MOTIVATION

People's motivation to learn is influenced by a whole range of factors. These include the enjoyment derived from learning; the rewards for learning offered in the general economy, through wages and employment prospects; the impact of learning providers' particular reputations; the impact of general wider cultural influences – often through friends and family – which turn learning into 'something that people like me do'; and the role of society itself and of government, in stimulating individuals' motivation to learn.

There is good evidence that many people find that learning is intrinsically rewarding. NALS'97 shows that three-fifths of adult learners and half of non-learners agree strongly that 'learning about new things is enjoyable'. But by the same token, 40% or more are lukewarm at best, and hostile at worst. Among young people at school: 80% enjoy learning new things, but 22% find learning positively boring;[16] over one-quarter of 16–19-year-olds do not enjoy learning at school;[17] and up to one-fifth of students do not enjoy their university experience.[18] The initial education system is not therefore seen as a pleasurable experience by a sizeable minority of those attending. It is likely that those who do best in the system, and who stay the longest, get the best intrinsic return. Those who are switched off as learners leave early, and obtain fewer leaving qualifications. These become the non-learners of the future, and are predominantly from the lower socio-economic groups.

Most primary schools are full of children keen to learn.[19] Difficulties start to mount in the secondary years. There are many influences at work, but the rising demotivation at the secondary stage has much to do with the inflexibility of the official curriculum, and the risk of failure in the competitive atmosphere which pervades many schools. The predominance given to academic values concentrates on just a narrow band of talents and intelligences. It does not naturally suit more than 40% of the age cohort. The sense of failure in poor examination results and in school selection processes runs deep, and causes many young people to truant and to leave full-time education early, in an effort to construct an alternative identity and build self-esteem by unofficial means.

The introduction of comprehensive schools has been in progress in the UK for 60 years, and is not yet complete. It is clear that the statistics on participation would have been even worse if this change had not been implemented. The current progress of the 'comprehensive project' indicates the strength of resistance to educational reform among those who benefit from the *status quo*. Whereas Labour once declared it would abolish selection, the first New Labour government has introduced new grounds for selectivity. Early selection by 'ability' (see Box 2.1) means, in fact, selection according to social class. The success of selective schools then blights the rest of secondary education.

The cultural process which leads to demotivation is like a searchlight. It highlights young people who do well at academic subject disciplines, indicating routes to success through universities which have a good reputation among employers, and thereafter into professional jobs of good standing. The price to society as a whole of that selectivity is that many other young people fall into the shadows of reduced motivation, where many – particularly those with less favoured family backgrounds – lose their way. They do not easily recover, nor are they in education long enough to develop fully as autonomous, self-directed learners, confidently pursuing a chosen learning path. They are likely to show little personal or social commitment to learning.

At the other end of the age spectrum, another major switch-off happens. As the memory of school experiences lessens, the deep ageism of contemporary culture begins to take a grip. Society has afforded so much status to breadwinners that, by comparison, people classified as non-breadwinners – especially older age groups – become relegated and patronized. Myths about older people's learning incompetence

- The 1988 Education Reform Act allowed Grant Maintained schools to control their own admission of pupils. They were allowed to select up to 10 per cent of pupils on the basis of *ability*. This was later increased to 15 per cent.

- The Specialist Schools Initiative allows any school to select up to 10 per cent of pupils on the basis of *aptitude for a particular subject*.

- A subsequent ruling ('the Greenwich ruling') said any local authority must allow pupils to apply for admission into its schools, regardless of where they live.

- A further ruling ('the Rotherham judgement') barred education authorities from 'ring fencing' their schools in order to create what would effectively be catchment areas.

- The effect of these legislative developments, under both Conservative and New Labour governments, is that all schools are open to all comers.

- The 1997 Schools Bill proposed that each LEA area should have a forum to co-ordinate admissions, under general guidance from the DfEE. If its members fail to agree, an adjudicator on school organization and admissions will make a decision.

Box 2.1 Creeping selection. Source: adapted from Whitehead (1998).

are strong in the current dominant culture, and the value of people in the 'third' and 'fourth' age[20] as a major resource to support other people's learning is largely ignored.

Economic rewards provide a different route to motivation. Vocational learning dominates the total picture of participation in adult learning. The progressive reduction in learning with increasing age, the thin pickings for learning in the lower socio-economic groups, and the poor learning record of flexible workers, all have their origins in a narrow and short-term approach by employers to investment in skills. This goes with an inability to structure wages and promotions to reward the learner in line with the value of learning to the business. If employers took a more robust, longer-term view it would enliven the whole learning system. But – as with individuals – employers' generally favourable attitudes towards lifelong learning do not translate well into day-to-day practice.[21]

There are really two routes for employers to follow. On the first, companies with sustainable success (not just short-term winnings) are those which aggressively seek new business on the basis that they already have highly flexible workforces or can assemble them quickly. These organizations are able to deliver quality high technology products and services in a very competitive time frame. Winning business challenges the ability of such organizations to marshal and bring to bear the skills and knowledge needed to fulfil the contract. Either employers find the skilled people they require in their organization, or if necessary they have to bring them in fast at premium rates. Either way, the employers are making strong signals to the labour market; and people with the necessary skills move in to compete for the jobs. Other individuals – and those who advise them – will start to see opportunities for personal development in the same or related occupations. This process underwrites speculative learning in the learning market. When the learning and labour markets both respond well, firms that have invested in skills make and hold their gains in product market share.

On the second route, employers remain stuck in the low-skills equilibrium. This is a depressed state, where employers *assume in advance* that they will fail to find the skills needed to capture the business, and do nothing about it, and where longer-term organizational development is not a priority. This inertia is currently the predominant condition for UK employers.

The effect on the learning market is deeply damaging. Individuals come under more and more pressure to recognize and interpret learning opportunities in an informational vacuum, and to make risky personal investments with unclear rewards. It can be an expensive pig in a poke. A 1993 national survey[22] showed quite clearly that vocational learning funded by individuals – 17% of episodes – was beginning to pick up. This probably reflected the fact that the job market was becoming more uncertain and that employers could not be relied on to pay for all the necessary training. But *only half the episodes of individually funded learning were seen as having any sort of economic pay off.*[23] This is significantly less than for learning which is employer-funded, still the predominant funding approach.

The national Investors in People (IiP) training standard was introduced in 1990 to help companies to tighten up their skills investment and management. It is slow but important work. A recent national survey[24] showed that 13% of organizations had achieved the standard in its first eight years. Culture change takes time.

A recent CBI consultation paper identifies the employer's role in a 'new partnership' to support individuals' employability[25] – involving individuals; employers; government and its agencies; education and training providers; and supporting bodies such as unions, trade associations and the voluntary sector. Workers' motivation would certainly be strengthened if the employers were to collaborate with them, defining joint strategies for personal development which would be properly rewarded, and which would benefit the employing organizations as well as individuals' employability. It would foster personal commitment, remove risk, and minimize the possibility of the workers leaving after undertaking the learning.

The latter is the main message of the 1993 Employment in Britain[26] survey: that firms which have good training strategies tend to attract and to keep good staff, rather than to lose them through poaching by other employers. Loyalty grows, rather than the opposite, as many employers seem to fear. There are good business reasons therefore for employers to be involved in general education for all workers, but especially for the least skilled. If the organization is to have the flexibility and the vitality which underpins success against global competition, every worker must be a lifelong learner.

These kinds of shifts in employment culture can boost learning participation by older workers and by lower occupational groups. The stimulus of that – working back through workers, their families and communities – would help to transform the current learning culture. Unless this happens, the economic rewards for learning will remain weak and contested.

This weakness is a particular feature at intermediate and craft level – the very area where the UK's skills profile is out of line internationally. While rates of return to individuals for university study are strong enough to enable graduates to service student loans, the average rates of return for lower qualifications (as a highest personal qualification) seem to be marginal. The playing field is tilted in favour of those with the most going for them. The rates of return for the others will only become more buoyant, and an open labour market with proper rewards for skill will only develop, if employers compete aggressively on the basis of being learning organizations.

Motivation and the impact of providers' activity
We have already seen how the supply side of initial education works – creaming off those with a head-start in personal development, while deflating and detaching many of the rest. As a system to produce lifelong learners, this is a fiasco. The process of deflation and detachment is closely bound up in government policies for funding the initial education system, and for managing the school choices made by pupils and their parents.

In state schools, money follows the pupils. Schools with healthy recruitment attract more cash; those which lose enrolment find cash ebbing away. The effects of this at the secondary stage are particularly significant for lifelong learning. The bulk of schools are comprehensive; but selective and self-managing schools include former grammar schools, with long histories and often a high reputation. This funding system allows parents to vote for the selective strand, forcing other schools to be less comprehensive than they might wish – for when these schools begin to lose money they try to raise their performance in the government's published academic league tables to redress the balance. This system produces unstable pupil recruitment patterns at local level, and a heavy emphasis on tests and examination results.

In many parts of the country, great stress falls on young pupils at the beginning of the secondary years, where the tension between selective recruitment and comprehensive education is strong. For those who do not meet the relevant criteria, the process of selection itself may be little short of traumatic (see Box 2.2). The effect is to exacerbate the switch-off effect for large numbers of lower-class children who, by default, find themselves clustered in weak and declining schools with a cultural imbalance. Thus the market processes, and the competitive funding system which goes with them, serve to widen the motivational gap, not to close it.

Similar processes are at work in initial further education and – less damagingly – in the universities. The competitive funding structures – supported for the government by funding councils – maintain a wide range of reputations among the institutions. This

---

In the Watford area of south-west Hertfordshire parents may apply to ten Grant Maintained schools, most using a selective test to choose up to half their intake, and to two council-run comprehensive schools. Parents have to apply separately to each school: some try for six or more, and their children may be offered places at them all. Others are less lucky:

> Rachael is suffering the after-effects of a road accident, and has problems travelling by car. Her parents applied to three Grant Maintained schools near her home. She sat the common entrance test for each school, but failed each. Further rejection letters arrived after the following three school selection rounds. 'She's devastated,' said her mother. 'It's worse than the 11-Plus, when you were told you failed [only] once. She's been through it four times . . . She can't bear to talk about it.'

Box 2.2 Parental 'choice'. Source: adapted from Whitehead (1998).

allows the middle classes to vote for selective academic education. Their decisions can be underwritten by cash flows pumped into the institutions 'through the back door' (as opposed to 'over the counter', when the learner pays) according to numbers recruited. So sixth-form colleges in further education attract high-achieving young people, on a narrow academic curriculum choice, premised on university entry. This leaves further education colleges with a generally lower status and a more vocational role. Very similar processes operate between the old (high status) universities, and the newer universities converted from polytechnics in 1992.

These processes add to demotivation in two ways. Firstly, the academic bias means that a significant proportion of students taking the academic route are not altogether suited to the demands that it makes. Secondly, those who seek to do well in the more meagerly funded institutions find that – irrespective of personal talent – their ultimate prospects in the labour market are likely to be adversely affected, by comparison with institutions accorded a better reputation. The demotivating effect is likely to diminish with the learner's increasing maturity. Whatever the damage done earlier, learners who have gained an advanced level qualification are unlikely to sink into 'Learning's not for me' attitudes simply because they are not at an institution with the highest reputation among employers and others.

The supply side in initial learning also influences motivation through gender and ethnicity. There is a general lack of role models for young males. The preponderance of staff are female, particularly in primary schools. This is an important aspect of the relative under-performance of boys evident in the early teenage years. Many research studies show that both 'whiteness' and 'maleness' pervade the ethos of higher educational institutions. This can prompt strong feelings of alienation among some learners in the last stages of initial education, especially those from groups whose own cultures do not strongly associate men with learning.

In post-initial learning, the impact of providers' activities is not always encouraging for learners' motivation. Figure 2.19[27] reveals *by clear implication* a serious degree of dissatisfaction with providers, across a wide range of different types of learning. It has three notable features. There is a widespread, basic unease about the standards of service, involving 30%–40% of the client group. If this were the experience of non-educational industry, these ratings would be seen as nothing short of a calamity. At first sight it is not easy to see why this position is endured. But there is an understandable tendency for students to rationalize their problems, for example by finding 'good' reasons why the wrong course was 'right' after all. This may well be a cultural legacy of school life, where teacher knows best and where grin-and-bear-it is the best strategy for personal survival. This is the precise opposite of the qualities needed to exercise personal commitment in the learning market.

Figure 2.19 also shows the lack of good care experienced by learners at the end of the course. At least 80% of all learners feel that they do not get good support from the provider of learning at the end of the learning episode. A survey of learning providers' attitudes undertaken by the government in 1994[28] made a related point. It revealed that only 9% of providers targeted previous students in their marketing efforts. So much for the continuity of learning; and so much for help in applying that learning effectively.

There is also a high level of learners' dissatisfaction with the standard of teaching. This reflects poor working conditions, the poor professional standing of teachers, and

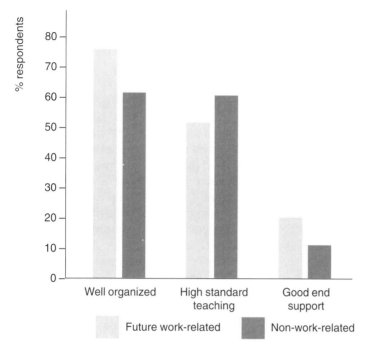

Figure 2.19 Positive perceptions of the learning episode: selected categories of learning. Population surveyed aged 16–69, in England and Wales. Source: *National Adult Learning*

– in universities – the influence of research activities which state-funding mechanisms strongly promote. High teacher motivation is needed if the learners themselves are to develop a self-sustaining momentum towards learning. Public respect is part of this equation. Survey work by OECD[29] shows that public respect in the UK for secondary school teachers as professionals is below the international average for a range of OECD countries, and very significantly lower than for the United States.

Many of these phenomena reflect the dynamics of current funding. Large parts of the system depend substantially on backdoor public funding through bureaucratic channels. In this situation it is the state – always seeking to squeeze the last ounce of economy out of the learning system – which to a large degree determines workers' conditions and rates of pay, and sets the scene for insensitive treatment of learners.

The effects of adult guidance should be added to these considerations. Many studies attest to the strong motivations towards learning which are created by guidance.[30] But NALS'97, despite weaknesses of definition, records that three-quarters of the adult population had never received any guidance; and some 13% of long-term non-learners said that they did not know where to go to get information and advice. These gaps reflect the long-term failure of the guidance industry and successive governments to find ways of making information and guidance readily available to all who need it.

The result increases the risks that learners will make expensive mistakes, and that the difficulty of finding suitable learning will dent their perseverance. Moreover the impact will be selective in its effect. In the learning market, evidence shows that learners depend heavily on information and advice from colleagues and friends. Those who become removed from these networks – through unemployment, or being single parents, or being retired, for example – find that involvement in learning becomes systematically more difficult.

Motivation and the impact of general cultural changes
The level of motivation in the UK's learning culture has to be seen against the wider cultural background. In particular it must be set in the context of the relativist storms of postmodernism, the globalization of the economy, and the homogenizing effects of footloose informational technologies. It is not that these pressures themselves undermine the will to learn – this is not like the effect of Darwin on the old-time religions. The opposite is true. The problem seems to be that in the current learning culture and its supporting arrangements, it is difficult for the curriculum to offer opportunities to people across all the age bands to consider and come to terms with the huge implications of these concerns and changes.

While institutions at every level spend time on heaving themselves into a position of relevance, or defending the indefensible – or (often) trying to do both – individuals will be looking for learning that helps them with identification and self-discovery in a postmodern environment. Already, according to a recent survey,[31] the most salient theme for encouraging learning is 'to discover the talents within you'. *This is now far stronger than economic reasons or 'fun' as a theme for the marketing of learning.* The official curriculum in the schools, and the stronghold of academic subjects in state education, are out of joint with this for most people. A new model is long overdue.

Motivation and the role of society and government
When the general learning culture is failing, it is for society – and most especially for government – to provide real incentives and encouragement. What is happening here?

There is little overt societal celebration of learning in the current general culture. Research[32] shows that about two-thirds of individuals think their relatives would encourage them, and be happy if they undertook vocational learning (see Figure 2.20). This proportion falls to 45% when reflecting the expected attitude of friends; 30% when applied to colleagues; and is almost halved (35%) for employers. For non-learners the fall-off in support is even more substantial. This is a glimpse of a rather aloof attitude to encouragement across society. It reflects the individualized, competitive educational traditions in Britain. In terms of lifelong learning principles, it shows low social commitment.

The government must therefore accept a heavy obligation to provide a lead and, if need be, the incentives. The provision of free educational entitlements to young people prevents a massive worsening in the socio-economic profiles of learning, compared to the current record. But the effectiveness of that intervention is greatly reduced by the ways in which government policy allows so many young people from unprivileged backgrounds to be squeezed out of the learning system. Even if that were put right, there would still be a need for major additional redistributive funding from government, to level up the learning playing field. But no such initiatives are on offer. Instead of redistribution, the emphasis in recent years has been on talking up the role of the employer, and on focusing on the individual to energize the learning scene. Though both employer and individual have key roles to play, this strategy cannot solve the problem.

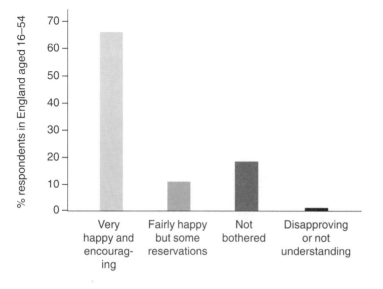

Figure 2.20   Attitude of family to vocational learning. Source: Individual Attitudes Survey, *Research Series 32* (DfEE, 1994).

NOTES AND REFERENCES

1. Office for National Statistics (1998).
2. Bynner and Parsons (1997).
3. National Child Development Cohort: a group of over 17,000 people born in one week in 1958.
4. Department for Education and Employment and the Cabinet Office (1996).
5. Sargant *et al.* (1997).
6. See: Hogarth *et al.* (1997).
7. Robertson and Hillman (1997).
8. Gallie and White (1993).
9. Baltes and Graf (1996).
10. Payne, Cheng and Witherspoon (1996).
11. Coffield and Vignoles (1997).
12. Confederation of British Industry (1994).
13. Social and Community Planning Research (1997).
14. Gallie and White (1993).
15. Metcalf, Walling and Fogarty (1994).
16. MORI (1998).
17. Beinart and Smith (1997).
18. Hogarth *et al.* (1997).
19. (1) National Commission on Education (1993); (2) Office for Standards in Education (1998).
20. 'Third age' = early fifties onwards; 'fourth age' = final period of dwindling energy in old age – exact age varies from one individual to another, but generally not applied before the early/mid-eighties.
21. Metcalf *et al.* (1994).
22. Park (1994).

23. Tremlett, Park and Dundon-Smith (1995).
24. IFF Research (1998).
25. CBI (1998). 'Employability' is defined by the CBI as, 'the possession by an individual of the qualities and competences required to meet the changing needs of employers and customers and thereby help to realise his or her aspirations and potential in work'.
26. Gallie and White (1993).
27. Beinart and Smith (1997)
28. Tremlett, Thomas and Taylor (1995).
29. OECD (1995).
30. Coopers and Lybrand (1995).
31. MORI (1998).
32. Social and Community Planning Research (1997).

Chapter 3

A Vision for Lifelong Learning

The current learning culture described in Chapter 2 runs very deep and is most unlikely to evolve of its own accord into a general lifelong learning culture. The fundamentals will continue to reassert themselves. The profound nature of the changes needed means that policy reform must be more radical than anything so far envisaged. Government's wrestling with this difficult truth was apparent in its consultation paper, *The Learning Age*, published in February 1998. This opened with an enlightened vision but the essential message of the substance, culturally speaking, was 'more of the same'. Subsequent developments have simply confirmed this.

A number of convenient reductions currently buzz around the idea of lifelong learning. These imply that it is just a glossy way to refer to adult learning; or to continuing education; or to an increase in the overall volume of learning nationally – irrespective of who is doing it and how continuously. They all avoid the uncomfortable fact that establishing a general culture of lifelong learning means turning the nation's learning habits, practices and systems inside out.

This is not a revolution in the sense that current systems have to be razed to the ground before their replacements are brought in. It does, however, mean an early revolution in attitudes, enabling the nation to make a determined, progressive attempt on a new course. It will take time to follow through, which is why this book looks forward across a generation.

LIFELONG LEARNING VALUES: SUPPORTING DISCOURSES

Our definition of lifelong learning envisages people learning consistently through life. The accent is on *continuity, intention* and *unfolding strategy* in personal learning. Beside these are the four principles of *personal commitment, social commitment, respect for others' learning,* and *respect for the truth.* These capture the vital spark of personal keenness, and the sense of delight in learning which can be so infectious that it helps others to learn. But they also include procedural values which create environments for others to learn; and they establish the paramount importance of truthful learning, rather than what is merely fantastical or politically correct. So there is a strong conceptual link between lifelong learning and the values of democratic debate. The occasional passion of the current debate reflects the potential of lifelong learning as *the learning dimension of democracy itself.*

This chapter examines four supporting discourses for these values: group learning; learning theory; economic externalities; and equality of opportunity.

Group learning

David Clark's work on the school as learning community[1] expresses a vision of learning which has strong affinities with the vision of lifelong learning presented here. For him, learning is best seen as a group activity. If the learning group is properly managed and constructed, the psychology of group membership reinforces the learning capacity of the individuals within the group. At the same time members of the group help each other to learn.

Research shows[2] that individuals have much to gain through learning collaboratively in appropriately structured and conducted groups. The most constructive dynamics works when individual members feel a sense of common purpose with the group, while at the same time feeling that the group recognizes their individual importance and potential contribution. This can be expressed as group identity, and as personal identity, respectively. At the simplest level, the learning group establishes a secure and comfortable environment which is highly conducive to learning. Such supportive group learning is more motivating for the bulk of learners than learning in an individualistic, competitive group environment, or on their own (see Box 3.1).

There is a drawback to this theory. The saliency of learning in the group depends on the group as a whole standing in contrast to – and, to a degree, in opposition to –

Research among college students in North America showed that collaborative learning promoted greater individual achievement than competitive or individualistic efforts in:

- verbal tasks;
- mathematical tasks;
- procedural tasks, such as swimming, golf, tennis.

Co-operation was also shown to promote:

- greater intrinsic motivation to learn;
- higher self-esteem;
- more frequent use of thought processes, such as rethinking knowledge, higher-level reasoning, flexibility and elaboration of thought, networking;
- greater long-term maintenance of the skills learned;
- social skills.

Box 3.1 Benefits of collaborative learning. Source: adapted from Johnson and Johnson (1993).

other groups. Any threat to the group itself from those other groups will enhance its members' sense both of their group identity and of their identity as individuals. In certain environments it is this phenomenon which turns the margins between distinctive groups and other groups into contested areas.

One way out of this in the learning context is to develop groups at another (categorically higher) level to which members of different lower-level groups also belong. Here they can work to resolve any tensions between the lower-level groups. According to Clark, schools should show young people how to learn in small groups, and also how to learn and negotiate within higher and wider groups for the common good. In this way, schools can mirror in miniature collaborative learning relationships between the diverse elements of a multicultural population.

In this model, there is a close overlap between our lifelong learning principle of 'personal commitment' and what Clark means by the individual's sense of identity as a learner. Similarly, 'social commitment' is very closely related to the individual's sense of group identity, which is the basis for co-operative and altruistic learning activity.

What this underlines strongly is that learning in properly constituted and well-led groups has a particularly valuable contribution to make to the development of a lifelong learning culture. This is especially true of learning groups mixed by age and background, closest to the mixed communities of everyday life.

Box 3.2, drawn from North American research among learners in colleges, shows that successful group learning in an institutional setting does not necessarily happen spontaneously. Teachers and students alike have to learn the relevant skills.

Research into collaborative learning identified five essential elements in achieving effective co-operative action:

1. Instructors must carefully structure positive interdependence to ensure that all students are committed to each other as persons and to each other's success.

2. Each student must be held accountable for exerting maximum efforts to learn by his or her peers.

3. Students must meet and promote each other's learning, face to face.

4. The teamwork skills required to co-ordinate efforts to complete joint assignments must be directly taught and mastered.

5. Finally, team members must gather data on their own progress and plan how to improve the process they are using to learn.

Box 3.2 Teaching group learning. Source: adapted from Johnson and Johnson (1993).

Learning theory and the brain

Further support for the definitions and values of lifelong learning lies in the biological learning theories of G. and R. Caine.[3] The human brain seems to be programmed to learn in group situations, where security, personal individuation and group identity all work together to maximize the efficiency of learning. The Caines hold that the would-be learner who feels under threat from the group – who does not feel personally committed to it or to its members, and who actively rejects the notion of being part of the group – will 'down-shift' to a psychologically lower level. 'Down-shifting' for the brain is very like what happens when the fire alarm goes off in a public place: a sense of danger prompts ancient circuitry in the primitive core of the brain to take over, posing simple 'fight or flight' choices for survival, and blotting other considerations out. This captures what happens when people 'freeze' over mental arithmetic. It also captures the quandary of alienated school pupils.

According to such theories, group learning initiatives can avert the antagonism of determined non-groupies. Experience shows that pupils who are aggressive in the academic environment of a formal classroom can co-operate willingly in an environment which they find comfortable. The most persistent young rebels have, for example, learnt self-discipline and co-operation in restoring old cars to drive competitively off-road. Even young people heading for delinquency can learn effectively – given the right kind of support, recognition of what is important to them. a non-threatening environment, positive role models, and good teaching.

This certainly does not mean that private, individualistic learning cannot be effective – only that it is something of a special case. Such learning is a refined skill, much more effective when the learner has had good experience as a successful group learner.

Externalities of learning

Another way of looking at much the same thing involves 'externalities' (incidental external effects). In Margaret Thatcher's neo-classical economic world, the optimum learning system would have personal commitment to learning expressing itself freely in a competitive marketplace. No other sort of commitment counts. So every individual person would learn for entirely self-regarding reasons, and any knock-on effects could quite simply be dismissed. If everyone behaved in this way there would be gross under-investment in learning, because it would completely ignore externalities.

There are two sorts of externalities connected with learning: those which directly affect learning decisions; and those which create public goods.

Externalities affecting learning decisions
Several possibilities exist:

- The learner becomes more skilled at learning as a by-product of a learning episode, and so it reduces costs to that individual of potential further learning. This may even open up whole areas of learning which have previously been unfeasible. It is an argument for encouraging people to learn more than they might initially seek to do.
- The greater the number of people learning something, the cheaper it is for each to learn it. One person's learning may produce new knowledge which, once recognized, can be made available to others without loss. What is more, the learning may lower the marginal cost of gaining access to stocks of knowledge and skills, for those other learners. With few exceptions, the access to knowledge shows increasing returns to scale.

- The learning which an individual does can be a demonstration for other potential learners. This can reduce the perceived risks or enhance the sense of the benefits associated with learning. It can even directly influence other learners' tastes and preferences.

All these are beneficial externalities relating to learning itself. They seldom feature in official policy discussion.

Externalities creating a public good
A public good is something which can be shared in use, and which cannot be sold for a price because there is no way to prevent people from enjoying it for free. Into this category fall public goods such as security, law and order, and good environments. Such goods, if not freely available, may well have to be provided by the state through general taxation (or in some particular cases by subscription clubs), because no one can make and distribute them through private market exchange.

These goods are vitally important to everyday social and economic life. John Gray argues[4] that they are even necessary for the operation of free trading markets, for without the trust and assurance behind market dealings, markets will work badly or not at all.

Learning creates valuable public goods of many different kinds as free by-products of the activity – for example, richer appreciation of heritage and culture; stronger social leadership; less prejudice and discrimination; greater vigilance against threats; greater social cohesion and inclusiveness; a sense of freedom. It is largely for these reasons that governments are ready to spend large sums on learning.

These two classes of externality link directly to the principle of commitment to learning.

- *Personal commitment:* produces private investors in learning who are keen to snap up the personal opportunities. Such people manage their learning in the way in which readers of the *Financial Times* manage their shares, along with the externalities which can be individually enjoyed.
- *Social commitment:* relates to the externalities which are public goods. It recognizes that in many cases the social externalities of learning can be fostered – that they are contingent on people looking in the right direction at the right time. People who are keen to spread their learning, and to make it work in the community, are doing much the same as the person who sets out her garden so that passers-by can also enjoy the flowers.

In economic terms, individual and social commitment need to work side by side to secure the proper balance between immediate private benefit and the externalities, particularly the public goods, which flow from learning. Efficiency is not only about immediate private returns. Lifelong learning and economic efficiency are not in conflict.

Equal opportunity

Every individual has what some call intelligences[5] – or, biblically, talents[6] – as a result of inheritance and nurture. Underlying our view of lifelong learning is the belief that every person should be able to discover what those talents are, find strategies to apply them, and be free to develop them. People will lead more fulfilled and creative lives if they do, and society at large will benefit. Moreover, the vast majority of individuals gain satisfaction not only from their own feelings of self-worth, but also from seeing relatives and other people developing their potential. These satisfactions seem to be universal across cultures.

Whatever its source and purpose, this interest leads people to *want* to even up the chances of self-development between different people. This is the *equality of opportunity* principle in learning, leading back again to social commitment. It promotes in individuals an active commitment to work which helps to even up other people's life chances for learning.

Overview of lifelong learning values

Summing up, it seems that the central principles of personal and social commitment to learning are sustained by four thoughts:

1. they are consistent with the doctrines of effective learning in groups;
2. they are in line with the implications of research into the way people use their brains to learn;
3. they show how the tension between personal and social commitment offers what is needed to reach efficient learning arrangements – once economic efficiency is properly defined to recognize external benefits, as well as immediate private ones;
4. they fall in with the widespread ethical concern for equality of opportunity in learning.

Two procedural values complete the picture: treating people courteously in their learning (respect for others' learning); and not obstructing learning by distortion and lies (respect for the truth).

Respect for others' learning is essentially practical. Experience teaches that unless we listen to others and concede their right to learn we place in jeopardy all the objectives which we are seeking: effective personal learning, efficiency in learning, and equality of opportunity.

Respect for truth is supported by a powerful argument, based on historical experience. People who have no respect for the truth are quick to stop other people finding it out – even at the cost of their own learning. They are the first to obstruct educational institutions and to persecute teachers. There is something here also of Paulo Freire's idea of learning as a *naming* of the world.[7] The pursuit of truth in critical learning is about learners breaking out of the silence of the oppressed state, and reaching the freedom to attach their own label to aspects of the world – saying, in effect, 'This is my truth. I have the power to name it, therefore I am free.' Our definition of lifelong learning centres on this fundamental assertion of the human spirit.

DEVELOPING THE LIFELONG LEARNING CULTURE

Developing a process for culture change means taking particular account of three influential features: biodiversity; cultural assimilation; and critical mass.

Biodiversity

A multicultural basis for lifelong learning has important implications. The passion behind the drive for lifelong learning can develop a dangerously patronizing bias, specifically favouring institutionalized, white male culture. Many people who attended the First Global Conference on Lifelong Learning (in Rome, 1994)[8] were uneasy on these grounds, for example.

The work on social identity by Michael Hogg and Dominic Abrams[9] identifies the danger. A widely held 'social mobility myth' teaches that individuals can move successfully from a socially subordinate group into the dominant group through assiduous networking and personal hard graft, without loss of identity. Politicians in the dominant group will go to great lengths to perpetuate this view, while doing little or nothing to change underlying economic and social barriers. But the individualistic strategies which socially mobile people need to pursue *necessarily* mean casting aside their subordinate group identity.

> Since this [individualistic] strategy leaves the *status quo* unchanged, in terms of the status and power relations between groups. and inhibits collective action such as riots and demonstrations on the part of the subordinate group, it is clearly very much in the interests of the dominant group to promulgate an ideology of social mobility. This is the 'myth' of individual freedom which characterizes some contemporary western capitalist societies ... Those few who do [make such a move], do so almost by special dispensation in order to perpetuate the myth, to become the token woman truck driver, or token black solicitor. (Hogg and Abrams, 1988)

It is easy to see why the myth of social mobility appeals to Western governments, and why a strategy by the dominant culture only giving *the appearance* of change actually reinforces the current culture.

As long as policy-makers stand on the ground presently taken by the educated elite in the UK – inviting other cultures in the community to 'come and join us' – it is unlikely that anything will change. This includes the underlying power structures which formed the elite in the first place, and similarly with a 'let us come and convert you' doctrine.

In this context, the educational commentator Michael Apple has written lucidly[10] about the New Right education policies now growing in strength in the United States. These seek an all-American 'melting pot' solution to the education of the diverse cultures across the States. This says that it is not for groups such as the Hispanics, the Jews and the Blacks to find what suits them best – that there should be a common curriculum based on the 'sound' values of the dominant (largely fundamentalist Christian) culture. The strain of such policy is sharp and painful. It sacrifices cultural biodiversity, and it leaves behind a trail of personal distress and psychological maladjustment as the unnecessary loss of personal identity and group-belonging takes hold.

This 'homogenizing' model of cultural development is inconsistent with our lifelong learning culture's basic tenets. The whole point of learning to listen and to pay respect is to avoid cultural colonization. It is aimed at preserving a diversity of viewpoints, rather than crushing those regarded by a dominant culture as 'crude' in the interests of promoting others labelled 'refined'.

Assimilation of lifelong learning into particular cultural settings

Much of the cultural diversity in the current UK learning scene tends to be submerged by the patterning of socio-economic status, and of employment status and age. A move to lifelong learning must be a culturally sensitive process. It will have to take account of the finer grain of difference.

Differentiated cultures of learning range across a wide spectrum. At one end are long-established, close-knit groups, whose cultural traditions have supported survival and prosperity in often hostile environments. At the other extreme are life-in-the-fast-lane cultures focused on youth, usually associated with short-term, loosely knit groupings. The first tend to value ancient texts, and to have traditions of didactic teaching based on a canon of literature. They also celebrate experience, and old people who embody it. Groups at the other end of the spectrum reject the need for teaching or mentoring, through a myth that the experience of the moment is unique. Accumulated experience and those who embody it are awarded correspondingly low status.

If people are not to be expected to migrate to some 'foreign' culture of lifelong learning, lifelong learning has somehow to mould itself around these differences. What does that indicate about promising or unpromising models for doing this?

John Gray in his analysis draws on the Cultural Revolution in China. He notes that Mao Tse Tung tried to graft modern Western approaches to agricultural production and industrial advance into traditional rural Chinese culture. The result was disastrous. Such profound changes cannot be effected by extracting elements of individual cultures that do not conform to certain principles, and replacing them with uniform cultural elements stamped (in the present case), 'Approved by the State Lifelong Learning Directorate'. Culture cannot, in effect, be dismantled and reassembled like some vast Lego construction. Quite the reverse. Cultures work in an organic way, through the interaction of all the elements expressed in people's lives.

In the learning context, the 'cultural engineer' cannot simply approach any of the individual learning cultures in the UK, unbolt the characteristic learning culture module, and insert a replacement. History shows that attempts to introduce lifelong learning need to be based on a process of voluntary assimilation and naturalization, adapting to the particular conditions in each case.

This process will have its own growing pains. Indeed in rarer cases it may not succeed, if there is a radical contradiction between the lifelong learning principles and the host culture itself. If, for example, the traditions of a host culture hold that learning opportunities for women should be restricted, the contradictions with the basic lifelong learning principles are likely to be exceedingly difficult to overcome. Where there is insoluble conflict, and the lifelong learning culture functions as a hostile invader, it could be rejected by some or all of the group and lead to the development of cultural factions. A look at the literature on black students in (and excluded from) British educational institutions shows that this view of the current culture is not overdrawn.[11] The way that educational institutions generally conduct their business is commonly perceived in black communities as expressing a white culture, which many find irrelevant or even oppressive.

Box 3.3 shows how black parents in a London borough saw the need to challenge the way that their sons, in particular, complied with common stereotyping for failure in predominantly white state schools. Creating a black Saturday school provides a place where black teachers can provide both support and challenge for the pupils: support in terms of an environment expressing mutual respect between teacher and pupil, in terms of black culture; and challenge in terms of the personal effort expected from pupils – both for achievements in learning, and for overcoming the power of racial stereotyping. Such initiatives are the green shoots of lifelong learning diversity, and it would not be surprising if relations between them and local state schools were initially uncomfortable. Cases such as this show the vital importance of social commitment in finding a workable solution for lifelong learning.

Family Friends is a black Saturday school in an inner-London borough, where each pupil pays £26 a term. The school's creation was prompted by a mother's frustration, when she felt that the mainstream school had low expectations of her children.

The atmosphere at the Saturday school is orderly but more informal than in the mainstream school. A 15-year-old pupil said, 'It's relaxed and we get on well. It's at ease here, it's like home.' Staff and pupils are all black. One teacher – who teaches both at Family Friends and at the local mainstream school – said, 'We can discuss black issues and no one is offended.' It also allows her to deal directly with excuses, lack of effort or lapses in behaviour. 'I use my blackness to get to the kids. For example, in a mainstream school if a boy who is difficult does half a page of writing when you know he could do better, the temptation is not to push because you don't want trouble. But here I can say: "Do you know what it's like out there for you as a black male?" I couldn't do that anywhere else.'

Box 3.3 A black Saturday school. Source: adapted from Julius (1998).

Critical mass in lifelong learning

An immanent general culture will be realized when there are sufficient lifelong learners to form a critical mass. This could mean two things:

1. reaching a point where there are enough lifelong learners, across all the varied groups which make up the population, for it to become a recognized general description of the national scene (and when that would be is a matter of judgement and measurement); or
2. reaching a point where the culture takes over and drives the pace itself. (It would be wise not to have too high hopes of this too soon.)

Even if they can be measured, these two points are not at all the same thing. It is possible to have the first but not the second. In theory at least, it is not even clear that the second exists to be found. Social theorists have not produced anything purporting to be a theory of cultural assimilation which could guide the policy-makers. In practice, however, we believe that the new culture *could* develop a log-rolling momentum. This follows the experience of individuals who warm to learning, and the persistence of learning behaviour among those who have already built up a portfolio of learning achievements.

Implementing a project to introduce a new general culture of lifelong learning is, for all its uncertainties, best seen as an open and adaptive process of learning – *itself fully in accord with the principles of lifelong learning.* A project of this kind can only succeed if it expresses true partnership, rather than the insistence of government. Its introduction needs to be clearly laid out if it is not to be interpreted as large-scale social engineering in the interest of cultural dominance. No strategy for this has yet appeared.

ELEMENTS OF A LIFELONG LEARNING SCENARIO

A lifelong learning society will be full of lifelong learning individuals, families, organizations and communities. It is important to be clear how these elements would behave, and what issues they would be facing.

The individual

Lifelong learning individuals learn consistently over time to an unfolding learning plan, expressing the proactive attitude and involvement of the committed learner. They make efforts to apply their personal learning fruitfully – perhaps through involvement in teaching, mentoring and supporting the learning of others. If this sounds like a description of missionary zeal, it is important to emphasize again the dangers of cultural colonialism.

Lifelong learning skills, at several levels, are needed for individuals to succeed in these roles:

- *Forward planning:* the individual learner is a forward planner of learning. This does not necessarily mean keeping elaborate documents; but having an achievement profile and an action plan in some form makes it easier for learners to review their progress (alone or with a mentor), to reflect on experience and changing needs, and to adapt their plans accordingly.
- *The ability to seek and benefit from advice and guidance:* it is important for everybody to be familiar with, and to have access to impartial information, advice and guidance on a regular ongoing basis – that is, to 'lifelong guidance' (see Chapter 11).
- *Lifespan development:* lifelong learners need a clear but flexible understanding of the lifespan and its learning possibilities. Over the years, influential analysts have attempted to break down the lifespan into a typical 'natural' developmental cycle. But much of this reflected a strongly gendered view of career and personal

development in corporate employment. A particular form of the 'life stages' myth is the belief that people become too old to learn. This view is now dismissed by scientists and psychologists as almost wholly misleading.

- *Need for assertiveness in the learning situation:* lifelong learners must develop a robust ability to assert their rights as learners. This is not as easy as it sounds. There is an inescapable element of directive teaching in the earlier school years and the resulting cultural imprinting cannot be ignored. People who are normally assertive are, paradoxically, often stoics in the face of poor services for learning. Chapter 2 showed a great need for learners to insist on proper and effective tuition. But the existing cultural environment is likely to label this 'making a fuss'.
- *Learning style:* lifelong learners need to know what learning style suits them best, so they can select the forms of learning opportunity most appropriate for them.
- *Learning skills:* there are five key learning skills which learners need at every stage, at a level which suits their learning plans. Box 3.4 describes the main features of these.
- *Influencing skills:* the lifelong learner will need special skills to exercise social commitment. It is very easy for learners to be seen as preaching to non-learners. It is important for the teacher or mentor to adopt the stance described by Paulo Freire as 'due modesty'. This is the very essence of the socially committed lifelong learner – a position halfway between teacher and fellow student.

Effective thinking concerns deductive, inductive, lateral, and creative logic.

Understanding culture means understanding the effects of culture and society on the way that people think, and helps people to get under the skin of an argument. This is a central lifelong learning skill.

Applying knowledge goes well beyond examination performance and technical skill, and includes the sharing and communicating of what is known. It includes 'implicit knowledge', which learners need to realize and to make accessible, as part of everyday learning. This is the *real* stock of knowledge and skills in a community, too often only revealed by the desperation of war and natural disaster.

Research techniques add to available knowledge, either through new knowledge or through improved access to knowledge. Lifelong learners need to research at all levels of learning, not just as a function of advanced study. In industry, for example, 'total quality management' and 'quality circles' are based on workers' research for piecemeal improvements to products or services.

Using resources covers, in particular, skills associated with fast-developing ICT.

Box 3.4 Five key learning skills.

The family and household

The family – and by extension the kinship group and the household – commonly takes a degree of group responsibility for the learning of its members. It is widely accepted in principle that parents have a direct responsibility for the learning done by their children in the years of their minority, and indeed that their responsibility is greater and more fundamental than that delegated to teachers at school. But in practice schools report considerable apathy, for example in attendance at school–parent events. Although family-based learning strategies have developed strongly in recent years, benefiting children and parents alike, OECD[12] indicators put the UK well down the international league in the extent to which parents wish to play a role in their children's schooling.

Recent immigrants have something important to teach in this regard. Evidence points to immigrant families and kinship systems being widely used as providers of money and of support for learning. The drop in personal status associated with international migration may make it very difficult for a newly arrived individual to gain access to an institutionalized support system. Immigrants without substantial funds or appropriate references, for instance, may find it extremely difficult to get a bank loan, or to gain access to grants which depend on long-term residency or home-ownership. Individuals' fates may largely depend on their contacts – whether they are 'network rich' or 'network poor' in this respect.

This illustrates the importance of families and households as role models and support networks in promoting 'migration' to a new learning culture, a lifelong learning culture. In addition to the educational benefits, the domestic unit can itself be a direct beneficiary – a work-related course may bring in more income; a financial awareness course may improve the budget; a child's learning about diet can even change a family's eating habits (see Box 3.5).

Marec's school is taking part in a research programme run by the University of Bangor, which has encouraged children not only to eat up their fruit and vegetables, but also to ask for them in preference to sweets.

Marec's mother, Janina said, 'Before the food programme the only vegetables Marec would eat were carrots and peas. Now he eats everything and asks for a bowl of vegetables when he comes in [from school]. When we went to the supermarket, I was astonished when he asked to try some fresh spinach. I'd never had it myself! It's good for us all, and we've cut down on sweets. I'm even eating healthier myself.'

Box 3.5   Smart kids eat greens. Source: adapted from Magnus (1998)

Lifelong learning organizations

In a lifelong learning society it would be normal for employers to act as lifelong learning organizations. There are two strands to this:

- The organization's commitment to its own effective learning. This corresponds to personal commitment at the individual level, and to the idea of continuous planned learning.
- The organization's commitment to the wider learning scene. This broadly parallels the social commitment principle at the personal level.

No hogging of knowledge – nobody sits on knowledge for positional advantage.

Everybody gives top priority to marshalling and sharing information – whatever their position in the organization.

A 'no-blame' culture – people are given time and space to work together in reflecting on mistakes and experience.

Flexible databases and communications systems:

- manage and present 'hard' and 'soft' market information;
- collect and organize staff members' experience, knowledge and ideas;
- are *the first thing to be interrogated* when there is a problem or business opportunity.

Internal, decentralized training complements the system for information management – more responsive than a centralized human resource department to the needs of the staff in context, and less likely to weaken shared responsibility for assembling knowledge.

A system of individual learning accounts caters for people's self-initiated learning.

Box 3.6 Characteristics of the lifelong learning organization. Source: summarized from Tobin (1998).

Effective learning in the organization

Daniel Tobin[13] has identified steps that organizations can take to become lifelong learning organizations and which are also vital for effective business activity and competitiveness (see Box 3.6). The model has strong affinities with the Tomorrow's Company vision.[14] Its particular effect is to loosen the bias against broader general learning, so evident in UK companies, enabling greater mutuality of interest in learning to develop between the organization and the worker. Establishing the appropriate kind of culture in an organization depends on board members and senior managers setting a personal example, and making an unambiguous personal commitment. Success depends on managers being more committed to learning than to status difference in the workplace.

However, leadership is not enough by itself. Chapter 2 showed how UK employers tend to be suspicious of investment in learning for staff below management level. The short-termism, which afflicts so much of the UK corporate sector, still throws a large cloud over these important learning possibilities inside companies. This can only be dispelled by adopting a more strategic approach.

An organization following Daniel Tobin's prescription will need to set out a proper strategic vision for its learning activities, and also for the knowledge assets which it will need to command. It is this broad sense of direction which lies at the heart of the national Investors in People standard, controlling the broad balance between the expensive recruitment of skills from outside, and the efficient fostering of skills and knowledge within the organization. Funding policies will also be needed to fill the individual learning accounts; and to give long-term commitment of expenditures for installing and running the systems which will make the whole approach work. Box 3.7 illustrates an early stage of learning, for businesses moving in this direction from a more traditional British business culture.

Managers at a Rotherham firm introduced the Investors in People standard through initiatives driven by a management-only steering group. There was slow progress until they formed a joint steering group, also involving union representatives. Results include the following:

- improvement in employees' understanding of the role of basic training in the company's success;
- the company published a training prospectus for the site;
- employees' right to training established – averaging about five days a year per employee;
- an annual training review and management/supervisory appraisals have shifted the focus of responsibility for identifying training needs from the training department towards the individual;
- union members designed a training scheme for NVQ Level 3, developing complementary skills among engineers and electricians;
- increased autonomy for employees;
- improvements in: levels of motivation; multi-skilling; flexibility; machine down times;
- work 'crews' now responsible for organizing their own holidays, time off and shift swaps;
- provision of confidential basic skills training for employees with numeracy and literacy problems.

Company managers associate improved training provision with:
- fall in absenteeism from 10% to 4%;
- improvements in productivity;
- improvements in accident rates and quality, measured by the volume of complaints;
- 'dramatic rise' in employees' understanding of business objectives.

Commenting on the initial failure to involve the trade unions in implementing IiP, a Chief Shop Steward said: 'If people buy into something they want, they will work with it. If it is imposed, they will kick back.'

Box 3.7 Culture change: lifelong learning in the workplace. Source: adapted from: *Investors in People and Trade Unions,* TUC/Investors in People UK (1997).

A key strategic issue for employers is the concern about 'poaching' – that is, that any investment they make in the skills of current workers may simply walk away, as rival organizations compete for skilled labour. Economists such as Gary Becker[15] have tried to deny that poaching is a problem, on the grounds that employers simply have no incentive to invest in general skills. It has now been convincingly demonstrated in theory that, in the imperfect labour markets which operate today, organizations can quite rationally choose to train staff on their payrolls.

It follows that the *fear* of losing such trained staff – and the investment value they represent – is not illogical in principle. However, evidence from case studies shows that the dangers of poaching are nothing like as great as they are often made out to be. This is due to the potency in employment of good psychological contracts, based on relationships of trust. The investment in skills can be shared between employer and worker – through the latter being willing to accept wages at less than top rates, as part of the contract. This sharing generates *loyalty effects* which are strong enough to act as a brake on employees' willingness to leave an employer they rate as 'good'. Such practices also attract better staff on recruitment. In general, far from learning emptying a firm of its talent, it is strongly enhancing over the medium term.

Organizational commitment to the wider learning scene
Any would-be lifelong learning organization will also have to show *social commitment, respect for others' learning* and *respect for the truth,* if it is to qualify for the name. Until recently this looked like heresy – but the attitude of many organizations is beginning to change.

There are two positive factors at work here. The nature of competition is shifting from *a focus on marketplaces* to *a focus on networks of loyalty relationships:* it is an organization's contacts and its rate of response that count. Businesses which are not at nodal points in networks are economically excluded. Firms wanting to maximize their own advantage need social commitment to learning. Organizations are also learning that *a society of lifelong learners will make for more discriminating customers.* They are therefore beginning to develop products and markets on that basis. Scandals over research into the effects of tobacco on smokers' health, or the promotion of dried milk for infants in inappropriate markets, leave their mark. They show the long-term damage a firm's reputation can sustain if its business is based on ignorance and on antisocial assumptions.

Lifelong learning therefore offers a growing, diversified market which is rich in opportunities for companies to use sponsorship of learning to grow potential customer loyalty – especially among young people. Even so, constant vigilance is necessary to protect learners' interests. The government in particular must guard against the influence of those who would push their support too far so as to monopolize the education system. Computer companies providing affordable equipment and services to meet government targets for ICT in schools is just one example of such a danger area. More generally, experience of the commercialization of education in the USA is a substantial warning. The attraction of heavily discounted educational materials contains potentially grave dangers for intellectual freedom.

Learning communities

Communities in the UK are already declaring themselves to be learning cities, towns, regions, etc. This is partly a reaction to the lack of co-ordination and market brokerage among local learning providers, and to high levels of competition on the ground in the various localities. It also reflects the concern of local communities to use education as one way to respond to social and economic development, in the face of economic dislocations and social exclusion. These initiatives will have an important place in a general culture of lifelong learning, alongside learning organizations, learning families, and lifelong learners themselves.

It is tempting to say that the basic principles applied by theorists to the learning organization should simply read across to learning communities. At this level, libraries would correspond to Daniel Tobin's data bases, and the activities of local education authorities in supplying largely free adult education would correspond to the human resource development in companies, and so on. But communities are not single-minded corporate bodies. They are – essentially – subject to democratic debate, in which there may be many distinctive and divergent voices, often reflecting cultural diversity.

For this reason there is very little chance of developing any sort of single view or concept of how learning communities should be constructed, and indeed what they should do. The key test in a lifelong learning culture is not so much whether communities are all working to a common template, but whether they have a thought-out strategy and the powers to carry it through. A lifelong learning community would develop its own strategy grounded in the lifelong learning principles. A second test, following on from the first, is whether the community links well with other communities, to spread the practice of lifelong learning on the broader scene.

Learning providers

In all cases the learning provider in a lifelong learning culture will be expected to foster lifelong learning as the top priority in its teaching and facilitating work, and also to conduct its own business activities just like any other lifelong learning organization.

Chris Duke has shown the importance of these two principles in the context of UK universities,[16] but their application is entirely general. If the second applies it will reinforce the first, and vice versa. This is particularly true in the face-to-face relationships between teachers and students. According to Carl Rogers, effective teaching depends on conviction and passion.[17] This is where the lifelong learning message gets across: if teachers are so distracted by bureaucratic and organizational requirements, and are so lacking in high-level support that they cannot be lifelong learners themselves, they will not come over as convinced and convincing learners.

In statutory education, the potential role of schools as lifelong learning communities in embryo needs to be exploited. They are the test-bed where young people learn how to live in and to support learning communities, *at any age.*

Learning schools will have a twofold mission:

1. teaching pupils *how to learn in mutually supportive groups,* in such a way that the individual pupils – regardless of capability – become adept at supporting each other's learning through teamwork, mutual tolerance and understanding (see Box 3.8);
2. teaching pupils in their groups *how to relate constructively to other groups or communities* of a wide variety of kinds.

David Clark stresses the role in postmodern culture of community-based action as a means for people to manage the increasing fragmentation in their lives. The group skills cited above are preparation for such action, and good core skills are essential for the task.

Schools will also need to prepare young people for life in lifelong learning organizations. Beyond the home, schools are the first workplaces that most children get to know in any detail. For better or worse, therefore, schools provide an early, influential role model of workplace relations.

Geeta has moderate learning difficulties, and easily gives up. Her class teacher makes sure that she always uses ICT with another pupil or an adult, because of her continual need for prompting and encouragement.

Jake has delayed communication skills. He is always paired with another pupil for ICT work, to encourage him to talk and discuss the program they are using. He is much more talkative and fluent in these sessions than at other times.

Jessica's hearing is impaired. In one session, she worked with another hearing-impaired pupil, using a multimedia program to add sound captions to a story. Jessica operated the program while her friend spoke into the microphone to form the captions.

Patrick has cerebral palsy, and relies on ICT to support much of his learning. School staff are conscious of the risk of isolation that this incurs, and make sure that he is included in group learning activities. On one occasion, for example, when his group was collecting information about shoe sizes and height, Patrick entered the measurements on his computer.

Emily also has cerebral palsy. When she is included in group work, her greater experience in the use of ICT makes her 'the expert', and boosts her self-esteem.

Box 3.8 ICT and group learning in mainstream schools. Source: adapted from Brooks (1997).

This vision for schools is likely to sit very uneasily with their current focus as curriculum-centred institutions. Many schools will find the objectives for the lifelong learning school at odds with aspects of the current formal learning culture. In particular traditional concepts of schools as special spaces – separated off from the rest of community life – will dwindle. More schools will take their learning activities out into the community environment; and more socially committed organizations will draw in people to help with the school's work, both inside and outside the classroom.

In higher education there has been much soul-searching about the ways in which universities conduct their business, reflecting a built-in dilemma: they are strung uneasily between maintaining on one hand the values of the current elite culture of learning and, on the other, pursuing high-volume supply, and responding to an increase in learners' instrumental motivation. The solution is to give priority to training students as lifelong learners. This restores the idea of universities as 'communities of learners'.

REASONS FOR CHANGE

No vision of lifelong learning can be persuasive unless it clearly displays its reasons. Recent reports on lifelong learning have acknowledged two reasons for making the change to lifelong learning:

1. the notion that economic prosperity depends on the UK's competitiveness, both at home and abroad, and that a key way to do this is by building up the nation's knowledge and skill;

2. the idea that rising social exclusion of disadvantaged groups can be alleviated by raising their participation in learning.

These two reasons are generally presented as interdependent to a degree. Both are responses to perceived threats. Useful though they are, they are not the only important considerations, nor could a solution to the learning problem be based on them alone.

The 'economic competitiveness' argument

At the heart of the economic argument is the notion of globalization. This has a wide array of possible meanings. Three influential ones among them are: the *global marketplace,* created by the emergence of much more open trading conditions, achieved by the General Agreement on Tariffs and Trade in its last days, and new high-tech communications available world wide; *unregulated world capitalism on the USA laissez-faire model* using the new global marketplace; and *global cultural invasion,* riding on the back of modern communications and these two economic senses of globalization. This section looks at the first two of these. The cultural threats are explored later.

Paul Hirst and Grahame Thompson[18] have argued that the present openness of the world economy is nothing new. It was matched during the 'Pax Britannica' period of the high gold standard in the years before the first world war. Nevertheless the fact that Britain survived and prospered in it, first time round, is not a cause for complacency now. Mega-corporations are scouring the world looking for low-cost opportunities to site goods and service production, spurred on by new technology. This will continue until real wages broadly equalize across the world. Corporations are increasingly footloose, and they may well choose not to come to Britain. Worse still, those already here may threaten departure, if they are not well served with benevolent tax, subsidy and regulatory regimes, and stable exchange rates. Much of Britain's attraction to such corporations is its 'offshore' position within the large European market, which has been favoured in recent years for its low real wage costs and flexible labour markets. But other countries in the 'Euro' system, and the low wage competitor economies further afield, mount a formidable challenge. World capitalists have the UK over a barrel.

Devaluation is no longer an effective means to shore up competitiveness. So, until real wages even out around the globe, the *only* way to protect the UK against serious dislocations to jobs and prosperity – while preserving society from a sharp worsening of social exclusion – is to raise the nation's skills. This means building up comparative trading advantage in high-tech, high value-added goods. It requires excellence in research and development, and well-qualified labour. Even these are not sufficient in themselves; they must be supported by a whole range of enterprise and financial policies.

It is not immediately obvious that a *mass* lifelong learning model is the one to adopt in this context. The Treasury could reason that all the UK needs is a larger (but still narrow) elite of highly skilled and trained development scientists, engineers and entrepreneurs. Those who succeed in business worldwide, however, do not accept this technocratic view. Research[19] shows quite conclusively that skill requirements are rising rapidly over the whole structure of the nation's jobs, for all but a small proportion of the very lowliest occupations. In this context companies succeed by maintaining a sufficient general level of skill – not just by having a few star performers. This is the 'learning fitness' model of the successful firm. It is analogous to a rowing eight: it helps to have some stars, but the effectiveness of the boat is a delicate matter of fitness, balance and timing across the whole crew. Races are not won by a few giants rowing their hearts out.

As a nation Britain can probably seek to keep abreast of the competition by relaxing the safety net of the welfare state, and by allowing real wages to fall further, as the USA has done. But, as Michael Apple has shown for Americans, the costs of such policy in terms of misery and death in deprived ghettos is unspeakable. It is only considered bearable because so much of middle-class America is becoming ghettoized, bunkered behind high walls and a gun-toting culture. From a UK perspective, the implications of that are nothing less than horrific. Ultimately, the costs of the social mess will feed back into the economic system, weakening the competitive standing of firms, and cutting into the prosperity of those who have retreated to the laager.

How much better if the UK could use lifelong learning to bolster competitiveness, sustain social cohesion, and by close assimilation hold social exclusion and its huge welfare costs at bay. This would not just be instrumental learning. The old idea that raising workers' skills makes them inappropriately ambitious is moribund if not dead. Government, organizations and institutions are now looking for ways to encourage motivation for self-improvement. The skills of radical thinking, creativity, communication and personal effectiveness are needed as much as old-style vocational competences.

The 'social exclusion' argument

Social exclusion is the second standard argument, but its real meaning is not self-evident. Bill Jordan[20] clarifies exclusion usefully in terms of the economic theory of clubs. This holds that clubs are set up to arrange for the supply of collective goods among their members *on a subscription basis,* rather than through the market.

The welfare state – or more generally, civil society – can be likened to a club, but one with rather unclear rules and boundaries. The 'moral majority' pay their taxes to benefit from the insurance which it offers: they are the fully paid-up club members who by and large behave as expected within the rules. On the margins of the club are members who want the services, but either cannot or do not wish to pay the dues and act according to the club's norms. They risk exclusion by being removed altogether from the collective; or they risk harsher terms of membership, and even sanctions. This is not quite exclusionary, but it is uncomfortable enough.

Those who are in this marginal position effectively form their own rival club – half in and half out of the wider club – providing mutual aid and support to their own members, in an alternative lifestyle. These can be very effective arrangements. The people involved form their own close-knit community with a strong group identity. But in important ways they still depend on the larger welfare state, and cause it heavy costs. These can become intolerably heavy.

So the moral majority debate what to do. Do they tighten the rules, and so deepen the exclusion at the risk of high costs in law and order, social services, education, etc?

Do they say that the diversion of costs towards marginal members is intolerable, so they will pay lower dues for themselves and look more keenly for private solutions behind the walls of still more select clubs? Or do they make strong efforts to bring excluded people back into the fold, where they are less costly to deal with? This is the stuff of modern national politics, seen in club terms.

Many people, fearing the worsening of social exclusion for reasons of economic globalization, advance lifelong learning as an appropriate response. But it is seldom clear exactly why. In club terms, is it because it will help the excluded members to return? Or because it will help to improve the alternative society of the marginal members? Or both? Or – more fundamentally (and in accord with Paulo Freire) – is it because it will remove the scales from the eyes of members of both clubs, so that a new order can replace all existing club arrangements?

Taking a narrow emphasis here can be damaging. There is, for example, a very real risk that lifelong learning can be captured by the moral majority and be put to work in an instrumental fashion to show the marginal population the error of its ways through narrowly-defined citizenship courses and the like. Such doctrines will fail, because they pay no heed to the cultural realities. According to the approach taken in this book, the rights of the different 'clubs' should be respected so that lifelong learning is not used to set up a cultural hegemony – to set one club above all others.

A better model is for lifelong learning to help to reduce the social friction at the ragged margins of society in a whole variety of ways. This is the 'oil on troubled waters' model. Some people may try to shift from one club to another as a result of learning and reflection – rags to riches (or the reverse). Others may apply their learning to dissolve problems of interface, or to improve the workings of the adjacent groups. What is important is that *it should be the learners themselves who decide*.

Clarified in this way, the social exclusion argument has heavy implications not only for the appropriate modes of learning and the supporting systems, but also for the *content* of lifelong learning itself. This is explored in later chapters.

Would any of this make a difference? *Real pessimists* would say that the boat of the welfare state is itself sinking. Pulling someone out of the water into the boat may be a zero-sum game, if someone else falls over the edge in consequence. *Lesser pessimists* would say that it is better to keep trying than to let the whole structure crack up and sink. This is the 'revolving stock' notion of exclusion – keep pulling people back on board, even if others are displaced in consequence. This aims to lessen misery by sharing misery.

Optimists have a different viewpoint. They see that the boat full of people can raise enough energy to row to land in time to rescue those still in the water. In this way social exclusion can be healed by national economic regeneration based on higher levels of skill and knowledge all round. In short, social exclusion is tackled best by a balanced strategy of learning across the whole population, not by giving priority *exclusively* to people who are socially excluded. This wider vision is the way to break out of the low-skill equilibrium, and then to be in a position to help socially excluded people from the fruits of new prosperity. In this sense the competitiveness and social exclusion motives have to be taken together, as the Kennedy report for the FEFC made clear.[21] The authors of this book incline towards the optimistic end of the scale.

Other arguments

There are four other important arguments to add: cultural invasion; environmental disaster; social cohesion; and human development.

Cultural invasion

There are two main candidates: *postmodernism,* which rejects the progressive rationalism of the Enlightenment, and sees culture changing towards lives which are unstable, relativistic and quicksilver in attitudes and beliefs; and *consumerism* which, in the learning sphere, would mean the replacement of intellectual and artistic expression with a diet of 'dumbed down' and pre-digested pap, launched at the population through every possible medium.

John Gray argues convincingly that the economic impact of modern open world trading conditions and capital movements does not necessarily mean that all parts of the world will be homogenized in *cultural terms* – whether it be via McDonald's, Disney, or some other manifestation. The most potent global cultural invasion is more likely to come through the airwaves and the Internet, than through the operations of capital shifters on the financial markets. The cultural factors can and will be resisted in different ways and to different degrees across the world. Comforting though that is, our thesis is that the best way to counter such threats is through lifelong learning, with a strong element of critical learning to deal with the invader, and a strong measure of community learning to help with any fundamentalist threat which it may ignite in return.

Environmental disaster

Stephen Yeo[22] has set out *harmony with the natural environment* as a major consideration, arguing that lifelong learning is nothing if it is not an instrument to ward off future threats to life. His argument, like David Clark's, is that if humanity is to deal effectively with global and local environmental threats, it will call for lifelong learning on a massive scale – particularly if the content and manner of that learning is weighted towards critical thinking and collaborative learning focused on resolution of issues.

Social cohesion

This is another important theme, also taken up by Stephen Yeo. Social cohesion is not in essence about inclusion and exclusion, although closely related to these concepts. It deals with the general state of social networks and relationships across the communities which make up the population, and how far they are conducive to the solution of societal problems. It is more about living *within* Bill Jordan's clubs than about the boundaries between the clubs, and the rules of transfer between them.

Societies, like economies, work well through the strength of their networks. This is a point made repeatedly by Manuel Castells in his epic trilogy.[23] The connectivity is social capital: an asset which can directly influence the economy and the quality of life. There is little doubt that in the contemporary culture such social connectivity is under threat. Fortunately, as the think-tank Demos has shown,[24] the evidence is that social pastimes and activities have, so far, kept up well in Britain compared to elsewhere. This is a major reason why our society generally has such stability in the face of recent major changes in the distributions of income and wealth.

Even so, social cohesion is not something to take for granted. This is where lifelong learning, particularly with an emphasis on social commitment, has a large role to play. Shared group-based learning, built around principles of tolerance between people of different backgrounds, creates social capital and adds to cohesion.

Humanity

Finally, and most fundamental of all the reasons for introducing a general culture of lifelong learning, is humanity itself. It is something which transcends all the doom-laden arguments above. Lifelong learning fulfils the conception of what humankind is for. The human is built and adapted for learning, and lifelong learning is the way to give expression to that fundamental identification.

NOTES AND REFERENCES

1. Clark (1996).
2. For example: Johnson and Johnson (1993).
3. Caine and Caine (1997).
4. Gray (1998).
5. Gardner (1993).
6. Parable of the Talents: Matthew ch.25.
7. Freire (1993).
8. Longworth and Davies (1996).
9. Hogg and Abrams (1988).
10. Apple (1996).
11. Bourne, Bridges and Searle (1994).
12. OECD (1995).
13. Tobin (1998).
14. RSA (1995).
15. Becker (1993).
16. Duke (1992).
17. Rogers (1993).
18. Hirst and Thompson (1996).
19. Gallie and White (1993).
20. Jordan (1996).
21. Kennedy (1997).
22. Yeo (1996).
23. Castells (1996–98).
24. Hall (1997).

Chapter 4

Review of Issues

Simultaneous action is needed on many fronts to establish a general lifelong learning culture. It is already apparent that many policy-makers and implementers are inclined to approach the task obliquely, and piecemeal. Such an approach is bound to fail. Neither can the job be done in one fell swoop. It will need to be a through-designed process of managed change. The end must be determined at the outset, by a process which identifies objectives and time scales across the entire field. Many of these can be expected to go against the aims and tendencies of the current, stubbornly resistant, learning culture.

Once the objectives are clear, a new interlocking system of institutions, procedures and funding arrangements must be introduced in parallel, to support the emergent culture and the process of managed change. This chapter maps the broad outline of this underpinning system and the issues it raises. At the highest level, those responsible for whole-system design and management work on *strategic planning* (examined in detail in Chapter 9). At the next level, the *infrastructure* provides the framework for implementing national strategy (examined in detail in Chapter 11). The day-to-day good practice arrangements for individuals and organizations at the operational level, which use the infrastructure to carry through national strategy on the ground, lie largely beyond the scope of this book.

THE STRATEGY LEVEL

Britain has never had any sort of overall, high-level strategy for learning – let alone one which has been declared to the public. It has relied on the time-honoured method of 'muddling through'.

Figure 4.1 maps the territory to be covered by a strategy for the shift to lifelong learning. At the level of the overall system, *policy* informs *design* and *development*, which indicates what is needed for *implementation*. The results of continuous *monitoring and research* feed back into adjustment of policy – and so on in a continuing loop. Strategic direction of a nation's learning systems and structures has to be set up as an open-ended learning task. It should constantly be unfolding.

A workable strategic system will not be as neat as this in use. If it is to be sufficiently responsive to real people's actual lifelong needs, the nature of strategy development will need to be organic – not mechanical. That will involve a degree of leapfrogging, cross-cutting and backtracking. What matters is the outcome, in the form of a decent, through-designed strategy *which works in action* – not the tidiness of the strategic planning process. In addition, the mode of implementation is as important as the design, for wide ownership of the strategy is imperative.

Strategic policy
At the time of writing, the UK does not have a true, workable national strategy for lifelong learning on this model, and will clearly not have one until the next general election and beyond. Government policy perpetuates the deeply damaging gulf between pre- and post-16 learning, excluding the schools from the lifelong learning territory. As long as this continues, there cannot be a holistic analysis of the problem, and any effective strategy for lifelong learning is hacked off at the knees.

Moreover there is little sign that the government is prepared to share its strategic role with others in a working partnership. Government will have to be the lead player, but it will need to be absolutely clear about partnership arrangements if it is to attract other parties with appropriate motivations for the task. The partnerships need to be even-handed to share real decisions. The partners should include: representatives of learners; representatives of providers; employers; trade unions; professional and voluntary bodies; and cultural and community leaders from across the social landscape.

Effective lifelong learning strategy should also run across several government departments. It will need to be developed alongside other major policies, if potential

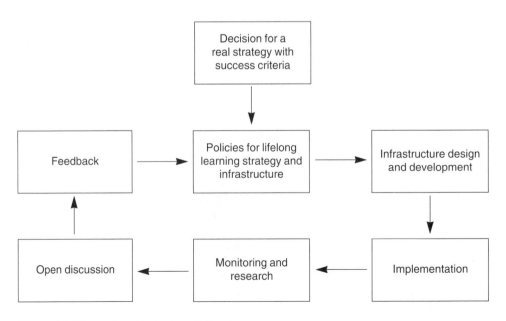

Figure 4.1 The cycle of strategic activity.

clashes of objective are to be avoided. A classic example of such a clash is the tension between the government's proposals for individual learning accounts, and for individual savings accounts and stakeholder pensions. Such potential clashes need to be reconciled through effective inter-departmental machinery.

Design and development
A national strategy has to have an all-through design and be properly worked out, planned and phased over time. Again, ministers and officials will need to show genuine commitment to their part in this, if the confidence of their strategic partners and the general public is to be earned and kept. There has been a recent tendency for the government to telescope the development process at early stages into consultative conferences, seminars and focus groups. These are not an adequate substitute for hard analysis and clear thought. Government machinery will need to change quite radically to produce work of the quality needed, and to maintain the essential contacts and networks of communication which produce effective partnership.

Implementation
The new strategy must centre on keen learners taking responsibility for their requirements and expressing social commitment. It will need to take a very different form from the present, state-dominated and provider-led arrangements. The implications for institutional and funding arrangements run very deep. The strategy will need to give high priority to building continuity and progression of learning into the infrastructure, and to reducing the gaps where people tend to fall out of learning. If learning is to spread wide, the strategies of the government and its partners need to run wide also, reaching far beyond the gates of educational institutions. This is an opening out similar to the Care in the Community health policy, and on no smaller a scale.

Monitoring, research and feedback
A greater sharing of responsibility for lifelong learning strategy means properly shared systems to monitor, research and feed back data for further policy development.

- *Monitoring and feedback* should be on-going elements of the system. Strategic assumptions, objectives and content need to be developed against clear criteria; and the implementation time for total strategic development must be specified.
- *Long- and short-term research* into lifelong learning, and to support policy development and implementation, is essential.
- *Advisory groups* which help in these processes need to be properly constituted. Groups which are created and dissolved by government on an *ad hoc* basis, which work in closed session and whose reports are not always published, seriously undermine public confidence. There should be no ambiguity about the status of people invited to serve on the relevant bodies. It should be clear to everybody whether senior officers of organizations are invited to serve in their representative or their personal capacity.

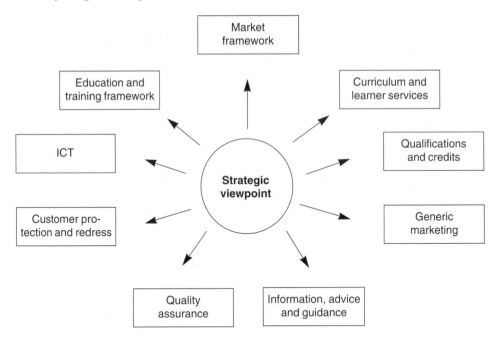

Figure 4.2 Aspects of infrastructure

THE INFRASTRUCTURE LEVEL

The infrastructure level (see Figure 4.2) is where the main elements of the support system are identified, in a framework which is maintained and developed by high-level strategists. It provides a common playing field for learners and learning providers.

Generic marketing

Generic marketing in this context is marketing the idea of lifelong learning. It is distinct from the marketing of particular schemes, or marketing which is undertaken by providers for their own purposes and market share. It may be undertaken collaboratively between providers, or on behalf of certain sectors. Or, more realistically, it is undertaken by government in the public interest. Generic marketing will generally be national. But marketing focused on specific localities and target groups can still be generic. Even individual providers can undertake generic marketing.

Generic marketing for lifelong learning is most notable for its absence. Marketing for learning in the UK has concentrated on providing a backcloth of awareness to support government educational and training schemes. It has usually been conducted by government as short-term advertising to coincide with the start of the relevant initiatives. This contrasts strongly with government marketing on themes like drink/driving and personal health, for example. The expenditure has been trivial by the standards of many industries and companies, and when set against the size of related budgets.

What marketing there has been has had particular undertones. Marketing is not culture-neutral and any marketing of learning – and more particularly of lifelong learning – must adopt a clear cultural position. Under the Conservative Government in the late 1980s and early 1990s the main thrust was instrumental and utilitarian, with strong images of ladders of success in executive occupations. Many people found this approach culturally and ideologically hostile.

There are important contradictions here. Left to government, the effectiveness of generic marketing may be sacrificed to political ideology or expediency; and any strongly partisan flavour inhibits the development of effective partnership approaches, and endangers long-term consistency in the messages to be conveyed. On the other hand, marketing supported by providers acting in common is largely frustrated by the incentive for individual providers to free-ride on the back of collective expenditure.

Joint arrangements between providers and government seem to be the best way forward. This will need a fully reasoned, culturally consistent, promotional strategy, one which is shared between the parties and pursued consistently over a long period. Nobody has yet published a complete and reasoned analysis on the objectives of a campaign for generic marketing of lifelong learning on these lines. Much hard thinking still needs to be done in partnership.

Information, advice and guidance

There is still no real agreement about larger questions such as how the guidance industry will be structured, and in particular how the public sector will deploy its funds in support of adults. This is a disappointment after so much effective developmental work in the 1980s and 1990s. There have been a number of useful developments in this area of the infrastructure, including the introduction of Learning Direct, the national helpline for information and advice; a clear framework of professional standards of staff training; and the work done by the Guidance Council, and by the Advice, Guidance, Counselling and Psychotherapy Lead Body, to introduce new service and organizational standards for guidance delivered in any setting. But there is a widespread sense that the time for development is over. Permanent infrastructure should be put in place.

At the time of writing, the possible impact of government proposals for a 'University for Industry' is not clear – either in relation to guidance for adults in general, or for the development of policy and practice for true lifelong guidance.

Information and advice

Much useful work was done during the 1980s to establish modern standards for collecting, storing and presenting data on course opportunities, and on support services for learning. But latterly there has been a serious failure to maintain the momentum of development. An effective, clearly visible 'information front line' for local communities and in workplaces is still lacking; the government has much to do to ensure that publicly funded providers conform to information standards, and that they supply up-to-date and reliable information on a regular basis; information has still to be linked effectively in nationwide computer networks, and new professional structures are needed to consolidate the work on standards.

Guidance

Some clients need more than information to resolve difficulties and choices. Where this involves young people, public policy and expenditure budgets for guidance have focused on free and effective arrangements for pupils and students in initial education (see Chapter 8). This has long been the priority of successive governments.

It is in the area of guidance for adults where there are still major failings in supply, and where there is much less support from politicians. The Treasury, in particular, has been reluctant to accept adult guidance as a free entitlement. It has argued that the results of guidance are primarily beneficial to the individual, so the individual with sufficient means should pay. Historically, the guidance profession has been very ambivalent about asking clients to pay. Guidance professionals have long seen their activities more as a public service free at the point of need than as a product which can be traded in the marketplace. The problem with this is that the putative paymasters do not agree, and are unlikely to do so. If the situation is to improve, the deeply rooted cultural resistance in the profession to a (part subsidized) market model will have to be overcome.

Members of the public will also have to adjust their attitudes. Many adults have only a hazy view of the advantages which guidance can bring. Most look for guidance first from relatives, friends or workmates; or seek advice from providers, which may in fact be biased. Only a clear, strong lead from the government can break this image problem down, treating guidance as investment in a national lifelong learning strategy, and determining, once and for all, just how much of a free market there can really be. Without it, there will never be a sound and integrated guidance industry, and a good proportion of the costs of marketing lifelong learning will be wasted.

Institutional framework

In the short term, the institutional framework which shapes the learning scene must be taken as given. But in the longer run the question of the suitability of the framework to the emergence of a new culture of lifelong learning has to be faced. A system which has evolved over centuries to develop an educational elite is unlikely to serve more democratic purposes, or to work for its own demise.

In Britain the framework of learning institutions is dominated by the structures built to support the entitlements of young people to initial education:

- public sector schools are established and run only under strict conditions established by Act of Parliament. Local education authorities can only do for schools what Parliament has decided to allow them to do, according to the long-standing provisions of British constitutional law;
- near-public bodies like TECs have rather more latitude, but can only do under contract to the government what Parliament itself has sanctioned, under powers granted to the sponsoring government departments;
- further education colleges and sixth-form colleges form part of a largely independent sector established by law, and managed and funded by the FEFC, whose duties are laid down by the 1992 Act;
- universities are set up by the government under Royal Charter, and are funded through separate higher education funding councils in England, Scotland and Wales.

- reintegration of Grant Maintained schools into the general secondary education sector

- independent schools' entitlement to benefit from their status as registered charities

- integration of institutional arrangements for age 16–19 education and training, bringing TECs together with the further education sector

- separate funding and a more specialized curriculum for school sixth forms, compared with the rest of the further education sector

- possible merger of higher and further education sectors

- the role and duties of local education authorities for further education, and for adult post-initial education in their areas

- freedom of entry for new universities in the publicly supported higher education sector

Box 4.1 General institutional change for lifelong learning.

The workings of these institutions of initial education and training are not only relevant to education in the years of youth, they are central to lifelong learning itself. The learning done through them is a crucial part of the whole; and the success which individuals have in the initial system profoundly conditions the success which they may have in later learning.

Box 4.1 shows key unresolved issues surrounding these institutional arrangements. Even a restless government would think twice before twiddling all these knobs. But it seems likely that a move to a general culture of lifelong learning would require major changes in at least some of these areas.

In the background is another issue: whether anything can be done about the gaps between institutions. The fracturing of roles and mission between institutions, and the separation of their funding arrangements, means in effect that no institution can relate to any individual as customer for lifelong learning as a whole. Once the learner has moved on to another stage and another jurisdiction, it becomes a case of 'out of sight, out of mind'. The one-stop-shop argument has not been consistently applied across the piece.

As far as lifelong learning is concerned this 'space between' problem may be the most elusive of all the institutional issues which need to be faced. In later chapters we shall look to see whether the concepts of a 'University for Industry' and learning accounts might provide the necessary linkage, reinforcing and connecting the established institutions with new *vehicular* means to provide continuity, mobility and progression for the individual learner.

Market framework

State-sponsored initial education and training, with its own backdoor funding structures, currently forms a complex set of quasi-markets.[1] This is the mighty institutionalized edifice where learners exercise their entitlements with a degree of choice, and the government – directly or at one remove – picks up the bill.

In the case of initial learning, the key questions concern the trade-off between the elements of central control which the quasi-market system provides, and the principle of individual responsibility which lies at the heart of the lifelong learning definitions. The full market approach works against state-imposed standard solutions, and allows diversity and choice to express themselves more strongly. The quasi-market solution sets limits to these factors because the market solution may produce inequalities and extremes which are generally damaging, which the government may wish to suppress. Much of the discussion of later chapters will revolve around this trade-off. The answers will be hugely important for the emergence of the new general culture of lifelong learning.

In the world of post-initial learning it is very different. The market is going to be the dominant factor whatever happens. But this leaves the institutions of further and higher education and training institutions – whose main business has normally been seen as initial education – in a quandary when it comes to post-initial learning. They are left standing half in and half out of a wider free market for learning. This does not create a level playing field between providers: some receive backdoor subsidy for market clients – others do not. Moreover, some state-sponsored learning providers are allowed to subsidize employers in their role as learning providers, while others are not.

All this is ramshackle to a degree which compromises developments for lifelong learning. This is partly because the complexities confuse the potential learner. But it is also because best use is not made of public resources in reaching the more intractable parts of society where the motivation to learn is at a low ebb. Sorting all this out in the name of lifelong learning means paying close examination to the principles and targeting of subsidy.

Curriculum

Not everybody calling for a new lifelong learning culture wants it for the same reasons. There is a multiple tug-of-war between groups wanting quite different contents corresponding to their different objectives. Humanists want individuals to unfold all their potential, corresponding to the whole range of intelligences and aptitudes which they have. Moralists want to establish core values for a civilized and well-behaved community. Employers want capable leaders, and employees who have sufficient core skills for them to be able to carry responsibility in the workplace. Artists want to develop everybody's potential for creative expression. Academics want to ensure the ability of the population to carry forward the task of academic enquiry and the creation of knowledge at the highest level, within and across established disciplines. Governments want to create a population and a social structure which is supportive of the causes which they favour, in their interpretation of the national interest. The extraordinary interest of discourse about lifelong learning is that it brings all these diverse forces to bear.

A key question is whether the advocates of lifelong learning have to adopt any particular stance on these issues. An early debate, for example, concerned the focus of individuals' learning: should lifelong learning policies aim to extend the range and influence the content of people's learning in particular directions? Or is any learning good enough, because it is better than no learning at all?

A rather different approach, explored in some depth in later chapters, is to argue that the essence of lifelong learning is that people should be able to take in appropriate knowledge quickly when they need it, and so maintain learning ability for the next stage of the lifelong journey. They do not need to strap on a pile of personal knowledge and skill at the beginning. This would place the emphasis on learning how to learn – or in this context, learning how to be a lifelong learner. According to this view, efforts by the state to impose a curriculum on the schools which does not serve this purpose would have to be resisted, just as strenuously as encroachments on academic liberties are resisted in the universities. People are entitled to be lifelong learners. Box 4.2 shows some of the issues raised by evident conflict between current curriculum requirements and the aims of lifelong learning.

- At what age should formal teaching of reading, writing and number begin?

- Should the school curriculum extend *routinely* beyond the boundaries of schools – into communities, the natural environment, and the world of work?

- Should the state use its influence in schools to introduce mandatory elements of content? Should these take over some of the academic subject concept of curriculum?

- How can the potential of ICT best be realized?

- Should the whole 16–19 curriculum now be restructured in line with the aims of comprehensive education?

- Does the curriculum in higher education need fundamental revision, to reflect the population's needs for lifelong learning?

- In the post-initial marketplace, should the state apply any content-related impositions on any free purchases of learning?

Box 4.2 Curriculum and lifelong learning: formative questions.

Quality assurance

The government has a full panoply of arrangements for quality assurance in the learning sectors which it sponsors. These purposes are costly: Ofsted alone costs over £100 million a year. The inspectorates have a major role to play in tracking down abuses, in promoting efficiency of delivery, in spreading good practice and necessary consistency, and in offering praise and reward. These functions are well recognized and supported in principle on all sides. Opinion is more divided on how well they are carried out.

A new general culture of lifetime learning will need new arrangements:

- Inspectors – including Chief Inspectors – will have to conform to the definitions and principles of the new culture.
- Inspections will have to be freed from the ideological grip of the government of the day.
- Current assumptions about proper learning methods and techniques will have to adjust to the involvement of new groups of learners, whose requirements are likely to be very different.
- General underlying theories about teaching will have to be more clearly stated, and their research base identified.
- The inspectorates will need to develop new measures and indicators, to reflect the importance of promoting continuity of learning at every stage.

Customer protection and redress

In recent years a major effort has been made by government and its agencies to develop charters setting out customer rights and legitimate expectations about the services of learning providers. In a parallel movement contractual protections have been developed for learners funded through government training contracts. But these arrangements – pursued through the power of the public purse – are patchy, and lack consistent standards across the piece. Progress may already be slowing.

For its own part, the learning industry is conspicuous in the weakness of its guarantees, money-back assurances and after-sales services, by comparison with other industries. What is more, it is held to be unthinkable and disloyal for learners to want these things. There is a fundamental cultural point here, marking the historical difference in the way that Britain has valued 'the professions' and 'industry'. Putting snobbery and prejudice aside, why is it inappropriate for those who pay for learning services to seek satisfactory outcomes? Even lawyers provide clients with information about client rights. Learning providers in a mature culture of general lifelong learning would be expected to do the same.

Underlying these difficult and contentious issues is the whole concept of what the service to the client should actually be. Are learning providers – like general practitioners, dentists, or lawyers – aiming to provide a *lifetime service*? Or just one-off episodes? How can loyalty concepts be seriously developed to help establish the continuity of the lifelong learning vision? Later chapters will show that these 'over time' concepts of customer service and protection are at the heart of the new culture.

Information and communications technology (ICT)

There are three main infrastructural possibilities for ICT: *protocols* which provide consistency in applications and enable separate facilities to be put together into compatible structures, and allow any combination of hardware and software to be used, with minimum aggravation and additional cost for users; *networked physical facilities,* in the form of high-rated communication channels – such as broadcasting facilities, or the National Grid for Learning;[2] *learning stations for all,* open for general use in the home, in the workplace, learning resource centres, in libraries or other public buildings, or in specially equipped community learning centres.

The issues here are highly complex. They bring together large-scale capital and operating outlays; difficult issues of the appropriate modes of learning for the new technologies; and a subtle cultural undermining of established activities and power relationships within educational institutions.

Many people believe that it should be possible to accelerate the maturing of the new culture, if the riddle of linking these three considerations together effectively can be solved. Some even argue that there is no option but to engage wholeheartedly with these computer-led learning possibilities, because the arrival of mass computing facilities redefines the whole purpose of learning. To do otherwise is like trying to teach soldiers the arts of modern warfare by prolonged spells at the Spanish Riding School.

Cultural analysis has much to offer here. It is imperative to get behind the technofascination to the real issues. A project leader at Sheffield University puts it well:

The National Grid sets out clear goals for the achievement of the technology infrastructure, for schools connectivity, ICT teacher training and the creation of learning content. But the vision . . . is technology-driven rather than learning-driven . . . Content must be designed around the concept of lifelong learning progression and be available in a wide range of interdisciplinary subjects with strong on-line learner support and guidance. It is the combination of high quality learning materials . . . with group communication and a delivery structure which supports effective on-line learning which makes learning truly accessible. (Banks, 1998)

Qualifications and credits

The ready availability of nationally accredited qualifications, credit accumulation and transfer (CATS) arrangements, and a standard format for learners' records of achievement are all infrastructural facilities which learners and providers can draw upon at the operational level.

The assessment of learning outcomes, and certification of the results, are necessary facilities for many people. In the labour market they do for learners and learning what house deeds do for home ownership in the housing market: they signal that the learner has *some* degree of reliable learning, known to be valued by employers in the labour market. The efficient distribution of labour within the economy needs this procedure. Half of all people in employment are in 'second-best' jobs, which they had to take in the circumstances in which they found themselves. Without qualifications to assist recruitment this situation would be far worse. Qualifications can also give important incentives to individuals, by giving social recognition and approval to the learning they have achieved.

But qualifications create problems for others. Particularly important is the fact that qualifications are very often a condition of funding by the state. This can be very off-putting for people who have been switched off from learning, to whom the very mention of qualifications can be threatening or irrelevant. It can also lead to 'creaming': biasing learning recruitment strongly in favour of those who have already achieved and who are more likely than others to add to their pile of educational trophies.

Serious problems also face those who seek recognition for the learning which they have achieved in a real-life context. They may well find that their learning achievements, which are genuine and valued, are incompatible with accreditation requirements set down by the awarding bodies. The example in Box 4.3 describes one of many ways in which inflexible institutionalized arrangements can seriously inhibit individuals' motivation to learn.

Establishing the new general culture for lifelong learning means facing funda-mental issues in these areas. There is a central dilemma between *qualifications as an incentive, and a useful source of information for third parties*; and *qualifications as the source of pass/fail judgements* on the learning outcomes of particular individuals. 'Pass/fail' is known to leave lasting scars on personal motivation. It is important to establish for all qualifications: how effective they are in the signalling they do; what serious and necessary purpose they have; and how their arrangements and design avert failure, or deal with its consequences, should it arise.

There is also the question of the kind of qualifications which would best fit and

Switching off the learner: A nurse's domestic commitments prevented her from taking in-service training offered by the hospital where she worked. Instead, she borrowed a 'carer's certificate' training pack from her local library. She found this invaluable, and said it changed her view of her work. The hospital was unwilling to pay for the tutor's fee for validation of the course which would have enabled her to gain a certificate – as an alternative to financing her attendance at the courses provided by the local college.

Adapted from Allred (1990)

Switching on the learner: A hospital that is a lifelong learning organization would be flexible about the provision and range of training that it offered. It would ensure that staff had the option of distance and open learning, and that they were not restricted to a limited range of courses offered on site in one college only. It would also recognize the paramount importance of encouraging staff motivation towards learning.

Box 4.3 Switching the learner off or on.

support a new culture of lifelong learning. The fact that qualifications must be respected, useful and flexible raises many issues. Is there room for 'gold standard' qualifications which serve to undermine the reputation of other kinds of awards? What about depreciation over time in the value of a qualification? And can credit systems be made to work?

The best-kept secret of the UK learning system is that qualifications depreciate in value. In the conditions of the modern economy it cannot be assumed that graduates, or holders of any other qualifications, will maintain and enhance knowledge after receiving their award. What kind of 'call-in' services would a lifelong learning society need to help people keep abreast of developments?

Moreover the need for flexibility means that it is essential for many learners to secure credit for prior learning, to avoid waste and demotivation. But widely-based credit accumulated and transfer systems (CATS) have acute problems in establishing equivalence between competences and skills on the one hand, and knowledge and academic prowess on the other; and in ensuring that the qualifications reflect an overall mastery of a subject or skill, rather than prowess in components as unco-ordinated and separable tasks.

A new culture will need major reforms in the relationship between qualifications and curriculum. The qualifications framework for 16–19 education and training currently sets the curriculum for the state entitlement to further education and training: the qualification conditions the course, not vice versa. This enforces a narrow academicism on the age group, benefiting less than half the students, and for the convenience of the universities. The arrangements exert a long-term influence, confirming the division of the population into learning and non-learning groups.

The National Achievement Profile (formerly the National Record of Achievement) has so far been used almost exclusively in the schools. A lifelong record of achievement concept has yet to be demonstrated. It would need to enable people to document their personal performance and learning throughout life, in a form that helps self-reflection and assessment of achievement by others.

Overview of the infrastructure

In all these aspects of infrastructure there is a great temptation to engage in the exercise of *piecemeal* improvement. Two groups of people pursue this goal. Some, despairing of resource increases, try to squeeze more throughput from the learning system. Output-related funding is attractive to this school of thought. Yet so often this results in loss of quality, and a counterproductive trade-off between increases in volume – in the same old patterns of learning distribution – and hopes for a new culture. Others scrape what resources they can get and set up exploratory and innovatory projects, all with commendable zeal. Yet so often this channels the energy for radical reform away into marginal and frankly ephemeral themes.

In reviewing these issues of strategy and infrastructure we have tried to keep to a more holistic perspective. Three essential questions will need constantly to be asked during development of the infrastructure:

- What has to be done in this infrastructural area to enable it to support the lifelong learning culture?
- How will it increase the probability that people will continue to press for learning over their life spans?
- How can this piece complement what is to be done in other parts of the infrastructure, so that the whole will be more effective than the sum of its parts?

NOTES AND REFERENCES

1. Quasi-market: has some of the main features of a free market, but not all.
2. Department for Education and Employment (1997: 2).

Part II

Chapter 5

Time for Lifelong Learning

Time is an essential input into the learning process, and people's responses to it are very important for understanding the implications of general lifelong learning culture. The impact of time on learning is much more than a matter of when courses take place, or how much 'time off' people can get. The first step towards a useful idea of time is to reject the reductionist view which focuses on 'clock time', and on ways of saving odd moments here and there for learning, and to take a wider perspective.

Barbara Adam[1] encourages this approach. She has helpfully highlighted the shortcomings of conventional theoretical analysis regarding time, which tends to disaggregate the complex set of dimensions that everybody has to juggle on an everyday basis:

> Time is understood . . . as either social or natural, as a measure or an experience, as cyclical or linear. It may be associated with the clock or the rhythms of nature, with ageing and entropy or with the timing, sequencing, and rhythmic organization of activities. With few exceptions, social theorists conceptualize as single parts in isolation *what bears on our lives simultaneously*. [Italics added.] (Adam, 1990)

In the same vein, Geoff Mulgan and Helen Wilkinson[2] have voiced the sobering thought that '. . . material progress has not brought much improvement in how we use our time . . .'. They predict that a new political agenda will have to be 'no longer about rearranging or redistributing time, but concerned rather with its qualities'. This is particularly true for learning time.

Two senses of time

Lifelong learning means lives filled with learning. This chapter will consider the implications of this in two interlocking dimensions: *lifespan time* and *diary time*. Lifespan time is time seen as part of an entire lifespan – the accent is on *when in life* things happen, *how much of life* is consumed by them, and *in what order* events occur. This is time measured in months and years, perhaps even in decades. Diary time is time which is juggled in the day-to-day business of getting through life, and is measured in minutes, hours and days.

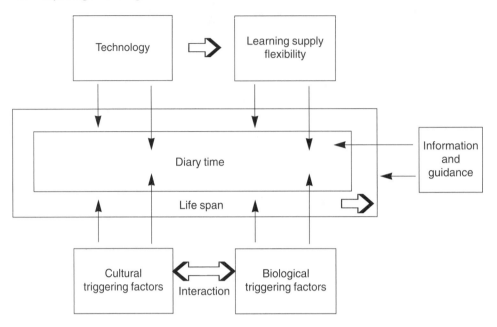

Figure 5.1 Time for learning and its influencing factors

Figure 5.1 shows how these notions fit together, and how they relate to a number of influencing factors. At the centre is the individual's learning experience in diary time. The outer box represents the lifespan time. Someone deciding to start a two- or three-year, full-time course, or embarking on a research project, is committing time in this high-level sense. Such decisions are about carving up the total lifespan (although they will certainly have acute implications for the diary also).

The inner box – diary time – is where time for learning competes with other uses of time, on a day-to-day basis. It is a measure of individuals' freedom that diary time – as an input – belongs to each of us. The state may currently take command of individuals' time for three things only: for learning between the ages of 5 and 16; on suspicion or proof of criminal and some illegal activity; or in war. Otherwise, people's diary time is their own to dispose of, or to make available to an employer in exchange for a wage. It is very significant that compulsory initial learning is in the list of state interventions. The social imperative for initial learning must be very great indeed for national policy-makers to require sequestration of time on such a scale.

A number of influences bear on people as they consider time, for learning in either of these two senses.

Biology

There are biological factors which influence the use of the lifespan for the purpose of learning; and there are also some biological influences which shape the ways in which people might manage their diaries from day to day for learning and other purposes.

The fertility cycle, for example, is particularly influential in females' lifespan decisions, because of the continuing impact of child-rearing on women's work and income. Age constraints may be important for the very old; while, for very young children, physical and social development play a significant part in determining how quickly they can be introduced to formal learning. Throughout childhood and adolescence, the pace of their continuing development also has a dramatic effect on learning possibilities. Variations in pace of learning achievement against the 'norm' can give rise to serious problems of adjustment, which may have a lasting effect on a learner's motivation towards lifelong learning.

Biology also affects diary time. Parents' nurturing roles, for example, take large slices from time potentially available for other learning; for older people, diminishing physical stamina may constrain the times of day when effective learning can be undertaken; and learners of any age may have learning styles requiring them to mix study with intermittent physical activity and relaxing breaks.

Biology has a fundamental effect, whether the emphasis is on how lifespan time is applied, or on the use of time per day. In many instances, biology applies the initial influence, and cultural factors then interact with it – often amplifying and complicating the initial effect.

Cultural influences

Cultural influences are similarly important in how people consider their time (in either of the two senses). An influential case, in terms of diary time, concerns children's travel to school. Society now expects that children will be accompanied any distance to and from school by an adult. For children themselves the process can impinge on the learning experience in a number of ways, affecting development of their sense of responsibility and independence; time management skills; peer-group relationships; informal out-of-school activities; opportunities for imaginative and creative play. Chaperoning can also represent a sizeable chunk of otherwise disposable learning time, for the adults who do it (see Box 5.1).

By 1990, 900 million hours were spent each year in accompanying children to school – reflected in the proportion of seven-year-olds going to school unaccompanied, which fell from 71% in 1971 to 7% in 1991. With the extra congestion caused as a result, it is estimated that the cost of seeing children to school and back was 1,356 million hours in 1990, or in money terms, £10,000 million.

Box 5.1 Chaperone time. Source: adapted from DEMOS (1995).

In terms of the lifespan, a pervasive ageism marginalizes and patronizes older people. Old age is still commonly treated as a period when people can be expected to give up their individuality, choose a fairly monotonous existence, and become mentally less flexible. This is very largely a social and cultural construct – often cloaked by a false biological argument – which dramatically restricts old people's opportunities for learning. For many, it reduces their inclination as well.

Technology

Technology is another factor appearing in Figure 5.1. This is taken here to mean any technique, equipment, or means of applying organization to the learning process. 'High' technology enables activities and processes formerly bundled together to be separated, and to be reassembled in endless combinations, at the user's convenience (see Box 5.2).

A class of 10-year olds visiting the House of Commons had notebook computers with them. During their visit, they took quick notes by typing in key words about the visit into these laptops. Later, back in the classroom, the notes were developed and finished, and transferred to one of the school's desktop computers for printing. 'The children found it easier to work like this because they didn't have to worry about spelling at [the first] stage,' said their teacher.

'During a 50-minute period students barely have enough time to produce a finished piece of work. With [a laptop] they can produce a paragraph or two, a spreadsheet or drawing, name and save it in a user area of [the school's computer network] to be assembled into one document later . . .'

'[This equipment] gives us access to one computer per child in a whole class, which we have found particularly useful for visually impaired pupils. Their worksheets on the computer are written in a large font so they do not feel isolated or separated from the main class . . . Even the less motivated students are really fired up by these things.'

Box 5.2 Time for improvement. Source: adapted from McTaggart (1998).

Information and communications technology can make time work in dramatically different ways: it allows more to be done in a given time; the ordering of events may be different; the risks of delay may be affected; and the separation and dovetailing of processes into efficient sequences may be enhanced. Metaphorically, high-tech time may be very different from low-tech time, and new technology (the 'knowledge media' in particular) can revolutionize people's experience and expectations of time.

In the learning context, Figure 5.1 shows the influence of technology working in two directions. Objectively, it affects how the learning provider can supply learning materials and experiences. This in turn has implications for the calls made on time. A test of this, relating to the diary, is to imagine doing without electric light, or a photocopier, or a computer, and the spectacular effects such events would have on the time it takes to carry through today's curriculum. Subjectively, it affects how individuals think about their options for disposing of personal time. The use of lifespan can also be radically affected. A new-found awareness of computer-based learning, for example, can encourage adults to re-engage with learning and to revisit the whole conception of their learning career for years ahead. This may result in their developing learning programmes for themselves, and for relatives and friends.

Information, advice and guidance

In much the same way, discovering time-flexible opportunities for learning through advice and guidance can strongly influence people's perception of time, in either of the two main senses (see Figure 5.1). Employee development schemes have shown, for example, that good guidance in the workplace, and information about systems for accreditation of prior learning and credit accumulation, can transform personal motivation. The realization that past learning has 'investment value' towards a new qualification – and that a learning provider is offering appropriate opportunities for busy, part-time learners – can prompt new ambitions or reawaken old ones.

PERSONAL LEARNING DECISIONS ABOUT TIME

Against this background people have to make decisions about learning time. They do so by weighing up *the offers of learning providers, with their costs and benefits* against *the opportunity costs of the time requirement.* This is the basic model of personal decision-taking related to time. In assessing this trade-off, attitudes and beliefs about diary time and the lifespan will have a major influence, working through their effect on *opportunity cost.* Opportunity cost has two aspects: the first (the standard technical meaning) is the loss of net benefit from alternative activities which would have taken place otherwise, were it not for the learning; and the second aspect focuses on the wider psychological and cultural cost which is often involved.

The following example shows both of these senses at work. Many women combine family care with home-working, paid at piecework rates. Typically, the work is low-grade assembling and packing; the rates of pay are very low indeed; and there are no employment benefits attached to the job. Many such workers speak little or no English. A worker of this kind may want to take up opportunities to learn in order to improve her ability to support her children (quite possibly as learners) and to increase the family's income through better-paid work. She faces the opportunity cost of completing less piecework; and, at psychological and cultural levels, she may also feel the cost of giving up aspects of traditional family roles which may be defined in the terms of domestic labour.

This basic model of decision-making can extend to three further features.

1. In the more technical sense of opportunity cost, learners' changes of preference or external events may shift dramatically to free up time for learning – or, conversely, to tie it up. If a dependant becomes ill, for instance, the opportunity cost of learning for the learner may suddenly rise and lead to an interruption of learning. Or, in a single-income family, one adult becoming redundant can free up the time of another adult in the household to do learning which they would not otherwise have done, and may also sharpen the incentive for that person.
2. Policy-makers interested in lifelong learning can develop policies which will strongly affect ways in which individuals consider the learning/time trade-off for diary time, or indeed for the lifespan.
3. The trade-offs tend to be highly complicated. Table 5.1 shows the typical allocation of time in the day in the UK.[3] The learning elements are hidden in the two residual

Table 5.1 Time use: May 1995. Source: *Social Trends 28.*

Activity	Hours and minutes per day
Sleep	8.42
TV and radio	2.33
Cooking, housework	1.35
Eating at home	1.01
Personal care	0.44
Garden and DIY	0.39
Care – child and adult	0.27
Other home leisure	1.08
Paid work	3.01
Travel	0.46
Socializing	1.03
Shopping	0.36
Eating/drinking out	0.31
Other out-of-home	1.03

categories, 'other home leisure', and 'other out of home'. It is clear that there is not much elbow-room for learning. What is more, time decisions become ever more complex – and opportunity costs for learning ever harder to face – as the result of contemporary changes, such as the rapid rise in households supported by short-term contract work and part-time jobs; the rise in the proportion of university students needing parents' financial support; and the shrinking of supportive kinship and neighbourhood networks.

In these circumstances individuals need a personal strategy for allocating parts of their lifespan to continuing and unfolding learning, and tactical plans for beating the constraints of the diary. Both of these demand particular kinds of skill on the part of the learner, and also the support of good domestic facilities and arrangements – such as the co-operation of other members of the household, or car ownership, for example. Learners also need external support through services such as child care (see Box 5.3). Most important of all, would-be learners need access to quality-assured guidance workers who can help them to pick their way through the thicket of personal constraints.

Finding time in the lifespan

This decision model can help to identify a whole range of factors influencing the release of lifetime for learning. Lifelong learning aims to spread learning across the whole of the lifespan. If this is to be realized the principal influences and constraints affecting people's use of the lifespan for learning must be closely understood. There are a number of specific ways in which biology and culture play important roles; but just as influential is the general view or idea which the would-be learner has of applying the lifespan to learning.

'Without depending on my mother, my sister and my mother-in-law it would just be too much. And they're not getting any younger. This morning my mum had [my daughter] twenty to eight. She walks up to the bus stop for her. To do that every day, to get me to work – I just don't think it's fair. They've had their time of this . . . I didn't mind so much when she was at the full-time nursery 'cos I felt no one was being put out. My sister came round quarter past seven yesterday morning for her to get me to work for eight and it's just not fair on people. Inconvenience to other people. It's just not practical.'

Box 5.3 Taking the strain. Source: adapted from Ford (1996).

Specific biological influences

At the young end of the age spectrum is a specific biological danger. If it is handled well, it can make lifelong learners virtually in the cradle; if it is handled badly, it can blight learning prospects for decades – if not permanently. It arises from the fact that the biology of human development is adapted to enable the very young to learn rapidly as a guarantee of reaching adulthood and of successful breeding. The behaviour of infants shows that learning is a basic instinct. Indeed in some respects – language development, for example – infant learning seems to be more efficient than adult learning.

This has important implications. Parents and other relatives have a corresponding natural teaching role, as part of nurturing. It is hard to overstate the influence on a child's future learning capacity if parents are imaginative and effective in this role. Middle-class parents generally seem to be able to give their children a head start over children from poorer backgrounds, because they are likely to have fewer constraints to contend with.

Lifelong learning policy needs to come to terms with the implications of this, and to give all parents strong support in this role. What happens in very early childhood can influence a person's learning behaviour and capacity for the rest of the lifespan. It follows that any physical or psychological problem that hinders a child's capacity to learn in early years needs to be identified early. Here again, middle-class parents typically have an advantage in dealing with professionals and initiating the necessary procedures. Local education authorities have often been slow to identify children at risk through the statementing procedure, and to promote effective long-term learning strategies for those with special needs.

Parents and teachers also have a responsibility to protect young children from the damaging effects of educational bureaucracy. This includes assessment and tests of the kind which put young learners under unreasonable pressure. There is a host of reasons why perfectly healthy and capable infants may not have the skills to sit still, manipulate pencils, and form recognizable alphabetic letters. Poor testing (under whatever name) which focuses on children's early attempts can mark them as failures, in the eyes of parents and others.

Adolescence is a similarly vulnerable time, when the blighting of future learning careers must be strenuously avoided. This is a stage when physical, emotional and social development; identity formation; energy levels; and the urge to grow up fast create strong distractions from learning for young people, over an extended period. This is where many of the learning needs of modern society have overtaken biology, and it is very important for lifelong learning that the contradiction is managed effectively and imaginatively. At this stage, the development of appropriate self-confidence can fundamentally affect attitudes to learning. If young people falter in terms of academic achievement for what are, in effect, biological reasons, they can become severely discouraged – often for the remaining lifespan.

Among young adults and into middle age, the biology of child-rearing comes into play again as a factor organizing the lifespan of many men and women. Current trends to later marriage and child-bearing may be loosening the biological grip to some degree, but family formation is still the predominant influence. This works in two ways. First, it is natural to put the child's needs first, and the imperative on every parent is to educate the child before updating personal knowledge and skill. This is where the disastrously simplistic doctrine of giving schools priority over adult learning really comes from. Second, children's immediate needs make such heavy demands on time that parents' own aspirations towards learning can easily be crowded out – pushed from the forward agenda, and down the list of priorities.

In this context the issue for lifelong learning is essentially new. Despite the dramatic effects of war, social change was generally slower across earlier generations: parents' own stocks of skills and experience served as a basis for teaching their children. The rapid changes in technology, and in social and economic frameworks, at the end of the twentieth century mean that *parents themselves have to keep on learning* if they are to fulfil the teaching aspect of the nurturing role. The policy task is to prevent the force of family responsibilities closing off large numbers of years from learning, just at the time when parents are still buoyant in their life expectations.

A counter plot runs alongside this theme. At any given time there are many adults who are not immersed in child-rearing. Some are childless; others are separated from their children through family break-up, or through the natural process of their children's developing independence. Policy-makers need to consider how to enable these groups to be lifelong learners.

Many people become freer of biological constraints on their learning as they move from middle age into the 'third age', than at any other time. But, for a growing proportion, nature is not content to relax its grip just yet. Given the ageing of the population, and the 'care in the community' policies of successive governments, many find themselves increasingly involved in the physical care of older relatives.

When final physical decline sets in at the 'fourth age', often quite rapidly, the interest and capacity for learning do start to fade away. But the onset of this final period and its length vary a great deal, and can be delayed by continuity in learning. Specially designed learning experiences, reflecting with others on life and experience, can give real meaning and satisfaction to the people concerned.

Overall, biological influences have very significant implications for the lifespan of learning, ranging from blighting effects if things go wrong, to serious preoccupations arising from natural caring roles. Many of these factors are intensified by cultural norms, and are often further intensified by public policy.

Cultural influences

Although there are periods in life when biology has a particularly strong influence on learning, the learning consequences are rarely *entirely* biological. Cultural forces often amplify vulnerabilities produced by biology; they may even invent false biological doctrines to rationalize the cultural bias, and generate new myths to support them.

There are also a number of influences which draw their strength rather more from culture than from biology. Some of these bear on children in early years and in preadolescence.

The greater support given to very young children by parents in middle-class groups has already been noted. It has long been held that child care in nurseries for pre-school years had lasting beneficial effects in later achievement at school. New research (still in progress on data from the National Child Bureau cohort) is reported to be finding a more fundamental effect that lies behind this: namely, that young children benefit hugely from parental learning support; and that, for a variety of reasons, middle-class parents generally do better at this than others, giving their children a significant head start.

But even here there is a downside. The current performance-related culture in schools causes many ambitious parents to be anxious, and to pressurize their children in ways which are counterproductive for learning in the long run. Bookshops and computer stores are now full of key-stage preparation and testing material for parents to use with their children at home. But children who have been pushed on too quickly merely learn to parrot answers in tests. The mistakes they make show clearly that they have not grasped the fundamental concepts involved in the use of the symbol systems underpinning literacy and numeracy. The disadvantage caused by such fundamental conceptual failure can become a serious handicap in later study. It explains much of the innumeracy and some of the poor literacy which afflict a high proportion of the population, with grave implications for lifelong learning.

Gender stereotyping in learning is also important. There is currently widespread concern about the lack of good role models for young boys in the domestic environment. The dwindling proportion of male teachers in schools compounds the difficulty. Many boys reject activities such as reading as 'girlie', in favour of physical activity (real or virtual). Media-promoted heroes and stereotypes reinforce the cultural message to boys that there are better things to do with their time – now and later – than school and book-based learning. Strong commercial and cultural expectations are also targeted on teenagers as 'young adults'. The results can be seen in primary and secondary schools, where many children (boys as well as girls) have become inappropriately concerned about their body shape and weight, in imitation of underweight role-models. All these factors affect future learning careers profoundly.

In the early middle years of life, very strong cultural effects intermingle with the biological factors to constrain people's options in allocating slices of their lifespan to learning. Many young women who fail or reject the academic route, and who slip away from further education into stereotypical jobs or unemployment, are drawn to motherhood as a familiar route to social status and authority. But this is often entry into a non-learning trap. This is likely to be confirmed later by the need for them to support family income through part-time employment – most of which may be spent on the costs of child care.

Women who do embark on professional careers must be prepared to face a series of possible dilemmas in balancing professional development and family development, despite progress on 'family-friendly policies' among employers. Although traditional gender roles in the home and in the workplace have been opened up for renegotiation, this is attempted more often than it succeeds. Men are typically less constrained. But they have been heavily hit by the insecurity of the labour market and by the long working hours, extensive travel and burnout now expected of the young up-and-coming male. The shift from 'nuclear families' towards 'serial families' means that increasing numbers of men have financial responsibilities towards more than one household. These pressures often make it difficult for fathers to support the learning activities of their children. As far as their own learning is concerned, the focus of this is most likely to swing towards vocational and functional learning.

Social and labour market changes have also profoundly affected men in the third age:

> ... the rate of activity of men between 55 and 65 has declined precipitously in the last 20 years in major industrialized economies, and in 1991 was down to 65% in the US, 64% in the UK, 54% in Germany and 43% in France. For these countries, be it by early retirement, disability, permanent unemployment, attrition, or discouragement, between one-third and over one-half of the male labour force *permanently* quits the labour market in their early fifties. (Castells, 1997)[4]

This ought to open up major new markets for learning, for many men remain active and fit enough to contribute socially through voluntary work well into their seventies. At one level, society would appear to support such learning. The Campaign for Learning survey in 1996, for example, showed that over 90% of the general youth and adult population agreed with the statement that 'you are never too old to learn new things'. Nonetheless, in practice a tenacious ageism sets in – part imposed and part self-imposed – which restricts the scope for learning by people in these age groups. The popular argument is that their wits are not sharp enough for learning; that they have short time horizons; and that any learning they might do will have only a short pay-off period.

These views are fallacious when taken as referring to general characteristics of the population. Recent research shows that the learning faculties of people moving through these stages of the human lifespan do not decline uniformly and steadily as the years advance.

> Two widely (though not universally) shared assumptions that have been held since the beginning of gerontology are, first, *that persons who have reached old age will be highly similar to each other,* and secondly, *that age-related changes are primarily a matter of decline.* The main determinants of ageing were often assumed to be sufficiently powerful and uniform, thus moulding each individual in the same manner. However, the scientific evidence from long-term longitudinal studies does not corroborate this expectation ... Death certainly is unavoidable, but the individual pathways toward death appear highly variable. [Italics added.] (Baltes and Graf, 1996)[5]

The lessons for lifelong learning policy are clear. Society needs to get rid of ageism masquerading as biological necessity – and use the experience of older people to encourage and support others' learning.

It is easy to see how public support for third- and fourth-age learning will falter in the battle for priority in public funding, when young people are denied the resources they need in the schools. It is also important to recognize that there may be something behind the view that many of today's old people struggle with learning, for many of them had far fewer educational opportunities than are available for people who are currently young or middle-aged. Sixty years of self-deprecation is bound to leave its mark. A sudden realization after many years that they might have untapped talents can seem very threatening.

What is forgotten however in the simplistic assessment of 'old versus young' is the fact that the social costs of supporting the health and well-being of third-agers in the community are very high indeed. They are likely to be calling for heavy public expenditures, and may be restricting the learning possibilities of their carers, if they are not keeping themselves active through learning. The economic case for learning in these groups is strong.

Making sense of the lifespan for learning

If people are to become lifelong learners they have to negotiate these biological and cultural pitfalls in ways which open up the lifespan. In pursuit of this, their general view of the learning life itself is very important – it is not just a question of action taken at specific vulnerable points in life.

In search of such general conceptions, and in the face of the endless variety of human life from cradle to grave, a number of assiduous psychologists have studied the life stories of individuals in an attempt to map lifespans into 'natural stages'. The assumption is that the natural stages of development clearly visible in children up to adolescence can somehow be extended over the rest of life. Such doctrines might be thought to support the argument that it is 'natural' to learn certain sorts of things at certain life stages, so that 'normal' people should stick to the path set by 'nature'.

In the learning sphere, as in many others, this sort of reasoning leads to dangerous exposure to crankiness. Happily, there are no 'natural stages'. A broad-band notion of 'normal' development is useful in early childhood, helping to alert adults to possible problems. But such stage models progressively lose any descriptive and normative force as the child grows older, and as biological and cultural forces interweave. People are not like clockwork toys, wound up in youth just to spend the rest of life unwinding. Such determinism can be broken.

A less 'scientific' hazard in conceptualizing the lifespan of learning is to surrender to the cultural stereotypes reflecting age, gender and notional stages of development which colour people's expectations about themselves, and about others. These stereotypes represent real barriers to learning. Many people still map their lifespan according to a model which says that youth is for education; young adulthood is for child-raising and earning; and old age is for retirement and dotage. This is despite the evidence of large numbers of individuals and families who develop their lives differently. Work on social identity indicates that the prevailing culture will tend to encourage others to classify such individuals and groups as exceptions.

A much better approach has been highlighted by Tom Schuller[6], who describes the way that people '. . . carry their pasts with them as they go'. This 'recursiveness' in progression challenges individuals continuously to develop identities which incorporate their experience and environments from the past and present. This view rejects the convention that life unrolls as a neat sequence through time, in linear fashion. It recognizes that people constantly revisit their past – weaving history and developing myth through changing personal and group narratives. Individuals' expression of personal identity can change markedly from one period to another through life. This is often described as people 'reinventing' themselves, in response to the influence of crises, new circumstances or environments.

There is a strong link between this process of reinvention and the practice of lifelong learning. A lifelong learning strategy which merely followed the gyrations of the clockwork learner would be a fundamental denial of the wish to learn afresh. A much better approach could offer every opportunity for people to reflect on their individual histories of learning, and to make new departures. This has deep implications for lifelong guidance facilities, and it also points strongly towards the importance of systems to accredit learning done by the individual prior to application for a place in institutionalized learning.

Tom Schuller identifies two further important elements:

> Less recognized is the importance of *opportunities to unlearn,* to escape from routines and habits which have become deeply embedded . . . Providing the appropriate environments in which routine can play an enabling rather than a stultifying role is a major challenge to adult educators, as it is for schoolteachers.

> . . . [multiplying] *the potential for human beings to learn from each other,* for older people to learn from younger generations, and for younger people to profit from the experience of their predecessors. But if people remain tied in to an age-stratified society, and one which in addition encourages individualism to an excessive extent, that potential will be lost. The challenge, in short, is . . . to achieve an integration between the learning patterns of different generations. (Schuller, 1992)

Taken together, these thoughts make a formidable case for a reflective, interactive approach for lifelong learners to make sense of their lifespan decisions on learning.

Provider flexibility

Flexibility in learning provision is the last of the main influences on individuals' ability to free up the lifespan for learning (see Figure 5.1, page 82). Learning providers can play a major role through their ability to customize their offerings; their efforts to structure the continuity of the learning experience; their responsiveness to 'just-in-time needs' for learning; and their response to critical events in individuals' lives. Assessing the performance of providers in these terms would require a major new study to be undertaken. In these areas there is always a difficulty in separating what providers say they do from what they actually do. Too many of the projects have short lives or do not get beyond the pilot stage.

Inflexible provision shows up in many ways. Too often providers oblige learners to wait for the start of the academic year to begin courses, and are unwilling and/or unable to customize the duration and timings of their courses. Or they withdraw courses at short notice once the group has dwindled to an uneconomic size. Or they do not offer unitized courses, to provide the flexibility that learners' circumstances may require. Or poor tracking systems mean that providers do not really know whether learners completed or failed to finish their courses. And, despite the known influence of family learning, providers generally still do little to weave together the learning of parent and child.

The contrast with other industries is stark. General medical practitioners take a lifelong perspective; insurance and pension services are also life-bound; solicitors seek to found their trade on lifelong loyalties; and financial services have long done so – for banking at least. But it is not so for learning providers. Too often they seem to regard themselves as 'stopovers', offering learning episodes as fragments of disconnected experience. It cannot yet be said that learning providers, taken together, are properly engaged on the task of opening up the constraints of the lifespan for business.

DIARY MANAGEMENT

Filling up the lifespan with learning is important – but it is only half the battle. Individuals have to make concrete decisions on diary time if they are to achieve their learning. Such decisions are also under significant pressure from culture and other influences.

Time management

The problems of managing diary time for learning are twofold. Regardless of its importance from a lifetime perspective, the learner cannot undertake a course unless it can be fitted into other day-to-day activities at an acceptable direct cost, and without unacceptable opportunity costs in terms of other activities and damage to cultural values. And, once the learning is under way, the time has to be managed so that the course can be successfully completed. It is not just personal time which has to be controlled in this way. People have to spend a good deal of effort gathering their time so they can do things together in groups. Time has to be sequenced, so that X can be done before Y. It may be necessary to spend time waiting, or time may need to be committed ahead of an event, or reserved on a conditional basis.

Time management is therefore one of the core skills for learning, just as it is for an efficient economy, and it has to be developed as a skill early in life. In a lifelong learning culture, finding diary time for learning will be a routine part of life – like finding time for eating and sleeping. Everybody will need to be skilled at finding it, and protecting it.

Three particularly important aspects of time management for learning are:

1. *Putting all the time needed into the account:* learners often do the equivalent of leaving a performance at the interval. When the 'reflective observation' and 'abstract conceptualization' stages of the learning cycle are concluded, they think that the learning is finished (see Figure 5.2). They forget the 'active experimentation' and 'concrete experience' stages. This failure is an important factor in ineffective learning. Another example is forgetting to include travel time.
2. *Learning can take place in parallel with other activities:* sometimes learning may have to be 'time out', secluded away from other activities and distractions (the music student in the practice room; the scientist in the laboratory), but on other

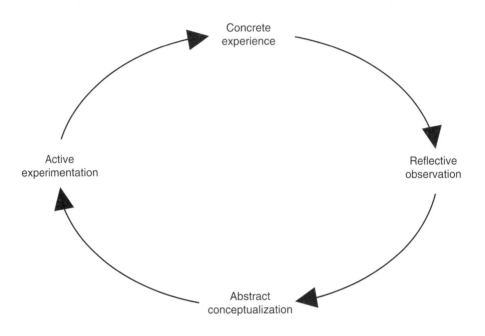

Figure 5.2 Kolb's Learning Cycle.

occasions learning time can be bundled simultaneously with something else (the driver listening to language audio tapes on the way to pick up the children from school; the literature student reading Chaucer in the doctor's waiting room). 'Parallel learning' can be very effective where the time cost for the learning is very small, because it shelters inside use of time on something else. It becomes time-on, rather than time-off.

3. *Learning time can be shaped to fit other activities:* A similar approach is for learning facilities to be sited with other activities commanding time priority. Sports facilities are now supplied at hotels aimed at the business-oriented customer, for example. Similarly, more learning facilities could be laid on in hotels, trains, airports, pubs, shopping centres – all places where people could do group or solo learning in the margins of a busy day. Efforts to make learning facilities more *portable* are part of the same picture.

Problems of time constraint tend to bite late in the process of planning a course of learning, as people approach the real problems of weaving learning into busy everyday schedules. Figure 5.3 shows data from NALS'97 on the *time squeeze* factor. It is clear that diary constraints are a major obstacle to learning. But the size of the effect is extremely hard to judge. Time problems often overlap with other constraints, and the particular effect of time constraints *as decisive in choices about participation* is almost impossible to untangle from survey evidence. Any such analysis would, in any case, depend on what respondents say or do not say – someone who is too poor to study may well prefer to say that he or she is too busy to study. People who are in learning can still

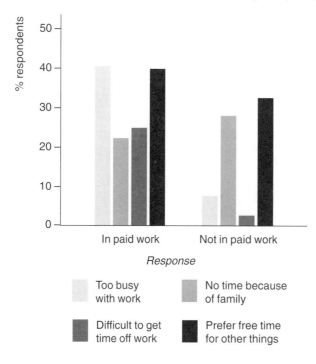

Figure 5.3 Time obstacles to learning. Population surveyed is aged 16–69, in England and Wales. Source: *National Adult Learning Survey* (Beinart and Smith, 1997).

have acute time problems, even though they are being managed at some cost and inconvenience. Providers are not always clear about how time-consuming courses really are, and it is a common phenomenon for learners to find out the hard way. This is where good advice and counselling are at a premium. Veronica McGivney's work[7] shows that time problems are an important element in student dropout from courses.

The UK learning system needs to provide more training in time management, as a core skill for learning. Much of what is currently done is supplied by employers. Colleges and universities are beginning to anticipate these needs of employers, and there are now demands for the schools to do more.

> Unless people learn the inner discipline needed to use time effectively, they cannot be truly autonomous. For schools, designed to teach people the external discipline of fixed timetables, this may require nothing short of a cultural revolution. (Mulgan and Wilkinson, 1995)

A problem in this context is the Fordist approach to time in the vast majority of schools:

> Even the most cursory look at contemporary school life reveals that everything is timed . . . the activities and interactions of all its participants are choreographed to a symphony of buzzers and bells, timetables, schedules, and deadlines. Layer upon layer of such schedules form the structure of our education system . . . Like the monastery bell, the

school bell secures conformity to a regular collective beat . . . it is neither questioned as a practice nor doubted as a principle: it is simply taken for granted. Without alternative vision and choice the participants surrender to the bureaucratically institutional beat. (Adam, 1990)

Importance of culture

There are two ways in which cultural and social pressures can impinge on the increasingly difficult job of finding the time for learning. At one level the task is essentially practical – just keep the plates spinning. But society may hinder some people more than others in carrying out this task. At another level the problem is not the practicalities, but the existence of cultural distractions – drowning out the efforts which people might otherwise have made.

At the practical level

Time constraints may be avoided, by swapping time around, or by arranging for someone or something else to substitute for the learner in commitments which would otherwise clash with learning time. Or they may be *bought out* through the purchase of a car, or automatic washing machine, or microwave oven, for example – making the crucial difference between a person having or not having enough time for learning. Frequently, time constraints are *ducked* by learners taking a 'second best' course which fits in without challenging the cause of constraint.

Much hangs on people's skills and resources to follow these remedies. But the 'playing field' is far from level across different social groups. An important factor in lower socio-economic groups is the high degree of illiteracy at documentary level (see Chapter 2). Access to information, advice and guidance can be crucial in offsetting this. Money is also important to help buy ways round the constraints, through time-saving machines and services, but public grant and loan support for learning focuses for the most part on fees, and hardly extends into these areas. Higher-income groups, on the other hand, can do more learning because they have greater access to the means of buying their way out of time constraints.

Cultural distractions

There is a limit to how far the nimble management of time can go in opening up diary time for learning. This is where cultural perspectives really bite, for they *fundamentally* shape the way that people are inclined to view their lives and direct their activities.

Many people are influenced by the consumerism of the current age, and by a cultural ambience which makes life seems too fragmentary, momentary and chaotic for long-term planning. Sociologists have written extensively on these themes, many describing a postmodern age where attention spans are short, values are provisional, and facts are true only as far as you can see them. These phenomena affect the young disproportionately.

People also often say that there is no time for learning. They feel that they are too busy, and that society in general is too hard-pressed. This is largely a misperception, similar to the popular view that society is much more dangerous than statistics show it to be. Studies of the use of time show significant amounts of discretionary time which could be freed for learning, even after allowing for the requirements of working and family life. Studies of these themes are badly needed, for it is important to understand why these general views have come to be so widely held. Until such studies have been carried out, it may be supposed that much of this is a polite way of saying that people are not confident enough in their basic skills to risk a course of learning; or that they are fatalistic about the chances that learning will improve their lot in the increasingly unstable labour market and social scene.

There also seems to be a sense of time unravelling, as regular patterns of time use break down. Rapid changes in the patterns of working time, for instance, can have a general deterrent affect on learning and on other uses of time which have to fitted around the margins of work. Full-time workers work longer hours in the UK than in most other European countries; shift working is on the increase, particularly in sales and security occupations; and only around a fifth of the labour force have flexible hours, which might in principle accommodate learning well.

The policy implications for lifelong learning of the diary time concept, and also of the earlier paragraphs on lifespan, are listed in Box 5.4. Many of these themes will be revisited in Part III.

Lifelong learning policy is needed which will result in:

- early-years education and experience in schools which does not blight motivation for learning;

- the state's contribution to learning to be fully flexible in time (postponable, stretchable, repeatable, and interruptible);

- a fully mature lifelong service of information, advice and guidance which helps people
  – to review repeatedly their lifespan strategies for learning; and
  – to solve the day-to-day time constraints;

- lifelong records of achievement providing individuals with a basis for reflection on learning progression throughout life;

- training in the management of time, for all learners from school onwards;

- learning providers to offer over-time loyalty and continuity-based services, offering a high degree of customization and divisibility in course arrangements;

- more prominent and systematic voluntary arrangements for workers to have time off for learning;

- much increased facilities and public support for older learners;

- extensive mentoring and support which draws older people into learning;

- improved support for family care, to encourage carers' own learning;

- focus on difficulties faced by parents during child-rearing years;

- financial and other support for intergenerational learning, including
  – family-based learning solutions which link the learning of parents and children;
  – complementary arrangements for children living in institutions.

Box 5.4 Life time and diary time: policy points.

NOTES AND REFERENCES

1. Adam (1990).
2. Mulgan and Wilkinson (1995).
3. Office for National Statistics (1998).
4. Castells (1997), Vol. 2.
5. Baltes and Graf (1996).
6. Schuller (1992).
7. McGivney (1996).

Chapter 6

Space for Lifelong Learning

Space cannot be accounted for in the same way as money and time, but it is an essential element in arrangements for learning. Space provides the arena and channels where money and time are expressed as resources for learning. Space and place are linked, since place – as location for events and relationships – is a key characteristic of almost all learning spaces. For convenience, people often use the single term 'space' when referring to the dual concept of space/place.

In the current learning culture, space for learning tends to be specialized for the purpose, and segregated from the basic activities of everyday life and work. Learners often have to break off what they are doing and go to the chosen space for the specific purpose of learning. The learning space also tends to be heavily institutionalized. This is similar to the way that mental health and public caring facilities were institutionalized and segregated away from the rest of society before implementation of Care in the Community policies.

Space is beyond doubt a central issue for lifelong learning. But it is one which cannot be neatly separated from questions of time or money. Time constraints may well be reflected in the places, and the kinds of spaces, used for learning; and learning space can significantly affect the cost of learning to the learner.

THE LIMITS OF LEARNING SPACE

The space/place duality has to be understood closely in developing ways of thinking about space for lifelong learning.

'Space' is used here to mean the designed learning environment – that is, the nature of the physical context for the learning process and its various activities. The environment consists of facilities, people, materials, stores of knowledge, buildings, light, sound and much else. The designer assembles this context because it is conducive – and perhaps necessary – to the learning which is intended to take place. Different kinds of learning activity (vehicle maintenance/desk research/singing, for example) need qualitatively different contexts.

'Place' is taken here to mean location. This is where, in conventional terms, the learning process is undertaken, and where the various facilities are positioned. Bamford Primary School is in the village of Bamford in the High Peak district of Derbyshire, for example. Place in this respect is a characteristic of the learning space – a map reference which establishes where the learning space is, and its distance from other locations.

In the most simple case therefore, learning space is a learning environment at a given location. But this simple case is rare. It is very commonly the case that the designed learning environment has elements within it which are at very different locations, some of which are not necessarily even plotted on the map. What makes these different locations part of a single learning context is the existence of various kinds of connections between them. The connections may be through a single learner, or they may be through various kinds of networks – such as telecommunications, broadcasting/narrow casting, postal services, travel infrastructure. People in different places share the same learning space when they communicate about learning.

The way that learning commonly spreads over different locations, and the potential of ICT in this, is beginning to be more widely recognized. In recent years, schools in some areas have taken initiatives to involve pupils and their parents outside school in learning compacts. The primary aim of these is often to improve school attendance, but they usually seek also to influence conditions for the young person's completion of homework. Nonetheless, learning providers in general (including most schools) still tend to be restricted to the organizational space for which they are responsible, and which they can control.

Learning cannot be narrowly located for another reason. Lifelong learning focuses on the importance of the learning cycle in its entirety (see Figure 5.2, p. 94).[1] This cycle means that it is inherently unclear just where and when learning takes place. The implications of information and ideas received in an encounter with a teacher, or with other learners, may not strike a learner until later on – perhaps when there is an opportunity to reflect or to try things out at home, at work, while shopping or in conversation with friends. This highlights the learning potential of all kinds of places where learners might find themselves at any stage of the learning cycle.

These considerations bring out a key issue for lifelong learning. If the learning provider's design of the learning environment does not cover the whole cycle, and its concern cuts off early in the cycle (at the organization's perimeter), whose responsibility is it to design and manage the wider environment? How can people who are not professional educators, in their locations, help learners to review and to 'fix' ongoing learning? How can public bodies and communities in a lifelong learning society work together with learning providers to ensure that public places provide opportunities for people to reflect usefully on what they are learning?

In the current culture the narrowing approach to design of learning spaces reveals much about the values of society. Learning activities – in common with undertakers' activities – are sanitized and removed from ordinary environments. It is as if the freeze-frame button has been pressed on the dynamics of societal development. In the words of Manuel Castells:

> Space is the expression of society. Since our societies are undergoing structural transformations, it is a reasonable hypothesis to suggest that new spatial forms and

processes are currently emerging . . . space is not a photocopy of society, it *is* society. Spatial forms and processes are formed by the dynamics of the overall social structure. (Castells, 1996–98)

RETHINKING LEARNING SPACE

The current disposition of learning space therefore reflects a learning culture and society in stasis. A lifelong learning society is a fundamentally new organism. It will be much more dependent on information technology than anything yet experienced, and will produce its own characteristic disposition of learning places and spaces. Such a society will drastically reshape and open out the learning environment that it inherits.

Traditional arrangements

Traditional arrangements for learning are offered in environments supplied by the provider, at a physical place or places in the community. Boundaries are clearly marked. The would-be learner goes to the provider's place to collect information, to enrol, and then to take part in a learning process as a member of a learning group led by a teacher. The provider may also send information and administrative documents to the learner's base. Within the learning group, communications between members and between members and teachers are verbal, visual, written and printed. They may occasionally be supported over distance by telephone, fax and e-mail.

The range of facilities provided within the learning environment tends to reflect the extent to which education is the organization's primary business. The paradigm model in the current learning culture caters directly or indirectly for:

- learning, teaching, assessment and associated support services – including ICT supply, technical support and maintenance;
- student support services;
- governance and management;
- meals and refreshments;
- sickness;
- socializing and entertainment;
- contemplation and worship.

Some providers also cater for the supply and upkeep of student accommodation and child care. This list is not exhaustive.

Distance learning

The basic arrangements for distance learning show marked differences, compared with the traditional model. Communications have a greatly increased importance, enabling a flow of information and materials, teaching and assessment processes, and teacher-to-learner, and learner-to-learner support. The learning group is likely to be dispersed in the wider community – possibly across the globe – with members mostly communicating by post or telecommunications. They occasionally meet with the teacher for tutorials, and/or for residential sessions at premises supplied by the provider. The community is more actively engaged as an aspect of the learning environment. The boundaries around the provider's environment are more permeable than in the traditional case.

Distance learning uses printed, broadcast and narrow cast, audio and video learning materials. It is basically of two kinds: *synchronous,* when teacher and learner(s) are in different places, but are communicating in the same time; and *asynchronous,* when learners collect and use learning materials at a different time and different place from where the materials were prepared by a teacher, or by a team of teachers and technicians.

In either case, the learners tend to be learning apart from each other, as well as at a distance from the teacher; or alternatively they may be in local groups physically separated from each other. Increasingly, with the development of ICT, learners and teachers will communicate with each other via telephone (conventionally or through teleconferencing arrangements), e-mail and fax.

Whatever its precise form, distance learning stresses the importance of providing support to individual group members. The aim is to enhance learners' sense of group identity, enabling them to offer and draw psychological support from each other, as well as from the teacher, whether they are together or apart. Importantly, learners value such arrangements, welcoming occasional face-to-face tutorials and group residential sessions, as a complement to their distance learning.

Hybrid models are common. A course may have a traditional element, but also have phases or elements of distance learning, both at one and the same time or in sequence. The permutations are many and varied. Each demands different skills of learners, teachers and learning providers.

Behind this variety an underlying sense of direction is clear. There are strong factors making for a swing towards the distance learning concept which are not likely to be reversed. Pressures on time, and the complexity of those pressures, point strongly to a model of learning which brings learning out of its segregation and into the more convenient locations of everyday life. Computers and the Internet are opening up ways where people can communicate reliably and cheaply at a distance. People are generally becoming more versed in new forms of retailing, where services are supplied direct – as in 'direct' banking, for example, or cold selling via the telephone. (Cold selling has been reported to be successful in an early 'University for Industry' pilot project in Sunderland.) Knowing how to respond to such approaches, and how to use the services offered, will rub off on learning.

That is not all. The power of computers in overcoming the costs and labour of accessing learning materials and information is increasing dramatically, and the availability of these facilities, still small across the population, will shortly be given a huge boost by the arrival of digital communications and cheap connections to the Internet along electricity cables. The realization that the learner is more central, and more in control, when using the new 'knowledge media'[2] is likely to be deeply appealing to people who have come to associate learning with being patronized by teachers and learning institutions.

Effective design of the learning space

For reasons such as these, people designing learning spaces for the emerging lifelong learning culture are certain to be preoccupied with ways to open out the learning environment. This will involve two elements: a shift towards distance learning models and a recognition that – whatever the model – the boundaries of the learning environment do not coincide with the physical territory of learning providers.

These shifts mean replacing a view of learning as a periodic event with a notion of learning as a continuous flow. What appears in the traditional model as periodic attendance for lessons, in a particular learning environment, at a given physical location, dissolves to include a flow of learning activities and communications across the virtual environment of distance learning. This coincides with Manuel Castells' view of social organization at large:

> . . . our society is constructed around flows: flows of capital, flows of information, flows of technology, flows of organizational interaction, flows of images, sounds and symbols. Flows are not just one element of the social organization: they are the expression of processes dominating our economic, political, and symbolic life . . . the space of flows is the material organization of time-sharing social practices that work through flows. (Castells, 1996–98)

The challenge for a lifelong learning society is to form associations between the flow of learning opportunities on the one hand and the flows of domestic life and work in society on the other. For the 'architects' and 'engineers' of learning environments the question is how best to construct these learning associations. An increasing proportion of time will need to be spent on constructing and managing learning networks and virtual environments, connecting all kinds of associations and communities; and adapting environments built for traditional learning. The providers of learning opportunities will be closely involved in this, but they will also have to share their responsibilities with others if the full extent of the learning environment is to be set up effectively for lifelong learners.

As far as the lifelong learner is concerned, the architectural and engineering work has to address three essential things: the feasibility and cost of the learning to the individual; the effectiveness for the learner of the learning experience; and the extent to which the learning environment fosters and expresses social commitment to learning. The particular design of the learning space, and the permutations of its elements, will have implications for the commitment of time and of money. In effect they set an important part of the overall price. If the permutations are restricted – making frequent travel for the learner essential, for example – the particular course may be unfeasible; or the opportunity may be reduced, because of inroads into family budgets for money and time. The constraints may even force the learner into taking a second-best learning course, or abandoning learning intentions altogether.

The permutations of the elements also affect the learning process directly. Some environments are better than others for effective learning. Some people find it more important to have a teacher than others do; or the social aspect of the learning pace, as reflected in the make-up of the learning group and in the quality of its communications, may be very important to individual learning success, and to building motivation and

'It was obvious that putting computers in classrooms unsupervised for significant periods in the day and used under the supervision of teaching staff who did not "own" the equipment or space could lead to problems of maintenance, security and vandalism. It would also be inefficient and inflexible . . . So we went for the creation of IT centres – at least one on all significant college sites. We started by combining classrooms to give a capacity of 50 to 60. When these rapidly proved inadequate, we removed more walls to take in the adjacent corridors and the other rooms opposite, developing centres with a student capacity of 80 to 110.'

'The atmosphere in the learning centres is generally purposeful and work-oriented. Students are encouraged to work together if they wish, so silence is not a feature – but excessive noise is not generally a problem either . . . The message we are receiving is that students like working in learning centres, volunteer to use them, respect the light supervision of learning advisers, and behave well. On the other hand, students do not volunteer for classroom work, need registering to motivate regular and punctual attendance and require firm supervision.'

Box 6.1 Transforming traditional college space. Source: adapted from Pitcher (1995).

a learning culture which extend well beyond the boundaries of the course. A lifelong learning culture assumes that learners want to share their learning with others. This indicates the need for a general social environment that enables groups of people to talk and to share their ideas. In the current culture, places such as clubs and pubs – which used to provide such environments – have increasingly been invaded by a culture of noisy entertainment.

The engineering of learning space in these terms merits the closest attention, both by individuals and providers (see Box 6.1). Just as the architect of a building negotiates the design brief with the client, so the learner, the provider and the community at large, need to negotiate with the architects and engineers of learning space. The usual assumption – that the learning provider holds the ring – may not be the solution in the lifelong learning context. Even if it were, it would be rare for the provider to lodge the responsibility for design of the learning space in all its aspects with any particular person or unit. Bursars, architects, engineers, teachers and administrators all have fingers in the pie.

Although some features of design will be fixed, learners will demand more and more flexibility as time goes on. A modern and efficient learning industry will have to respond to this challenge, which will be every bit as demanding as the changes sweeping over the retailing sector in the wars between major supermarket chains.

The implications are profound for all parties in the negotiation. Learning institutions whose primary business is delivering learning opportunities may need to reconsider a whole host of basic arrangements and provision. In a society where learning is distributed across communities, how can responsibility for the learning environment be shared among stakeholders? What implications does this have for the role of the institution as a source of professional expertise and support for non-specialists? Individuals and non-educational learning organizations catering for learning need to think hard about learning spaces and their attributes, and about communications in homes, workplaces, and in public and private spaces in the local community. Public bodies will need to protect the wider public interest in the negotiations, seeking common infrastructural solutions, if they do not emerge from competition in the marketplace.

In one form or another the emphasis in the negotiations on learning space will continually turn on issues of association and communication. The good design of group arrangements at every level is essential, especially in the context of groups whose members need to communicate more often than they meet face-to-face. The negotiations also need to have in mind the dynamics of learning itself in the wider social context. The ultimate goal will be to turn what is a complex of individual, flexible solutions to the learning space issue into a new society-wide nexus of learning, which knits the whole community together in a conducive set of interdependent and interconnected environments for learning. This constructed 'learningscape' is directly analogous to the concept of landscape for the architect or town planner.

ASPECTS OF LEARNING SPACE

People who reject the idea of learning do so for a variety of reasons. Important amongst them is the rejection of the learning environment, as it is perceived.

Distance and location

Many influences shape learners' perceptions about locations for learning, and the distances which they involve. Practical considerations about the time and money costs of travel, or of living away from home base, are commonly important in deterring the learner.

The strong traditional association of learning with educational institutions segregated from other activities may discourage some people from thinking of learning in places such as hotels, pubs, airports, trains, etc. Some learners are also discouraged by locations which are unfamiliar and risky, both to get to and to negotiate, once there. In the past, youth trainees from Toxteth were sometimes reluctant to travel to central Liverpool, because they regarded it as dangerous territory for them. Many people avoid going through the gates of a college for fear of the unknown, and because of anxiety that they will not be able to find their way around. The architecture and general environment may also recall school and other public buildings which they have experienced as hostile.

Cultural, social and physical considerations may limit travel options, or the possibility of living away from home, for members of some ethnic and religious groups, and for some people with physical disabilities. On the other hand, some learners, particularly university students, have traditionally been keen to find a learning base which involves living away from home. Recent changes in funding are forcing a radical reassessment of this. Time-shiftable and time-stretchable entitlements could work to the same effect.

The content of some learning programmes limits them to certain specialized spaces and places. Marine biology, for example, needs access to maritime spaces; most scientific study needs access to laboratory space. The lack of choice may create an insurmountable constraint.

The learning environment

Whatever the location(s), the environment for learning itself raises complex and inter-related issues. These reflect concern for personal safety, social and cultural values, and all the physical, intellectual and technical needs associated with learning. In general terms, 'learning in the community' should have a noticeable impact on the management of indoor and outdoor public spaces, to cater both for quiet and for noisy learning.

People's social and cultural conditioning have very important implications for the learning environments which they seek, and which providers want to provide. Individuals will tend to be drawn to environments which express, as far as possible, values similar to their own. Grand architecture that impresses tourists and sponsors may be hostile to learners who are not used to it, and be rejected by those who find the values it expresses inappropriate to present-day conditions.

A learning environment must provide personal safety and security at the very least. Beyond that, a decaying environment can seriously impair the attitude and motivation of learners, and poor design and function can waste learners' time and exhaust their patience. These problems express themselves very forcibly in the case of learners with disabilities, and some older learners, but they apply in varying degrees to all learners.

A provider must also offer – directly or indirectly – the kind of social and intellectual environment that will encourage cross-fertilization of ideas. Group loyalties are fostered by social contacts, and the effectiveness of learning groups is reinforced by the wider social ambience. This is just as important in distance learning as it is in other forms of learning, and may need more attention and structure as part of provision. A provider wanting to promote successful learning (and hoping to attract repeat business) will make sure that appropriate social spaces are readily accessible to all learners, whether or not they provide them themselves. Similarly, the provision and quality of learning services, and of technical support services, will condition the quality of learning available.

KEY FACTORS FOR LIFELONG LEARNING POLICY

Analysis can too easily produce lists of factors, like those above, which create a huge jigsaw of policy pieces – obscuring clear messages for lifelong learning. A number of important general themes do, however, emerge.

Good information, advice and guidance

Advisers and guidance professionals have an important role in helping the learner to weigh up choices of learning locations and environments on offer. For some time, people who manage databases of learning opportunities have been trying to develop standardized descriptions of locations and environments to help in this process. This remains a relatively underdeveloped aspect of the information and guidance services.

Partly because of this, but partly for reasons of their own, learners are still inclined to be over-casual in their assessment of spatial choices. Many young learners do not even read the prospectuses of universities which they eventually join as students

ECCTIS, which runs the national database of higher education courses, conducted research in 1997–98 among just over 1,000 second-year UK undergraduates (excluding students who had dropped out during or at the end of their first year of study). This showed that:

- 22% wished they were on a different course or in a different institution;

- 15% expressed disappointment or regret about their choice of university or college;

- only 37% had referred to the institution's prospectus before applying for a place;

- only 32% had consulted an 'alternative' prospectus (not the institution's official publication);

- about 20% had used the institution's course databases;

- about 12% had used other information systems.

Box 6.2   Buying an expensive pig in a poke. Source: adapted from Carvel (1998).

(see Box 6.2). The speed of the admissions procedure may be partly to blame, but this lack of basic research is a sign of profound stress in the choice-making system, given the size of the financial commitment which students are making. It is certainly not in anybody's interest in the long run.

Customization

Even if designers of learning environments extend learning beyond specialized spaces, such open solutions will still involve a host of trade-offs. No one solution will be good for all purposes and for all client groups. If the aim of the new culture is to extend participation by working over and around the constraints which have blocked learning in the past, it is likely that learning environments will have to be customized in very particular ways. Lifelong learning implies customization in large quantities. Openness by itself is not enough.

The convenience of learning at home may appeal to many lifelong learners, even if it means that they have less support from fellow learners. For some, indeed, it may be the only option. But it would be dangerous to assume that conditions in the home will necessarily be conducive: it may be too noisy and crowded. In a lifelong learning society, community-based learning centres would be a common feature of housing estates and residential areas, possibly as part of shopping centres and health centres. They would offer customized arrangements for quiet study, as well as facilities for group learning. After-school homework clubs already cater for this need for young people.

Customization should be pressed as far as the needs of the learners warrant. For some groups the process has to be unique to the particular individuals, who may need investment in special learning equipment and/or tutoring. This will be the case for certain people with disabilities, to others with exceptional abilities, and for pupils excluded from school. According to Her Majesty's Inspectorate, this facility is not always forthcoming from local education authorities.

Such customization has always suffered from the burden of high costs. But much of that cost is due to the rarity of customization, and the lack of process engineering which enables customization within mass production systems. As it helps to push the numbers of learners up, the cost of customization will come down.

Learner–teacher communication

Design of learning spaces needs to stretch far beyond considerations of the built environment, and of travel. Learner–teacher communications are a radical part of the design brief. This is where, for example, the proportion of face-to-face communication is determined, and where the amount of time for communication is fixed. The use of technology also features highly. To put all these matters into proper context there has to be a realization of what the teacher–student relationship should be, both for children and for adults, in a general lifelong learning culture.

The fundamental importance of this is reflected in Paulo Freire's firm rejection of the 'banking' concept of education,

> . . . in which the scope of action allowed to the students extends only as far as receiving, filing, and storing the deposits of knowledge. They do, it is true, have the opportunity to become collectors or cataloguers of the things they store. But in the last analysis, it is the people themselves who are filed away through lack of creativity, transformation, and knowledge in this (at best) misguided system. For apart from inquiry, apart from the praxis, *individuals cannot be truly human.* Knowledge emerges only through invention and reinvention, through the restless, impatient, continuing, hopeful inquiry human beings pursue *in the world, with the world and with each other.* [emphasis added.] (Freire, 1970)

This view presents the interactions at the heart of learning as defining humanity itself. The model of the facilitating teacher contrasts strongly with the didactic model, where the aim is to transmit information for people to file away in knowledge vaults. Design of learning spaces depends crucially on which model is used.

The facilitating model is common in adult learning. But when the primary aim is to stimulate and maintain lifelong learning it also suits teaching for younger people in schools. People who teach in this context may have to be more directive than in the case of the adult learner, because lack of self-discipline among younger learners can ruin the learning process. But discipline should not be allowed to slip into a didacticism in the teaching process itself. Power relationships used for keeping order can easily infuse and undermine the teaching process itself. As schools shift their focus away from 'schooling' and testing, and towards skills and motivations of lifelong learning, teaching roles will change. Managing this change will make new demands on teacher training and development, and on parents and other adults, in taking a greater share in the task of raising generations of young learners.

The designers of the learning space should be working to implement the facilitiative model. But good communications, encouraging the growth of trust, require more than bricks and mortar, space layouts, or telecommunication links. They have to work in practice, and they have to be maintained. Even in an impeccably planned learning space discomfiture can come from the teacher or the learner, or may directly intervene between the teacher and the learner – as a function of poor basic skills in using the environment.

The reasons for poor communication sometimes lie with the teacher's oral delivery, or with the teaching equipment. But, at a deeper level, teachers themselves may not really want to communicate; and they may not have the skills to get comfortable with the groups whose learning they are seeking to facilitate. On the learner's part, this is one very practical area where illiteracy and lack of confidence leave a deep mark, and where cultural divides may appear as chasms.

Learning groups

The design and specification of learning groups are crucial aspects of the learning environment. Indeed no learning environment can be judged for its effectiveness without considering the groups which will use it. Whether in face-to-face or distance learning, in small groups or in large classes, research shows that learners draw important psychological support from the sense that they are members of a learning community. This is true even for those who function for most of the time as members of a 'virtual' group, through electronic contact with teachers and/or other learners.

> [Students registered with the Open University], many of whom are otherwise isolated say that viewing the programmes makes them feel part of a learning community. This explains why many of the students who record programmes on videocassette recorders (VCRs) also watch them at the time they are broadcast. (Daniel, 1996)

A learning group has to keep in balance potentially conflicting factors. Ideally, group members need to be able to stimulate each other to learn in the most effective ways, as well as learn effectively for themselves. The 'best combination' in any situation will be strongly affected by the aims of the group, and the experience of the learners.

In some contexts designers may need to set up groups *within* distinctive cultural settings – but not all learners will be equally comfortable with the same groups. In other contexts the 'best combination' might mean consciously recruiting for cultural mix – if, for example, one aim of the learning group is to promote a sense of community in a newly built estate.

There are major difficulties in making best use of grouping:

- *The fallacy that learning time is only time spent on formal classes and assignments.* The designers of learning groups need to think beyond the context of formal attendance. Students at all ages in full-time initial education, for example, are increasingly taking to part-time employment for financial reasons. Some far-sighted teachers are seeking to organize this as learning experience.
- *The problem that organized group projects may cause difficulties with assessment.* Institutions are finding ways round this, but the problem of giving average assessment results to all members of a collaborating group remains acute.
- *The continuing ethos of personal competition* makes serious impact on the possibility for effective group communications.
- *Habituation to independent learning often runs very deep for older learners.* Good communications within and between groups has to be learned. This implies training, and in the case of the older learners, retraining.

- *The invisibility of people with specific learning disabilities and serious lack of skills.* This includes those who are socially unconfident, and those without Internet capability. It should not be left to chance, or the good will of individuals, to ensure that there is an inclusive approach to group communications.

In all this, the important point for lifelong learning is that design of the group aspects of learning environments is in its infancy. There has been a deep neglect of a whole dimension of the learning space. Indeed, there are dangers in pushing ahead with learning environments of a more open kind if this neglect is not tackled.

Networks of learning groups: a new university

If learning in groups is so effective, there can be major added benefits from linking learning groups in wider learning networks which can stimulate each other and cross-fertilize each other's learning activities.

This comes close to the classic theory of a university: a civilizing community of minds, covering the whole universe of knowledge, which grows and preserves its knowledge by mutual support, cross-fertilization, and specialization. Freed from its monkish origins and its latter-day association with higher knowledge, this idea captures precisely the connectivity which a lifelong learning culture would require. The 'University for Industry' is a doubly dreadful misnomer, but if it can enhance this connectivity for the wider learning society it will have justified at least the first half of its title. And what goes for universities should go for the whole learning apparatus of the country.

NOTES AND REFERENCES

1. Kolb (1984).
2. 'Knowledge media', or 'third generation' distance education technology represents the convergence of computing, telecommunications and the cognitive sciences. It promotes 'rich and rapid interaction between members of a learning community' (Daniel, 1996).

Chapter 7

Money for Lifelong Learning

The new general culture of lifelong learning cannot float on hot air, or on the good intentions and rhetoric of its protagonists. If it is not properly financed, it will not happen. If there is to be a large increase in the volume of learning across Britain, that volume has to be paid for by one or more of the main stakeholders: the individual, the state, the employer, the learning provider. Yet recent authoritative and influential reports, including a government Green Paper,[1] skate over the funding issues. The larger volumes of learning also have to be spread across the population in favour of poor people, socially excluded people and old people; and towards groups whose learning has been impeded by direct or indirect discrimination.

Just any volume of learning will not do. What is wanted is specifically a volume of learning evenly spread across the whole of society. This means that, whoever does the financing, the purchasing power has to be spread as well. Piling up learning outcomes is no comfort if those outcomes are predominantly channelled to a privileged minority. On the other hand, while 'more money – better spread' is a necessary condition, it is not in itself sufficient. If the goal is to be accomplished, there has to be an all-round strategy for culture development, with all the systems support it needs.

CURRENT FINANCING SYSTEM

Reform of funding has to start from an overview of the current financing arrangements, which are chaotic and complex. In the interests of clarity we have chosen to capture their essence with a series of simplified diagrams and commentary, rather than include all the detail.

Figure 7.1 shows the main stakeholders in learning, together with the principal links in the current system. A stakeholder here is any party active in resourcing learning. The links have different settings for different classes of learners, and indicate responsibility for paying the learning provider. Sometimes that responsibility is shared.

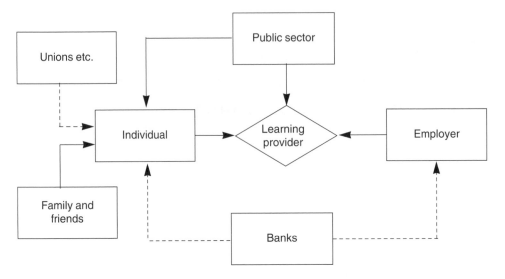

Figure 7.1 Main stakeholders: responsibilities and links.

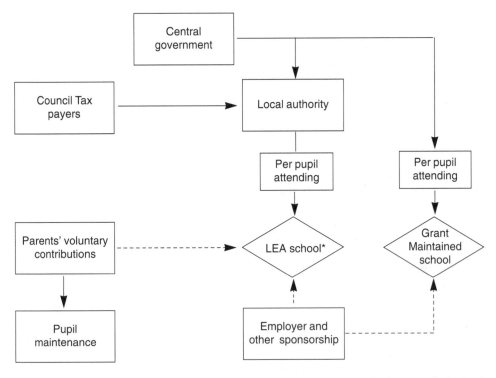

* Various types of local education authority-controlled school

Figure 7.2 Schools to age 16.

———— Significant funding routes   - - - - - - - minor funding routes

Initial education

Figure 7.2 shows in outline the finance system for state initial education up to age 16. These arrangements cover all but the 7% of pupils who are at private schools. The state pays for nearly everything out of general taxation, in effect buying the learning direct from the learning providers (state-regulated schools). State money intended for schools maintained by local authorities is fed to local government as a non-earmarked (unhypothecated) slice of the large Revenue Support Grant. Local government then decides whether to subtract from it or add to it – and on average they add to it. In these arrangements there is no direct government control on the particular sums of money which local education authorities actually spend per pupil.

After some deductions the money is passed to the schools on an age-related 'per pupil' basis, responsive to actual school recruitment. Individual pupils or their parents are not called upon to pay anything more, although they may be asked to contribute voluntarily to school funds. Parents may get some help with children's school travel fares, and child benefit is payable for most children at school under 18. Otherwise, parents meet all maintenance costs.

Grant Maintained schools are more independent, and have been getting their money direct from the Funding Agency for Schools – a central government agency – also on a per pupil basis. This agency is however in the process of being abolished; schools in this group are being renamed and are due to return to new categories of local authority responsibility. These will leave former Grant Maintained schools with a measure of independence, but tie them more closely to the basic local authority funding mechanism and recruitment policies.

A child's entitlement to full state support for learning during the years of statutory attendance reflects the principle of compulsory attendance, and the broad social judgement that this is the best way for all future citizens to get a good basic grounding in the skills needed for modern living. Without it the state would face innumerable constraints on its actions, and much higher costs in civil administration.

The entitlement is for free state-provided primary and secondary education. The only element of choice open to parents and children is some influence on where to go to school; it is not time-shiftable, beyond modest limits. Young people who play truant at a time when they have an entitlement to free education, for example, do not have an unrestricted right to return to finish foundation schooling for free after the age of 16, and no credit is given to the parent who arranges education for a child outside the state education provision. The nearest any UK government has come to that was with the recently-abolished nursery voucher scheme.

There seems little doubt that this entitlement approach (as opposed to the education which it provides) works well overall in support of lifelong learning. If parents were simply required to educate their children in a private market, with means-tested support for families with scant resources, a good deal of money would be soaked up in learning providers' profits and it would be a perpetual battle to see that foundation knowledge and skills were secured by people who are poor or struggling. There would also be gross excesses in social polarization. Giving every citizen a cash-worthy credit for school education would help the affluent minority to buy exclusive institutional reputation along with the learning. On the other hand, the rigidity and standardization of the state offering are serious drawbacks which the wealthy can overcome by using private education, but which others simply have to tolerate.

From a lifelong learning perspective, the main points of financial criticism appear to be that schools can spend less than central government is allowing on something which is an overwhelming national priority; the entitlement is not based on the achievement of a standard against a lifelong learning curriculum, and is not clearly time-shiftable if the standard is not met. The simple 'per pupil' funding regime still encourages polarization, and discourages the weighting of funding within a local authority area according to the degree of deprivation or educational problems of the pupils at different schools. This is a problem which some hope will be tackled by local 'education action zones', currently being piloted by the new Labour government.

Initial further education: 16–19 years

Figure 7.3 shows the position for education 16–19. There are three categories of public provider: the sixth forms of all-through 11–19 schools: sixth-form colleges; and general further education and tertiary colleges. The first of these is funded under the same general arrangements as in Figure 7.2. The last two are funded by central government through a further education funding council (FEFC) for each country in the UK. In either case, the state continues to be the predominant funder.

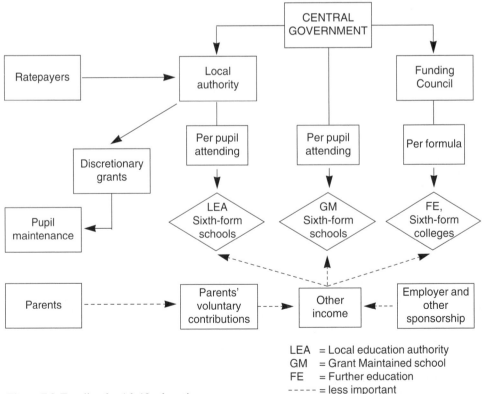

Figure 7.3 Funding for 16–19 education.

The sums of money and principles of funding for the sixth forms in schools are different from the rest, for no very apparent reason other than history. In schools there is an age-related sum per pupil. In colleges, under the funding councils, there is a massively complicated formula based on a matrix of tariffs, giving values to 'units of resource'. Students win resource units for their college depending, broadly speaking, on the kind of programme which they follow; whether or not they have any personal disabilities; and (in the near future) whether or not they reside in deprived local areas. The units are mainly for tuition costs, but there are also units for entry – including initial guidance – and extra units for completion, reflecting whether or not the learner has successfully completed the programme.

Local authorities on the sidelines have powers to make discretionary grants towards student maintenance costs, and do so in small, ever-diminishing, and highly idiosyncratic ways. Apart from child benefit and some help with fares, the assumption is that parents remain responsible for maintenance costs.

The public funding principles are very different for those who have left education and then undertake training (mainly Modern Apprenticeship or Youth Training) with a learning provider. This is shown in Figure 7.4. Training and Enterprise Councils (TECs) contract with the government to place trainees in training under a formula

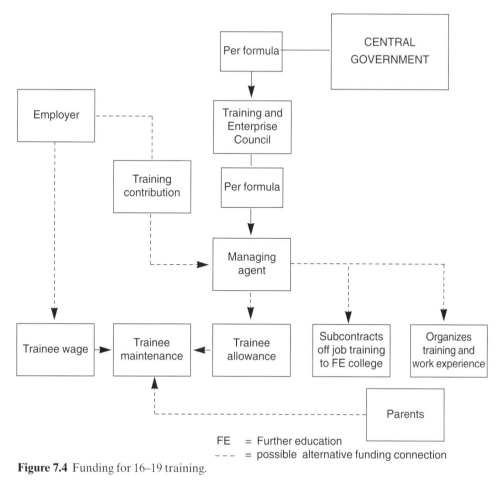

Figure 7.4 Funding for 16–19 training.

which reflects course starts, attendance and, in particular, achieved qualifications (as outputs). They do this through managing agents, usually paid on a similar formula. The managing agents provide the training either directly, or by subcontract, if they are not learning providers themselves. They will normally subcontract the work experience to employers, unless they are themselves employers, and in most cases secure a contribution towards training costs. They sometimes contract the 'off-the-job' learning element of the training to other providers, notably further education colleges. The colleges get a small subsidy from the FEFC, if this happens.

There are three important points here. The first is the extended lines of communication and responsibility inherent in this system, which leave an inevitable question mark over quality. The second is the employer's role in contributing to training cost, which contrasts strongly with the totally state-funded full-time further education route. The third point is an important difference on remuneration for the learner. In full-time further education there is no allowance or wage, but not so in training. The managing agent may pay the trainee an allowance, which has to be at least a given (small) amount per week; or the trainee may be paid a wage by the provider who is arranging the work experience and on-the-job training. Parents may choose to supplement this remuneration. Most trainees live in the parental home, and their parents lose child benefit payments for them. On the other hand, barring minor exceptions, none of the costs of training fall on the trainees or their parents.

For some years youth trainees have been issued with a credit covering their entitlement to youth training. The theory has been that the young person places the credit with the managing agent/learning provider of choice, and that agent then redeems the credit with the TEC, to cover costs of training. Redemption payments are, for the most part, made on the output-related funding arrangements just described.

This credit approach introduces the notion of the learner as customer, and is in marked contrast to the free entitlement-based funding model of the schools and further education. Although in both cases the funding 'follows the learner', in the training case the funds come under the trainee's personal control. This is intended to increase the sense of ownership and choice, and to promote competition for trainees between training providers. In reality however, studies have shown that, for these age groups in this learning culture, most young people do not have the maturity or bargaining power to trade actively in the marketplace, so that in many cases the credit tends to bless a decision already made by the young person under the directive guidance of the schools careers service. The lesson from this is that funding devices of this sort are not likely to be good instruments to lead culture change by themselves. They need to be set in a wider framework of complementary policies.

The main problem with the whole set of 16–19 arrangements is confusion and fragmentation:

- There are three quite different funding regimes: schools, funding council and TECs.
- Very similar courses can be pursued under all three formulae, at very different rates of funding.
- Each regime covers all the learning fees, but the maintenance regimes are very different between training and the rest.

- The training entitlement can be postponed, and can be time-shifted within quite large limits. The free education entitlements are not, in practice, legally effective after age 19.
- Trainees in initial training have to be offered a course at or above Level 2 or equivalent on the NVQ/SVQ scale, with the exception of young people with special training needs. There is no strictly comparable requirement in further education.

The confusion and fragmentation has important implications for lifelong learning. The separation of training and education makes it more difficult to offer an integrated curriculum for the 16–19 age group, with flexibility to span the academic, general-vocational, and training options with free choice. Training, being separated off, loses the chance of gaining comparable respect because people say that it is 'not educational enough', and that it is aimed at rote-training for particular – often menial – jobs.

The different financial arrangements not only bolster the problem of so-called 'parity of esteem', they also put pressure on the learner. They create a strong atmosphere of internecine competition between the colleges and the managing agents, who all compete for the young people who will attract payments from funding bodies for recruitment and for outputs achieved. This puts young people on the spot over the important learning choices which they have to make, at a time when it might be wiser for them to unfold their options carefully and progressively.

Higher education

Figure 7.5 outlines the position for higher education. The state will pay a large proportion of tuition fees – charged at a standard national rate – for first-time students

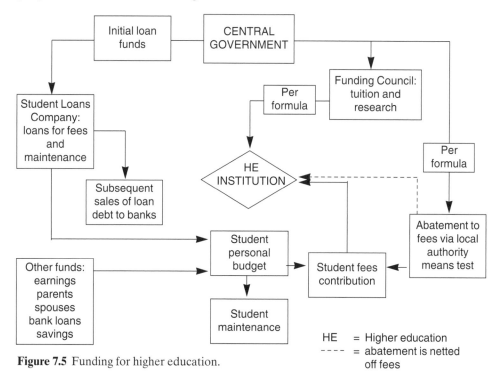

Figure 7.5 Funding for higher education.

of any age. Under new arrangements, the student is required to pay up to £1,000 annually towards fees (around 25% of the average full fee). This is means-tested by local authorities on a sliding scale against the income of the student's parent(s), for students under the age of 25 at the beginning of the course. A married student's fees are means-tested against their spouse's income. Students from very poor backgrounds will pay nothing.

To cover outlays on fees and maintenance, the government has up-rated its system of special 'soft' loans. These are issued up to given limits by the Student Loans Company, and the debt is in due course sold off at a heavy discount to financiers in the City of London. The state assumes some parental support towards maintenance in fixing the loan limits. The new loans are to be charged at zero real rate of interest and are income-contingent – that is, repayment by the graduate is suspended when their income is below a threshold amount.

In these new arrangements the state is no longer the sole funder, but requires a personal contribution. This is because in the fullness of time, for the average learner, there is a clear private return from having a degree, in the form of enhanced earnings. Before that advantage accrues, increasing numbers of students work part-time to earn money to contribute towards maintenance and the tuition fee, and/or borrow substantial amounts from the financial sector, in addition to any borrowings under the official loan scheme.

The central government puts its contribution to tuition fees into the system through separate funding councils for England, Wales and Scotland. In essence each council funds agreed numbers and mixes of places at agreed standard rates, reflecting the wide spectrum of normal costs for different types of course. As with all the other funding systems for initial learning, this is 'back door funding' – that is, it goes from government or its agent to the institutions and is not paid 'across the counter' by the learner as client.

Universities get the bulk of their income to pay for teaching through this route, but about 15% of revenue is distributed by a formula for research funding, according to a periodic Research Assessment Exercise, reflecting the research productivity of academic staff. This marginal funding has had a disproportionate and pernicious influence on the way in which research and teaching are being carried out in the universities. Instead of removing the bias, there is latterly some interest in giving a matching incentive to good teaching performance, to balance things up. But this brings serious difficulties in comparing efficiency of teaching across institutions, and in deciding whether to support those with low standards in the hope of improvement, or, in contrast, to reward the successful.

Overall, these arrangements have some notable features. Although institutions compete strongly for students, the students themselves have no direct cash entitlement, or voucher redeemable for cash, with which to 'buy' their places. There is little emphasis on consumer power in the university–student relationship. There is therefore a tendency for many students to be treated by the institutions as if they play second fiddle to the research funding exercise. Moreover, most students are recruited to universities very rapidly during August each year, shortly before the beginning of the traditional academic year. For those who do not get the places of their choice, this involves relegation to a pool to receive offers from other institutions very shortly before the academic year starts. It is not easy for these students to research their range of choices adequately.

Universities are controlled according to national overall fee structures, so that those offering enhanced services are not able to charge an enhanced price in the marketplace. This dampens competition by quality and content, and produces a cash shortage for universities attempting to uphold a high world status – in competition for internationally mobile star academics seeking high salaries and the best facilities. By the same token it inhibits students who want to obtain a respectable but low-cost higher education in finding a suitable course with fees substantially below the £1,000 norm.

In terms of lifelong learning, the whole funding regime gives serious cause for concern. Built-in biases move in quite the wrong direction for spreading learning across the population, and have the effect of reinforcing higher education as the preserve of the middle classes.

In particular, the changes being made will bear disproportionately on students from less wealthy backgrounds, because their ultimate indebtedness will be greater than that for students from more favoured family circumstances. It will be difficult to increase the proportion of lower socio-economic groups among students, despite the fact that the repayment of the loan is income-contingent. There is also an inherent assumption that students can still depend to a large extent on parental financial support, even well into their twenties. Such dependence can undermine the student's sense of personal autonomy, and prevent students' parents from returning to appropriate learning themselves.

Strong disincentives work against part-time students. The whole system is geared to full-time study. Although the entitlement is time-shiftable until well into middle years, most part-timers have to pay full fees and cannot obtain loans from the state student loan scheme. Many students, who would be better off as official part-time students, find themselves undertaking full-time courses as effective part-timers – spending large amounts of time and energy on casual jobs, to the detriment of their studies.

Post-initial learning

The 'learner' in post-initial learning might be a private individual, or a worker supported by a learning provider, or an unemployed person on public support. Funding for such people is very complex, and a minefield for learner and adviser alike.

Individuals

Figure 7.6 covers the post-initial part of the learning market for individuals arranging their own learning. There is a dramatic dropping away of state funding, but there are still significant public funds from the FEFC channelled directly to further education colleges, as institutions, to support adults. Community provision for a wide range of mainly non-vocational courses is provided by the local education authorities, usually at reduced fees. Again the money is pinned to a particular providing institution.

The cost is defrayed by other support instruments going to the learner. Support for vocational learning can be provided by the publicly assisted Career Development Loan scheme run by selected high street banks; and from vocational training tax relief (VTR), which comes in the form of a discount on purchase by the individual.

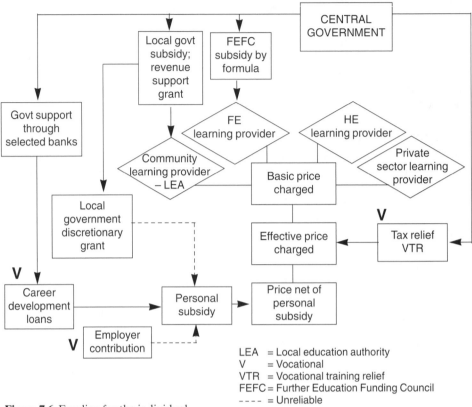

Figure 7.6 Funding for the individual.

Maintenance costs and fees can be covered by local authority discretionary grants, but these are difficult to find and are highly varied across the country.

Employer-supported workers
Figure 7.7 covers employer-supported workers. Again there is some access to public subsidy, although restrictions have recently been introduced into the further education subsidy possibilities for franchised schemes. The learning provider will have access to personal contributions from individuals, but these are not common. Training for employers' business, and on certain sorts of education schemes, is a recognized cost and reduces the employers' taxable profits.

Unemployed people
Figure 7.8 covers the unemployment case. Prominent on the left are the arrangements for unemployed people to learn under the 16-hour rule without loss of state benefit[2] – this applies mainly to learning with further education colleges. Their charged fees are paid for by the FEFC, and colleges can draw down mainstream state funding from the FEFC. This works on the same formulae as for the 16–19 age group, within the agreed overall planned volume limits for any college. In higher education, by contrast, there are as yet no subsidies for post-initial unemployed learners, although some are in the planning stage.

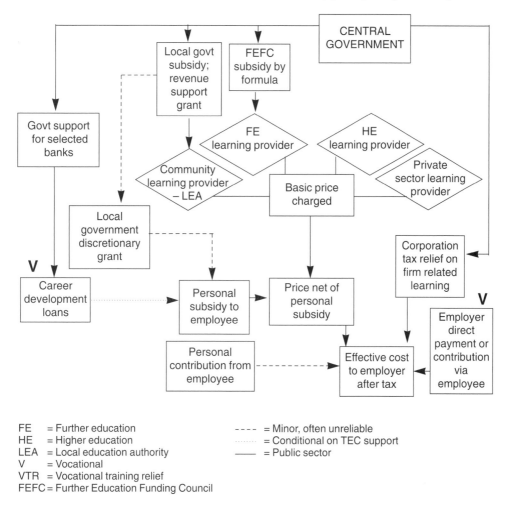

FE   = Further education
HE   = Higher education
LEA   = Local education authority
V   = Vocational
VTR   = Vocational training relief
FEFC = Further Education Funding Council

---- = Minor, often unreliable
······ = Conditional on TEC support
——— = Public sector

Figure 7.7 Employee funding through employers.

Unemployed people can also be supported through the government's diminishing Training for Work programme, which for the time being is still provided through the TECs on the basis of course starts, outcomes and progression; and through the New Deal programme arranged and contracted through the Employment Service. In these applications there can be work providers' contributions, and state benefits are commuted either into a subsidized wage or into a training allowance equivalent to benefits, with a premium to cover travel costs and to provide an incentive to attend. Large numbers of training places are also provided through European Union funding which has its own quite distinctive arrangements (not shown). In theory, also, there are local education authority discretionary grants – but their award is a virtual lottery, fast dwindling in availability across the country.

Supported Career Development Loans are available for all kinds of vocational learning, but not in principle for non-vocational academic courses. The latter are often just as significant as the others for employment, but bank managers have to bend the

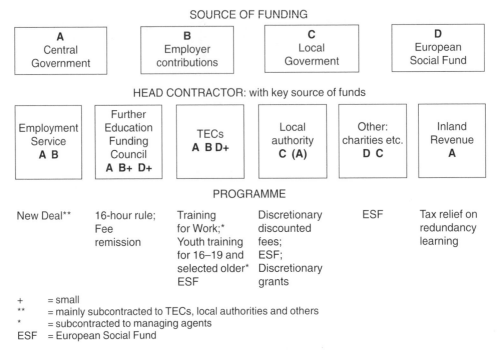

Figure 7.8 Learning for the unemployed: main possibilities.

rules to get them in (which, mercifully, they sometimes do). Nearly a third of these loans go to people who are unemployed at the start of their courses.

Student loans in higher education are denied to part-timers, including the unemployed, for no apparent reason. Moreover these loans are made out of government funds in the first instance, and the whole outlay is a charge on the public purse. The Career Development Loan, in contrast, is funded from selected banks in the financial services sector, and the call on the public purse is accounted for on terms said to be impossible for Student Loans. These and other differences are difficult to fathom.

Depending on how the count is done, there are at least four quite different funding arrangements for unemployed people, and quite possibly six. The scene is worse than chaotic. Many of the approaches have complex interactions with the welfare benefit system, which is still very reluctant to allow people to concentrate on learning instead of job search and an early return to employment. Fear of disruption of benefit has a strong deterrent effect, as Veronica McGivney[3] has shown. Many of the schemes have poor morale, perceived poor job placement rates and high drop-out. Most trainees are not treated as valued customers, and their training plans are often makeshift.

An overview of post-initial funding arrangements
From the viewpoint of lifelong learning the conceptual cloudiness, complexity and fragmentation of these structures are cause for dismay. The heavy vocational twist to personal subsidies is founded on a fundamentally false distinction, which is profoundly damaging to lifelong learning. Moreover, in a lifelong learning culture the recycling of skills should work more smoothly. It should happen for the most part while people are still in jobs, but if not, then through well-understood, non-punitive, relearning

mechanisms for those out of work. There is little evidence here of a simple, consistent approach that will do these things. Above all, nobody seems to be addressing the question of where public funds should go if they are to have the best effect from the lifelong learning viewpoint.

Information, advice and guidance

The funding arrangements in this area are also fragmentary. The schools can draw upon independent careers advice, to which pupils are entitled. This is supplied to them by careers services, which are companies under contract to government in the English regions and to other countries in the UK. The further education colleges can also draw on the careers service companies for some services, mainly for the 16–19 group. University students also receive free guidance services from universities' own careers service units.

Adults seeking advice which might lead to post-initial learning are not generally entitled to these free offerings. Further education colleges are required under the funding formula to give initial guidance and advice on recruitment for all their students. For the younger learners this overlaps in a vague way with the careers service responsibilities. In any case, the advice and guidance arrangements in further education often lack the full degree of independence which is needed if clients are not to be pushed into courses which the colleges offer, regardless of suitability. Similar problems attach to training, where there is also a requirement for initial advice and guidance. Such services are not now separately resourced. They are notable neither for their availability nor their objectivity.

Most adults seeking advice and guidance have either to buy it in the small, expensive 'executive' guidance market, or they have to look to a variety of patchy and *ad hoc* facilities. Some of the latter are charged; some not, being supplied through networks sponsored by TECs, and very occasionally through LEAs. In each case they draw on a wide and unstable miscellany of funding sources. These services have long had a poor image, and are much confused in the public mind with the unpleasant bureaucracy of state services for unemployed people. They are a conceptual battle-ground between guidance counsellors – who think the service should be free – and others who think that there must be a subsidized market framework. The upshot is a widely varied, often shabby, numerically inadequate service across countries and regions.

Local information services sit alongside advice and guidance, collating and supplying information on learning and on other opportunities for clients, mostly through advice shops and databases. These services have few opportunities to charge clients and they have no stable funding arrangements, despite their importance. Slowly, they are linking together into a voluntary national network – to be developed further under the 'University for Industry', but data quality and geographical coverage remain under constant threat.

The upshot of all these arrangements is that there is no integrated, economically sound guidance and information industry, which has the capacity, professionalism, and resources to underpin a strong move to planned lifelong learning on a mass scale. This is a major gap in the infrastructure and in the funding system.

FINANCING UNFIT FOR PURPOSE

If the current finance system does not work towards the greater volume and wider spread of learning it is not fit for the lifelong learning purpose, and will need to be replaced in the transition to a new culture. Unfitness is visible on every side (Box 7.1).

- There is no general mechanism to support *continuity or loyalty.*
- The system for information and guidance for adults is flawed and very patchy. Failure rates in learning are very high.
- The conspicuous complexity and inconsistency in the arrangements give learners an advantage over non-learners.
- Funding councils' formulae for resource allocation fail to spread learning into the parts of the population where learning is underdeveloped. Experience gives very little hope that these complex formulae can be turned into finely-focused instruments for targeted incentives on the scale required. Pressures for redistributive targeting tend to be offset by other factors within the formulae, and 'losers' lobby very vocally against new 'weightings'. There are strong institutional reasons why the incentives get lost at the level of the individual tutor and course.
- Colleges and universities are tied so tightly to central funding formulae that they are wide open to Treasury financial squeezes.
- There is a comprehensive failure in the adult market to overcome low use of the financial services sector for learning.
- Direct funding through funding councils makes institutions insensitive to customer needs in the marketplace. This undermines personal commitment.
- Much of funding for adults is linked to formal qualifications, impeding the gradual approach needed to build up the learning habit among new learners. It also hampers social commitment involving collaborative, community-based learning.
- There is no clear doctrine about stakeholders' responsibility for supporting post-initial education.
- There is inconsistency in funding relating to age: Student Loans and training programmes have age restrictions; further education and Career Development Loans do not.
- There are strong biases against formally designed part-time study, particularly in 16–19 further education and higher education.
- The doctrine of incentives for the state contributions is unclear.
- There is no clear view on centralization or decentralization. Duties of local education authorities are fundamentally unclear for adults.
- There is a general incoherence about support for the costs of access for adults. Support is often linked just to fees – it does not universally extend to child care, travel, and other expenses.
- There is a constant flux in the shape and names of different elements in the funding structure.

Box 7.1 Current funding arrangement: unfitness for purpose.

For reasons like this the whole system, as it has grown up incrementally over the years, is overdue for a refit. It is not just that it fails as a system: it also expresses and actively reinforces the whole current culture of learning. Almost all the features in Box 7.1 have the consequence that the longer-term learners – who are overwhelmingly from the middle classes – end up in a better position than anybody else.

There is not much comfort either for the learning providers who are dependent on the state budget. A majority of colleges and many universities are in financial deficit, with debts rising fast year on year. Many small TECs are struggling to survive. Shockingly, many schools are reduced to spending less on books than they spend on the government's performance tests, or on official inspections by Ofsted. These are all symptoms of failure in the financing system.

In these conditions, learning providers are living hand-to-mouth, with no real hope of taking a long-term view. A sure sign of failing finances is the non-replacement of productive assets. A company is sound only if it charges itself for depreciation on the basis of continuing business: how many colleges and schools, and how many training providers and providers of guidance are maintaining their asset base? How many are seriously investing in staff skills for the future? The 'system' has run itself ragged.

DESIGN BRIEF FOR FUNDAMENTAL FINANCIAL REFORM

A design brief is needed for financial reform. The following paragraphs identify main objectives, and Box 7.2 summarizes main design criteria. Chapter 10 will refer to these again.

- An overarching system which expresses and reinforces the definitions and principles of lifelong learning. In particular the continuity and planning of learning; commitment to learning; and support for all, cradle to grave.
- Principles clearly stated, and applied consistently and fairly.
- Strong enough to support much greater volumes of learning, and capable of funding the socially excluded.
- Lasting long enough for people to get familiar with it.
- One-stop-shop arrangements.
- Based on voluntary participation rather than on compulsion.
- Allowing learning investments to be funded through time-shifting of cash, and making greater use of banking mechanisms, such as savings and borrowings.
- Integrating different stakeholders, and facilitating joint funding and leverage arrangements.
- Permitting the funding of weak points in the infrastructure, e.g. information, advice and guidance, and marketing.
- Efficient in terms of administrative and transactional costs.
- Having full coverage of all types of learning, and of all relevant expenditures.
- Common throughout the UK, and with no artificial boundary problems.

Box 7.2 Main design criteria for a new national structure.

Raising additional financial resources

It is no use having a new overall financing system if it does not draw in large additional funds from the stakeholders. To do this the new system must make the most of existing private incentives to learn. This means helping people to see the returns, and not loading unnecessary specific subsidy onto learning which carries good incentives. It also means new general background incentives, provided by the public sector for the long term, to tackle the widespread underinvestment. Tax relief is the most likely method. It has had spectacular success as a permanent part of the household finance scene for two generations.

Decentralization as a major theme in funding

Two reasons behind the state funding of learning are the purchase of public goods and the redistribution of wealth. Public goods include stable communities, effective citizenship, and a sound base for a market-led economy. Redistribution in this context means giving every citizen a fair start in life through foundation and advanced education, irrespective of means. In a democracy, the use of the public purse in these two ways needs to be regulated by public opinion, expressed at and between elections. But things go wrong when government or local authorities lose touch with their electorates, and start treating as public goods things which the bulk of the population does not recognize; or when they start redistributing in favour of particular groups which are not widely recognized as 'deserving'.

On matters like these, the main concern should be to prevent an all-powerful central government riding rough-shod over local interests and judgements. This argues for an arm's-length arrangement in funding, under which local and regional authorities would have the ability to influence the precise public goods and the precise redistributive policies to be pursued in their areas. Nothing will destroy social commitment to learning faster than dictation on these matters from the central state. Even twenty years of assertion that local authorities have failed in the learning game, justifying all manner of centralizing tendencies, does not belie this simple truth.

Personal commitment to learning

'Personal commitment' (sometimes called 'individual commitment') means that the learner, and no one else, should normally have the roles of active seeker, purchaser and arranger of the learning. This would need to be a major principle of any new system, bringing with it efficiency and moral advantages.

People with personal commitment can find ways to tap resources which would not otherwise be found, and they can press the investment home. The commitment theme reflects efficiency through the economic idea of individuals and organizations being energetic in identifying opportunities, and in obtaining all possible private returns to investment in learning. The moral advantages of commitment have been advocated by many writers – ancient and modern – including Samuel Smiles, the nineteenth-century guru of self-help. Restated in appropriate terms, they have very important messages for policy today.

Focusing on redistribution

The dominant British learning culture, working remorselessly through educational advantage, has marginalized large numbers of people, leaving them under-provided, under-skilled and under-motivated. The middle classes currently do the bulk of the post-statutory learning, and secure large-scale public support for doing so. In such cases the value added through public funding is poor, for if public funds were not available, much of this learning would be funded from private means.

At the same time, more disadvantaged groups with lower incomes are learning much less. A significant reason for this is the lack of money for fees, for learning equipment and materials, for transport and for other enabling services. A lifelong learning society would have to find the means to enable people in these groups to participate. Even if the learning they choose to do eventually brings good financial gains, these people would still have difficulties in raising lump sum amounts ahead of the payback from the learning investment. This means redistribution: putting more money at the disposal of reluctant learners in lower socio-economic groups. Yet current financing systems have been designed to be the very opposite of redistributive.

Empowerment for learning

Any new redistributive system will involve national and local government, employers and others acting as sponsors (that is, putting up the money) for people in other groups, particularly those on the margin, to spend on learning. This is empowerment, and it is best done through personal commitment, by putting the learning budget into the full charge of the learner. The 'easy' approach to this seems to be to give people cash budgets to spend on learning. But governments and employers are understandably nervous of putting money up-front into cash budgets which may be abused, or to keep cash idle when it could be earning or saving interest for the donor. So the fallback solution is to resort to some form of voucher or learning credit.

Using this approach, the various sponsors would not necessarily give up all their interest in the learning activity. They can attach some general conditions to the use of the funding, relating to aspects of the learning content – such as gaining a new skill or qualification, or travelling abroad, or managing and undertaking a personal challenge. The aim would be to give individuals maximum scope for decision on their intended learning, while still meeting the essential requirements of the sponsor.

Vouchers or credits are not without their challenges. They are more suited to adults than to younger children. Yet even young people must learn how to make complex learning choices for themselves. This points to solutions for them which do not necessarily entail the use of vouchers at every stage of learning provision, but where some aspects of learning expenditure are approached through the empowerment route. The key point remains: that redistributive educational programmes which are 'done to people' are very poor vehicles of learning. Empowerment – not paternalism – is the proper way forward for most purposes in a new lifelong learning culture.

One-stop, user-friendly services

In a lifelong learning scenario all learning services will have to be re-engineered to offer easy, low-cost ways through the maze of stages and processes. An implication of this is that the heavy transactions costs faced by many learners need to be reduced. These costs include trailing to and fro seeking information; filling in forms; visiting endless offices; waiting for letters; and running risks of course cancellation. Nothing destroys morale or motivation faster than the feeling of being 'mucked about' for administrative reasons.

Compulsion and cultural transformation

It cannot be said too often that the aim is long-term culture change, not short-term volume targets. In the world of post-initial learning it will be counterproductive to try to force individuals or learning providers to pay for or to save for learning. It would raise defensive attitudes, drawing warnings from all sides that compulsory learning is nothing but a manifestation of a nanny state. If, as we argue, a test of the arrival of the new culture is that people and organizations are prepared to contribute voluntarily, it is totally contradictory to introduce a financing system based on compulsion. This does not exclude applying strong moral pressure to learning providers, or even to individuals.

Time-shifting expenditure through financial services

Banking services help to smooth out the cash requirements of 'lumpy' investments. Individuals or groups can save ahead of the investment, earning interest, or they can borrow when the money is needed and pay back later with interest, when the benefit of the investment should be in hand. In a new learning culture, even where bite-sized investments in learning are more common than now, there will still be an important role for such banking services. Yet there has long been a conspicuous lack of these facilities, reflecting deep-set market failure.

Few people seek out borrowing facilities for learning. The facilities are not offered on any scale; people do not see others making visible use of them; guidance workers fight shy of talking people into debt; and a default may queer the pitch for other more significant borrowings.

There are difficulties for bankers too. There is no collateral in the investment itself, and learning cannot be 'recovered' if the loan goes sour; the risks are difficult for ordinary bank staff to assess, and yet they are not large enough to justify banks resorting to specialists; the risks cannot be sold on to the insurance market, because they are not objective fact, like death, illness or the weather; if loans default, the bank manager collects black marks against promotion; and the recovery costs are very high, and unpleasant if sold off to debt-collectors. It is easy to see why – with the exception of the government's own subsidized Career Development Loan scheme – banks have preferred to lend for learning only very selectively.

Special learning schemes have been used to some extent to save for learning – for example, by affluent people preparing for private school fees. Although many non-learners are poor and would not have a surplus to save, there is nevertheless much scope in other sections of the population for learning-related savings to grow. The revision of university funding, and changes in career expectations, are just two examples. Many older people also wish to make learning savings for younger relatives.

Taking borrowing and saving together, opening up the savings and borrowings approach to buying learning would find extra purchasing power. Every little bit will help, and – over time – small changes can grow into very significant effects.

Time shift through flexible entitlement

Alongside the banking reforms, changes would be needed in the rules which insist that state entitlements to education should be taken at fixed ages, and that their use is a one-shot game. The sense of bleak finality which faces the unsuccessful pupil on leaving school lies at the heart of the demotivation process. Funding structures will have to overcome this fundamental barrier through a system of fully time-flexible learning credits.

Joint funding

Joint funding between different stakeholders can benefit all the parties. Current funding arrangements do not encourage joint solutions. The fear of 'substitution' lies behind much of this reluctance: that stakeholders – even 'committed' ones – might try to push the financing of learning investment onto some other party, before making their own commitment. This would cause friction, delay, and ultimately the loss of significant funding streams for learning. Under current funding arrangements it can be very difficult to reach the co-operative arrangement by negotiation. A new funding structure is needed which, although not free of all game play, would nevertheless provide a stable and conducive context for joint agreements.

An important special case of joint funding is using one contribution – normally from the public sector – to lever other contributions. An effective overall system of financing would make leverage schemes easy. These might, for example, help to make learning investments fit into complex economic regeneration schemes in local areas. For example, the costs of training new workers for new jobs might be shared across a number of different stakeholders. The TECs have a good record at finding imaginative ways to tie up public money in wider developmental schemes; but, importantly, money passed down to providers from funding councils tends to be insulated from leverage deals.

Multi-sourcing

If there is to be a significant personal contribution to learning investment, learners need to be able to bring together all the different sources of money – however small. They also need to be able to make multi-sourced investments – that is, to make the best use of money which may be available from a range of different sources. This may, for example, cover some savings; some credit from an employer; the prospect of a gift from within the family; and a voucher from the TEC. Individuals' ability to raise resources from the family circle, or within their particular community, is often underestimated. A high proportion of people whose applications for a government Career Development Loan fail, subsequently raise resources within the family. It is also common for adults to help younger family members with the costs of learning, such as tuition and equipment for music or dance or sport.

Other financing needs

In other industries, the needs for generic advertising, and for information, advice and guidance, are addressed by the providers. When customers buy a product or service, they are paying retrospectively for the advertising and information which they themselves enjoyed and used in deciding on the purchase. More than that, they also pay for all the other people who considered a purchase but who did not make one.

Learning providers need to take the same approach for their own cost of sales. But difficulties arise when the aim is to provide generic marketing to benefit the whole learning industry; or to supply independent information and guidance across a range of learning providers. Providers might be happy to pay, but studies have shown that, when they do, they tend to advise people to use their own courses. New financing arrangements will be needed to find ways of funding these things which are consistent with independence, yet reliable enough and focused enough to meet the learning need.

An inclusive outer boundary for the system

Any new system of financing has to avoid boundary problems, whether relating to geography or to definition. Geographically, there is much to be said for a UK-wide system, with common principles applied throughout. This would allow mobile learners to confront a broadly similar system wherever in the UK they go. The key aim in agreeing wide boundaries of definition is to close the present gap between fees and other supporting expenditures and services. Many present arrangements for public support for learning focus exclusively on fees. Learning-related costs – such as child care, fares, computers, materials, living costs, travel, and clothing – are covered in a sparse and inconsistent way across programmes. Including these necessary expenses raises sharp technical issues.

Another challenge will be to see that all the learning interests of all relevant government bodies and agencies at all levels are brought to bear on a common system. These include the DfEE itself; the Department for Culture, Media and Sport; speaking for the major national libraries and museums; policies on libraries, museums and sports facilities run by local authorities and other bodies; the Department for Trade and Industry, which has oversight of research and development for innovation in industry and business, and responsibilities for professional development of business leaders and managers; the new Regional Development Agencies; local government; the TECs; the national training organizations.

NOTES AND REFERENCES

1. DfEE (1998: 1) 'The Learning Age': Green Paper on lifelong learning; Kennedy (1997) FEFC report on widening participation in further education; and Fryer (1997) NAGCELL report on continuing education and lifelong learning.
2. 16-hour rule: An unemployed person can enrol for up to 16 hours of supervised tuition per week, without losing unemployment benefit.
3. McGivney (1996).

Chapter 8

Learning and Teaching

The move to a lifelong learning culture has vast implications for the curriculum, qualifications and state of teaching in the UK.

CURRICULUM AND INTELLECTUAL FREEDOM

In the first place, someone or somebody has to decide what will be learnt in a general culture of lifelong learning. Should this be a decision of the marketplace, negotiated freely between provider and learner? Or should it be determined by the state?

Who decides?

In the present culture of learning, the state intervenes extensively in the schools, imposing by law a National Curriculum covering statutory primary and secondary education. In education for ages 16–19, the state limits the curriculum by linking funding to a list of state-approved national qualifications. These are overseen for government by a quango – the national Qualifications and Curriculum Authority (QCA) which vets qualifications for general use. In higher education, each university has the power to award its own degrees, the contents of which are – currently – a matter for the university alone. The QCA, through its grip on qualifications, also determines the limits of post-initial learning which is supported through the FEFC in further education colleges. Colleges are free to offer other learning for unsubsidized fees. LEA or private post-initial provision offers a wide range of courses, most freely chosen between learner, learning provider and fee-payer.

There is more state control at the young end of the system. With the exception of higher education, this pattern follows the public money, as the state seeks to control the content of the learning it pays for. The universities are in a special position. By tradition they are seen as guardians of the stock of knowledge and upholders of the truth, established by royal charter for the purpose. It would not do for the state – no matter how generous its funding – to determine what was or was not officially 'true', or to direct what people learn in universities.

> Academic freedom is incompatible with the use of State authority over Universities to bring about a change of culture. This, of course, does not mean the Governments will ever stop wanting to change cultures . . . The two important points are that there must continue to be some patronage independent of Government, and that Government engaged in this process must use persuasions and not authority. (Russell, 1993)

There is, of course, persuasion and – persuasion:

> What we are seeing are the conditions of academic work so tightly framed with reward structures that academics find it easy to read the signals. In this situation, the opportunities for the realization of academic freedom are effectively reduced. (Barnett, 1997)

Such arguments raise the issue of state control over what is learnt in higher education. But such a danger does not arise at that level only. The existence of academic freedom in the universities – in principle at least – does not mean that the dangers at other levels can somehow be excused or tolerated. A lifelong learning society would recognize the dangers for what they are, and be prepared to deal with them wherever they are threatened. The entitlement of the state, as the principal provider of money, to control the content of what is taught, needs to be very closely questioned. If the universities are exempt from such arrangements, why is the rest of initial education supported by the state not also exempt? These are fundamental issues which the 'lifelong learning debate' in the UK has not yet seriously addressed.

A national curriculum for schools

Legislation establishing the National Curriculum was passed in 1988. Since then, something of a consensus seems to have emerged in favour of the view that a national curriculum is a good thing in principle for schools – but the current model is seriously flawed. We argue that a detailed national curriculum is bound to be seriously defective in the context of lifelong learning; that it should be replaced by a framework of output-related entitlement for learners; and that schools should have a statutory duty to provide education to meet that entitlement – but with much greater freedom in deciding the content of the curriculum.

The arguments put forward for a national curriculum reflect the struggle of one school of rightist educationists over another, as Clyde Chitty has shown.[1] On the one hand were people who believed in freedom of choice over the content and location of school learning; on the other hand were people who believed in a single learning agenda, and in regularly testing young people against it. Their aims were variously to raise standards; to root out inefficiencies; to help children in moving between schools; and to ensure that traditional subjects and the essential skills were not neglected in favour of 'trendy' subjects. In the end all made common cause, because the proposed National Curriculum could produce comparative performance information between schools. This could serve as a basis for parents to express their choices in the marketplace as well as for politicians and inspectors to pursue a certain sense of efficiency in schools.

These misguided policies are having a corrosive effect. They inhibit the professionalism of teachers, and restrict their action in developing a curricular range which would be relevant to all children from all cultural backgrounds. The pressure of 'teaching to the test' may have been effective in producing more results, opening up the pathways for more young people to advance to higher educational levels within the current culture. But it shores up an education system which conforms to – and confirms – the current dominant culture at the expense of lifelong learning for all.

The National Curriculum has also removed the latitude that teachers need if they are to help children express and maintain the natural drive for learning. The 1998 Annual Report of the Chief Inspector of Schools indicates that teachers concentrate on the standard tests at ages 7, 11, and 14, and tend to overlook the performance of children in the years between. The whole system becomes a sordid race for test results and credentials. It provides a very poor indicator of educational achievement, and does little to help young people identify and develop all the various intelligences in their individual profile of aptitudes. Chapter 2 looked at the way performance ratings of different schools, linked to the National Curriculum, promote social polarization and selectivity in the schools. This is a condition which occurs again at later stages in the educational system and which helps to relegate a quarter of the population to non-learning.

There are other serious problems. The existence of a national curriculum secures a large space for the government of the day to condition the curriculum to suit itself. For some subjects, such as History and English, the current National Curriculum reflects the personal preferences of particular Conservative politicians; and a vital subject like music has become peripheral. The review of this National Curriculum for the year 2000 provides another chance to redesign the curriculum for particular subjects, and to adjust overload in the whole specification. But it does not remove the danger of political influence in the longer run; nor is it likely to provide a clear view of the appropriate principles which would guide the construction of a national curriculum.

All of this is why professional bodies react as they do when government initiatives threaten to encroach on the prerogatives of teachers, in the name of a national strategy. Recent initiatives promoting teachers' use of ICT and government-originated teaching materials – now proliferating through the National Grid for Learning – take the government right into the classroom.

State schools should no longer be merely for 'schooling', in the sense of producing pupils who are good at performing tasks blessed by government. The UK needs citizens who can think for themselves. If schools are to play their part in raising generations of such citizens, and to produce able graduate teachers in the numbers needed to staff the schools, the principle of intellectual freedom must be extended to the whole state-funded education system. Universities can be responsible for defending the stock of knowledge. But the other essential wing of intellectual freedom – enabling developing minds to see beyond politically convenient 'official truth' – must be applied in schools. How else will every pupil have the chance to grow into a rounded person with the skills and courage for critical living?

Essential lifelong learning skills

Dropping the mandatory curriculum leaves the question of accountability. For all the public money put in, is there to be no assurance for the taxpayer that young people are to emerge well prepared for civic and economic life by the age of 16?

The answer to this depends on what statutory school experience is really for. In our view, it is for developing and confirming lifelong learners; that is, self-motivated people who learn continuously throughout their lives, working in society like a yeast which enriches and raises the profile of learning. School is not, in essence, about getting pupils over hurdles on the way to high academic honours, or for developing the sort of quick-response skills and regurgitative facility tested in examination conditions instead of understanding, reflection and persistence; or even for sorting them in order to determine their future positions as winners or losers in society.

> . . . what young people most need [is] the ability to detect bullshit and the courage to expose it. Students of all ages need to develop a critical faculty to enable them to challenge the hype of advertisers, the excessive claims of experts/researchers, the pretentious promises of politicians or the latest educational buzzword . . . A prosperous and cohesive democracy is most unlikely to result from the two segregated educational systems in England. The new knowledge economies require all citizen workers to be (and to remain) as highly educated as possible and to be able to ask pertinent (and impertinent) questions of the powerful. (Coffield, 1998)

This clear articulation indicates an urgent need for a curriculum that develops essential lifelong learning skills (see Box 8.1). The relationships between academic subjects and crosscutting themes in various kinds of curriculum have been much discussed over the years. The fixity of the school day and the demands of the National Curriculum mean that crosscutting themes come under pressure – not least because the testing and performance regime bears on them less directly. Yet most of the skills listed in Box 8.1 are thematic. An absurd position is reached if they are to be pursued as themes through the filter of subjects in a subject-centred National Curriculum.

- Ability to communicate and calculate above a basic level.

- Ability to use computers effectively.

- Self-awareness and self-development skills.

- Financial and consumer-rights awareness.

- Ability to understand the values of lifelong learning, and the courage to apply them.

- Ability to think inductively and deductively.

- Ability and confidence to find things out, and to take a reasoned critical view upon what has been considered.

- Ability to learn together with others, in mixed groups.

- Realization (as far as it can be determined according to age) of an unfolding personal profile of aptitudes and intelligences.

- Ability to apply learning usefully to creative or socially responsible ends.

- A basic knowledge of planning a learning career, and basic awareness of systems for learning and guidance.

Box 8.1 Essential lifelong learning skills.

The most important things play second fiddle, while the subjects continue to serve as stepping stones for selective academic advancement. This situation needs to be turned inside out.

Taking a lifelong perspective, the school curriculum should concentrate on laying firm foundations for a life of learning centred on personal attitudes and values; on discovering and developing individual learning styles and intellectual preferences; and on developing sound learning skills.[2] In the statutory years, subjects should become means to achieve the essential skills of lifelong learning rather than being ends in themselves. Every child should have a foundation-level entitlement to essential lifelong learning skills.

According to this approach, schools will be free to set their own curriculum in detail, so long as they prepare children to secure a Foundation Certificate in Essential Lifelong Learning Skills, on or before the age of 16. The essential skills can be assessed by portfolio-based methods, using a record of achievement. As soon as pupils are ready to graduate against the standards set, they can move into initial further education or leave school, according to their choice with the benefit of guidance. There is no case for requiring compulsory attendance at secondary school beyond that point. Not only will the Foundation Certificate of Essential Skills satisfy the needs of the state, it is likely also to meet the basic needs of employers (see Box 8.2).

- A significant proportion of UK employees' skills are a constraint on business development, particularly in terms of 'generic' skills such as computer literacy, customer handling and communication skills. These skills are in demand in both service and manufacturing industries.

- The UK has a deficiency in people with appropriate vocational skills at level 2/3, particularly in comparison with our major international competitors.

- Technological and organizational change and international competition have led to a shift in skills from repetitive manual work to knowledge-based 'thinking' jobs emphasizing problem-solving and cognitive skills.

- Employers are looking for employees with an ability to learn so that they can cope with the need to update their knowledge and skills. Teamworking skills are in widespread demand, particularly in manufacturing organizations which have adopted cellular production processes and just-in-time practices.

Box 8.2 Learning deficiencies: employers' views. Source: adapted from DfEE (1998: 4).

Critical thinking is a notable element in the essential lifelong learning skills list. Just as it is wrong for higher education to be seen as the only place where issues of academic freedom arise, so it is wrong to regard critical thinking exclusively as a high-level intellectual function. This is one of the great educational fallacies of the current culture. The development of critical skills is delayed in the British system because of the authoritarianism, paternalism and spoon-feeding of the gold-standard school culture. There is no reason why young people cannot work at the skills of critical thought, word and action.

The entitlement to essential lifelong learning skills will be a compulsory requirement on schools. It could replace GCSEs.

- The entitlement will provide any learner with redress if it could be shown that a school had not met its requirements in their particular case.
- Inspection will concentrate on the lifelong learning approach. This will not discard the need for stringent standards – it will simply require different ones.
- The curriculum to deliver the entitlement will have to be clearly specified by the school, but it will be neither common nor imposed. This is because it must conform to the values of lifelong learning – respecting the rights of learners to find their own voice and interests, without being overridden by a dominant agenda.
- Subjects will remain a valid way to approach the curriculum, but more direct curriculum materials can also come to the fore. The curriculum will also become more 'footloose', reflecting learning beyond the classroom.
- The entitlement will be time-shiftable, so that learners who do not achieve the Foundation Certificate by the age of 16 will be able to make repeated attempts to secure it. This will be subject to a limit only where it can be demonstrated that a particular learner has no further prospect of gaining the certificate.

Initial further education: 16–19 years

The curriculum at 16–19 years has to be more coherent and integrated than formerly. A single identi-kit national curriculum would be even more unsuitable and dangerous than for the schools. These are the years when young people continuing to learn do so voluntarily, as they take on the full responsibilities of adult social and economic life, including the suffrage. In addition to strengthening their skills further, students will need to begin specializing in particular subjects or discipline areas – most of them for the first time – to make the best of their prospective progression into the labour force.

The curriculum should be expressed as an array of modular possibilities across the spectrum, to meet all these needs (see Figure 8.1). To get an advanced qualification (Baccalaureate), at least 18 units will needed, chosen from across the structure and all assessed at pass grade or better, plus an Advanced Certificate in Lifelong Learning Skills. All components would be separately assessed and certificated. There should be an unconditional, time-shiftable entitlement for all 16- to 19-year-olds to pursue such a Baccalaureate, embracing both elements. It will have the same ultimate restriction on repetition as will apply to the Foundation Certificate.

This goes beyond the Dearing three-track solution, by building a single integrated field of choice, which will help to encourage those with academic skills to avoid excessively narrow specialization. It will therefore serve as a measure of insurance for an uncertain world. Students can make their choices, under any quality assured advice and guidance they care to commission. Learners' entitlement to preparation for the Foundation Certificate in Essential Lifelong Learning Skills will – if necessary – be carried forward from the school setting into further education, or beyond initial education altogether. Any young person still short of the relevant standard by 16 will be entitled to pursue learning suited to their particular needs, on demand.

Under the entitlement for the Advanced Certificate in Lifelong Learning Skills, a new list of more advanced essential skills would apply (see Box 8.3). The state can reasonably require all students who are supported by state funds to undertake study modules in these elements, as a condition of funding. A student would therefore undertake a mixed programme – some essential skills and, except where inappropriate, more specialized advanced modules across the academic–vocational spectrum. The integration of the curriculum helps to ensure that neither strand would be given any undue prominence.

Leavers at age 19 would therefore normally have a solid grounding in the values and skills of lifelong learning, and be knowledgeable or competent at advanced level in a number of chosen specialized topics. The latter would not enforce breadth, but breadth would be available for choice. The general principle should be to encourage lifelong learners to follow the learning path which they feel best motivated to follow. The Baccalaureate would be the standard university entry certificate.

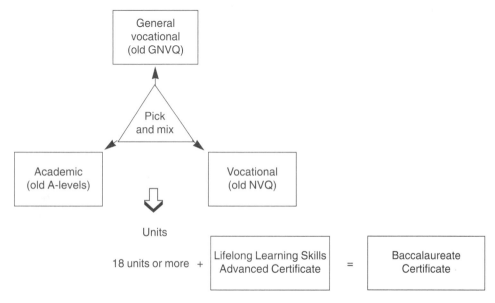

Figure 8.1 Qualification-based curriculum structure for 16–19 (and others).

- Involvement as a citizen in a community learning project.
- Personal financial skills.
- Use of basic statistics.
- Assertiveness and self-presentation skills.
- Competence in Internet learning and research.
- Labour market and careers awareness.
- Advanced critical thinking.
- Overcoming challenge to personal capability.

Box 8.3 Advanced lifelong learning skills.

Initial higher education

The financial terms available should entitle any learner who has achieved the Baccalaureate to pursue a higher-level degree and other higher qualifications in state-supported initial higher education. This entitlement would be time-shiftable, but not repeatable on a state-supported basis. This is because the Baccalaureate will establish the learner's ability to succeed at the higher level. Higher-level qualifications would increasingly become unitized. It should be left to the student – advised as necessary – to choose sequences of units freely.

It would also normally be possible for students to pursue a Higher Certificate in Lifelong Learning, designed to develop skills of teamwork, mentoring and leadership in the lifelong learning culture. This could become a valued qualification for professional development in the public, private and voluntary sectors. Deference to academic liberties means it should not be a mandatory state requirement.

TEACHERS AND TEACHING

Fears about indirect government encroachment into teachers' professional domain are running high. In higher education, the welcome new emphasis on effective teaching does not allay anxieties about a determination to pin funding to assessments of teacher quality. Academics – who have seen the deep cultural implications of the funding regime for research – have a right to be apprehensive. In further education, the resource squeeze is intensifying the casualization of teaching staff and threatening standards. In schools, the National Curriculum and administration has put enormous pressure on teachers' time for thought and for professional development.

The risks are reflected in an article by the Chief Inspector of Schools on government-approved materials published on the Internet by the DfEE.[3] The article proposes that downloading will give schoolteachers more time, and asserts the Chief Inspector's personal opinion that teachers would not be interested in using that time for thinking.

> The notion of the autonomous teacher reflecting in splendid isolation on best professional practice is a romantic but highly dangerous myth . . . Teachers need support. They need tightly-defined definitions of approaches which really work . . . Pious exhortations and vapid generalizations are hopeless. For too long we have been precious in our deliberations about professional autonomy. Academics agonise: teachers teach. The latter do not always want to wend their lonely way to their individual holy grail. They have lives to live out of school, children to play with, hobbies to pursue. (Woodhead, 1998)

The implications for a lifelong learning culture are clear. To reduce teachers to technicians, purveying standard government materials, contradicts all that is known about effective teaching in the critical tradition. Yet this is what is threatened as the new technology and the National Curriculum come into close alliance. A lifelong learning society will offer teachers high and independent standing, in return for which they will be expected to make the lifelong learning culture the focus of their professional commitment.

Teaching as a process

The vast majority of learners depend on teachers and teaching. Even distance learning is normally supported, although it makes new demands on teachers and those who train them. Teaching must be designed to fit the lifelong learner and the principles of lifelong learning, whatever the mode of learning. Institutional arrangements which leave no room for the best of lifelong learning approaches imply failure at the very first hurdle.

In a general lifelong learning culture, every teacher's prime goal will be to trigger and nurture lifelong learning in every learner. This is a vital skill for teachers. It is not the same as the skill of keeping order in class; or of being effective in assessment procedures; or of imparting a body of knowledge; or even of 'knowing the subject'. This ability to inspire is partly a natural-born talent and partly hard work, good humour and determination.

Current conditions in educational institutions of all kinds and levels tend to be hostile to these principles. This is one reason why, according to NALS'97, people on average end their initial education, or their adult course, expecting to do less learning – not more. In the secondary schools too, it largely explains why so many young people turn away from further learning. Teaching mechanically for predominantly instrumental reasons is certainly not going to reverse that trend – though it may be a way to survive the experience of teaching overcrowded classes of reluctant learners day in, day out.

Teacher training and development

Those who select and train teachers at any level need to be able to recognize and develop the talent to inspire and encourage continuity in learning, and to ensure that it is not destroyed by the thousand frustrations of teaching life. Yet there is currently little sign of a strong element of lifelong learning theory and practice developing in initial or in-service teacher training in the institutions.

An important factor behind this is the lack of hard research into the methods and approaches of teaching which increase the probability of continuing learning. There is, on the other hand, much research devoted to the efficiency of teaching methods in terms of qualifications. That is no substitute for looking at the lifelong learning perspective. A link with the proposed Higher Certificate in Lifelong Learning would rectify this. Would-be teachers who had not acquired this Higher Certificate in taking their first degree could be required to take it as part of their professional training.

Teachers: conditions and incentives

Talent and training alone will not make a good facilitator for lifelong learning. Good teaching conditions and equipment, good terms of employment, and good incentives are crucial. Here the chronic lack of money in the state-funded system and politicians' misguided policies come home to roost. If it is true that lifelong learners take their cue from the enthusiasm and sensitivity of their teachers, there is trouble in store.

Teachers' stress levels are commonly running very high, across the whole initial learning system and beyond. Pay is poor; class sizes are high; and the hours worked are generally excessive. Chances of promotion are also poor, and the system of funding by average salary units has worked against the more experienced teachers. Little wonder that unprecedented numbers of schoolteachers were retiring early – until, that is, the previous government closed a pensions loophole and trapped exhausted teachers inside the profession.

Matters were exacerbated by the current government's 'name and shame' policies directed at failing schools. Constant public rehearsal of a grossly exaggerated estimate of the number of inefficient teachers has diminished and demeaned the professional standing of teachers, both in their own eyes and in the eyes of parents and pupils. The stress levels for school staff associated with inspections by the Office for Standards in Education (Ofsted) are commonly high. All these contribute to a crisis – in numbers and in quality – in the recruitment of new teachers.

Things are little better in further education and much of adult education. There is considerable casual work amongst lecturers and tutors. This casualization makes it very difficult to tackle questions of curriculum and staff development, and to raise standards further. Staff contracts are a source of unrest, and the complexity of the funding structures causes endless problems for internal administration.

It is a similar story in higher education. Tenure is rare; salary levels are low; and contracts often carry onerous waiver conditions which deny workers basic rights. The recent large volume increases in the student body have not been reflected in staff/student ratios. This has put serious pressure on staff at the same time as the Research Assessment Exercise – which determines the allocation across higher education of £600 million of general research funding – has pressurized academic staff to publish research, thick and fast.

In any scenario of lifelong learning, problems originating in overload and inappropriate expectations will have to be addressed. Incentives and rewards for formal teaching are a particular concern:

- *In schools*, funding arrangements under the annual increment system have worked against the experienced teacher. Promotion normally means that good teachers move out of the classroom. To counter this, the government has proposed a new grade of 'super teacher' paid at management rates of pay. The 'super teacher' would get extra pay to remain an active teacher, for part of the time at least, and to act as a mentor to less experienced teachers. The suggestion runs directly counter to the culture of the teaching profession. As members of a team – whether at the level of a department or an entire staffroom – teachers tend to be suspicious of systems which will introduce comparative assessments, rivalries and additional budgetary tensions among them. The force of these objections is very strong. For the same reasons the idea of performance-related pay for a minority of teachers runs against the current professional culture, and does nothing to move it towards a lifelong learning culture.

  Just as important as good incentives are easily accessible and supportive escape routes for teachers who are approaching exhaustion. 'Burn-out' is now a familiar professional risk among exactly the kind of committed teachers that schools need. Teaching unions report real despair among teachers in their late middle years at the recent tightening of the criteria for medical early retirement.

- *In further education colleges*, the delivery of courses is so complex, and the teaching force so casualized, that there is relatively little accent on identifying and supporting good teaching. The funding structure does give a measure of reward to successful outcomes against intended student learning goals, but it is unknown how far this filters down to rewards for particular teachers under current staff contracts. Many staff members are not salaried, but are paid at an hourly rate.

* *In higher education*, the evidence is that rewards at the level of the individual staff member are generally insensitive to the quality of the teaching. Promotion and security are more commonly related to success in the publication criteria of the Research Assessment Exercise. There is a growing recognition that this bias in reward needs correction. But there are acute problems in getting proper incentives to bear – both on institutions for their average quality of performance, and on individual teachers in those institutions.

Gender and lifelong learning

Gender difference may be expressed differently in different cultures, and among people of different ages and generations. But there are some constant factors – biological and cultural – which have a strong bearing on individuals' propensity and opportunities for learning, and to continue learning. In a general lifelong learning culture, sensitivity to the influence of gender on learning will need to spread beyond professional teachers. The gender implications of social commitment and respect for others' learning are likely to challenge current practice, in and beyond educational institutions.

The curriculum and environments for learning should provide learners with stimulus and challenge appropriate to their needs, including gender-related needs. It is known, for example, that boys and girls tend to respond differently to opportunities for individual collaboration and competition in learning. While boys seek external and often overtly aggressive competition, the kind of competition that stimulates girls' learning tends to be of a more introspective kind: not so much a matter of, 'How much better did I do than X did?' but 'How much better did I do this time than I did last time?', or 'Did I do as well as I might have done?'

But these generalizations do not obscure the fact that there are boys who are intimidated by aggressive competition, just as there are girls who are motivated by it. A straightforward segregation of the sexes in education, on a short- or long-term basis, is not an appropriate solution in the context of establishing a lifelong learning culture. Males and females need to be capable of learning, and of supporting the learning of others, in environments which are mixed by gender, by age, and by any social or ethnic difference.

Learning environments – in and beyond educational institutions – therefore need to be constructed to include some competitive elements at the group level which can encourage some learners, but which are not so aggressive or personal as to discourage others. The curriculum must aim to develop co-operative behaviour and proper assertiveness in every learner.

ASSESSMENT: FORMATIVE AND SUMMATIVE

All learners need assessment, whether at the start, during, or at the end of a spell of learning. Chapter 5 looked at the accreditation of prior learning; here, the formative assessment which runs through learning, and summative assessment which leads to formal qualifications, are reviewed. 'Formative' means 'used to shape the ongoing learning experience'. It is interwoven with the learning. 'Summative' means 'summing up' the learner's performance and achievement for a part or the whole of a learning course. This is normally carried out for the award of formal qualifications.

Formative assessment

Running assessment: recent research by Paul Black and Dillon Wiliam[4] reflects serious weakness in the form of assessment used in many schools. The current school emphasis 'on competitive testing and achieving national targets may actually be counter-productive because it reinforces low-achieving pupils' sense of failure', according to Paul Black, who is Chairman of the government's Task Group on Assessment and Testing. Teachers' workloads are such that parents are lucky if they get more than one report a year on their children's progress – whatever the basis of assessment.

Achievement profile/record of achievement: every school pupil also needs an achievement profile, maintained jointly by the pupil and school staff. This record is a crucial adjunct to formative assessment. Records of achievement started in school are an important preparation for reflective and self-directed learning later in life – a process at the heart of lifelong learning. The basic principles of running assessment and records of achievement should apply to all formal learning, whether in initial or post-initial education. There is a general lack of systematic thinking and practice on this issue.

School/pupil agreements (sometimes misleadingly called 'contracts'): the use of these is a growing practice. Parents and school get together to create learning plans for individual children, leading to agreed joint action on a shared educational and developmental agenda for the child, together with regular assessments of progress. This is an approach which sits very well with running assessment and the maintaining of records of achievement.

Summative assessment

Summative assessment for qualifications raises two particularly relevant issues for lifelong learning: a concern about gender and cultural biases, and the contribution of marked course work towards final qualification. It is well known that reform of the GCSE allowed girls to express their abilities more effectively than previously. It is still thought that the A-level examination system, and the intensive examination systems still practised in older universities, have a masculinity of design which creates problems for some candidates. Such biases would have no part in a lifelong learning culture.

The role of marked course work in qualification is another sensitive matter. The last Conservative Government reduced the contribution of course-work assessment on the final award in 16–19 qualifications. This was done in spite of evidence that continuous assessment was beneficial to students; raised incentives for successful completion; and corrected for gender differences, while using a more compelling definition of learning excellence. These modes of course-work assessment are much more compatible with general lifelong learning – despite their cost and openness to abuse than trial-by-ordeal, 'sudden death' examination methods.

QUALIFICATIONS

Beyond assessment, there are important questions about qualifications themselves. The key issue is the link between qualifications and lifelong learning culture. There is a real dilemma here.

On one hand, a lifelong learning community treats all learners with respect. No one should be so elevated in honours that they cannot own up to ignorance, and learn from others. Also, highlighting success casts a shadow on those who are more modest achievers. This effacement can permanently damage the motivation to learn. This argues against the overt badging of achievement.

On the other hand, it is right for people to want to increase their achievements in learning, and there are strong arguments for signalling such achievements to society and the economy through a system of recognized awards. Without it the incentive to learn would be less, because it becomes more difficult to realize the benefits of the learning – both for the individual and for wider society. Qualification badges make the labour market work more efficiently. Without them, caution in making appointments on imperfect information keeps wage levels low, and slows the exploitation by employers of employees' full potential.

The overall advantages of qualifications must be acknowledged, despite the fact that some individuals find an emphasis on them acts as a learning deterrent. It would be wrong and futile to try to get rid of qualifications in the move to lifelong learning. Even in a general lifelong learning culture the demand for qualifications will be strong.

Enhancing the efficiency of qualifications

The task for policy is therefore to learn how to enhance the efficiency of qualifications as signals of achievement, and stop them being an inhibition and a deterrent through the pain of odious comparisons. Much can be done. For example, qualifications can be designed so that even people who fail can accumulate credits towards ultimate success. Awarding bodies can also seek ways to minimize the erratic effects of written examinations. Learning providers, for their part, can take greater care over entering candidates for qualifications by asserting the principle that no teacher should commit a learner to certain failure.

Depreciation of skill

The depreciation of skill is another aspect of qualifications which needs to be more clearly visible. A degree in computing or in engineering, for example, is likely to be out of date in three to four years. A general lifelong learning culture will need to give much greater recognition to qualification decay, and to promote the steps that counteract it. The current approach to university degrees raises acute problems in this area. According to the 'once a graduate, always a graduate' view, the qualification proves that the holder can achieve at a certain level; and that the abilities which led to a given award will continue to be available throughout life for tasks of equivalent difficulty, subject to the usual wear and tear. Depreciation is therefore not a central concern.

In fact a degree is typically a mixture of general competences, which depreciate only slowly, and subject mastery, which will drop away rapidly, if not reinforced by new learning. There is a link here with the earlier discussion about lifelong learning entitlements, and also with the qualification structure for age 16–19. Degrees need to make two kinds of signal: to mark the learning capabilities of the learner, as exemplified in the course; and to mark the learner's specific competences and knowledge. Degree certification needs to recognize both these points, and the decay factor in the second should be clearly recognized.

Credits of learning achievement

Incremental signals are a further issue. Employee development schemes have shown that information about systems for accreditation of prior learning and credit accumulation, combined with good guidance, can literally transform personal motivation. The realization that past learning has 'investment value' towards a new qualification – and that a learning provider is offering appropriate opportunities for busy, part-time learners – can prompt new ambitions or reawaken old ones.

More progressive and cumulative approaches to gaining qualifications through unitized, step-by-step achievement can be expected in a lifelong learning culture. Separately assessed and certificated units allow learning to be progressively signalled. This is useful as far as it goes. But for many qualifications the award in its entirety needs to be more than the sum of modular assessments. There will need to be extra units expressing some overall 'coherence criteria', which show how the learner can put the whole body of learning to work in an inter-related way.

In its full form the unit approach becomes a call for a full-sized credit accumulation and transfer system across providers, allowing extensive modular pick-and-mix options across subjects, levels and providers.[5] This is tailor-made for lifelong learning. The flexibility it provides is potentially immense, offering individually picked courses at all levels, with a multitude of built-in pathways of progression. The difficulty lies in the detail.

- The proposal of a national system immediately raises questions about the role of the government in fixing the principles and values of the value-points attached to learning. There are serious questions of academic freedom involved in this, not only for higher education but for providers and awarding bodies at all levels in the system. It would be essential for a permanent body – quite separate from government – to be set up to hold the ring.
- Even before values are attached, every qualification to be included in the system has to be broken into 'units of assessment'. Each unit would have to be described and lodged in a database on standard terms across the whole system. This is a major task, although it would be highly beneficial in its own terms, as Geoff Stanton has shown.[6]
- The attachment of values has to reflect not only the module/unit itself, but also the role the module fulfils in a wider scheme of study. In some circumstances, the value of a given unit may vary according to context. Valuation may also stumble over the 'apples and pears' problems created by different kinds of assessment systems, and the varying concepts of grade of performance across different types of course.

NVQs, for example, have pass/fail judgements of competence, whereas A-levels are graded on a scale from A to F.

- At the point of assessment itself the problems are also challenging. The assessment of units becomes divorced from the reputation of particular providers. A university, for example, is concerned, almost above everything else, with the integrity of its degree awards. If it issues a degree to a learner on the basis of accumulated credit 'points' largely amassed from study with other providers, how can anyone tell whether the degree really has the full standing of the awarding university?
- CATS imply a large-scale increase in facilities for the accreditation of prior learning, to recognize uncertificated learning.

It will take a major commitment from government and providers across the whole learning scene to solve these problems – especially in the context of the international comparability of awards which enable lifelong learners to use qualifications in an international labour market. *The Learning Age* shows the current government edging towards a separate CATS system for higher education; and a partial system applying to learning in the further education sector. This falls well short of what a lifelong learning society will surely demand.

'Parity of esteem' in qualifications

Finally, the problem of respectability looms, as it relates to qualifications. This is otherwise known as the parity of esteem problem – the high-flown language itself expressing the pure snobbery attaching to certain academic qualifications. These are popularly held to maintain the 'gold' standard for learning at their level, compared with those which are mainly vocational.

A widely accepted principle is that qualifications which are set at the same 'value' level in terms of learning achievement under the CATS system should have equal respect, with no attention paid to irrelevant criteria. But it is difficult to get the principle across to employers and others. Attempts have been made to stop the expression of prejudice by official declarations of equality. These have proved entirely futile. In the current culture, no amount of official pronouncements about the respectability of vocational qualifications can counter the cultural shadow cast by their academic equivalents. The problem lies not in the values of the official signaller, but in the values of those to whom the qualification is signalling: employers and the parents of young learners. The lasting solution depends on the creation of a new culture.

While the cultural transition takes place, and to minimize the problem in the meantime, it will help to remove the unnecessary features of qualifications which provide a purchase for prejudice. This can be done by losing the academic/vocational distinction in a broader unitized qualification structure; avoiding the label 'vocational' for a qualification, if it can be at all avoided; giving all qualifications a grading structure, so that a qualification cannot be dismissed as ungraded; and by unifying assessment procedures as far as the subject matter permits, so that they look and feel the same.

LEARNER SUPPORT OUTSIDE THE CURRICULUM

There is commonly a need for two kinds of learner support in a wide range of matters not directly related to course work: internal support, which is provided within an episode of learning; and external support, which is provided between and across episodes of learning. The need for either might reflect personal difficulties with attendance, illness, child care, money and a host of other matters. They might involve educational choices – over which units to take, perhaps; or when to take a break in study. They might involve induction at the start of courses, and debriefing and 'after-sales service' at the conclusion. The main point for lifelong learning is that the current standard of learner support is seriously inadequate for the future.

Internal support

Learners currently face a medley of diverse arrangements depending on where they are in the system. A general charter of client's rights is needed, which will include under its terms a number of support provisions and warrants to run in common across the whole of the learning field.

It cannot be said too often that accessible and impartial educational advice and guidance is essential. Experiments with guidance vouchers in the past have shown a tendency for providers to make high rates of self-referral, and similar forces operate in keeping 'staying-put' rates high at age 16 in 11–19 schools. Standards of independence in advice need to be applied to this situation, extending to all staff who give advice and guidance to learners.

External support

The importance of information and guidance services for lifelong learning has already been discussed, but two points need to be stressed:

1. Provision of information, advice and guidance needs to be lifelong. This involves much more than the ready availability of these services when they are needed at any point in a person's life. It involves a different service, with a different emphasis. It will focus on continuity of learning, on pre-empting problems, and on a running reassessment of personal and family goals. The emphasis will not be just on an individual's next career or learning step, but on carrying through a flexible and unfolding strategy over the lifespan.
2. There needs to be much more mentoring. The theme of mentoring is gradually becoming more familiar, but in a lifelong learning culture it will come into its own. There will be major problems in raising mentoring from an occasional facility into a mass provision.

NOTES AND REFERENCES

1. Chitty (1992).
2. The 'Pathways to Adult Life' project has developed similar ideas across part of the field. Developed by the London Enterprise Agency, it was piloted during 1996–7 in schools in Cheshire, Doncaster and Lewisham.
3. Woodhead (1998).
4. O'Connor (1998).
5. For a thorough exploration of CATS in British higher education, see Robertson (1994).
6. Stanton (1997).

Part III

Chapter 9

Strategy for Lifelong Learning

This chapter considers what needs to be done to set in place an overall strategy for leading the transition to a general lifelong learning culture. A robust strategy (see Figure 4.1, p. 66) will need to be developed by a partnership of government and major stakeholders. It will need clear success and failure criteria, and an unambiguous statement of tasks set against a definite timetable. No such strategy can be complete unless the resourcing issues have been closely explored. This means thorough strategic planning, and the commitment of resources to drive the processes involved.

FORMATION OF OVERALL POLICY

The overall strategy and its key policies must be fit for purpose, and the machinery which support them must work effectively. Good systems require attention to lifelong learning definitions, government departmental structures, governance and partnership.

Definitions

Responsibilities for lifelong learning are currently held by the Secretary for Education and Employment. He or she is supported in this by officials who act alongside but, for the most part, separately from officials responsible for the schools, the further education sector, and the universities. This means that the definition of lifelong learning stands in perpetual danger of being limited to 'adult continuing education' and 'continuing professional development', as current practice shows.

Government rhetoric occasionally acknowledges that lifelong learning is more than this, but key documents give no clear definition. This is a critical weakness. When it comes to actual policy, lifelong learning is telescoped into adult learning; and the division between initial and post-initial learning remains as profound as ever.

The repercussions are a set of false dichotomies which pervade the entire policy scene. These reflect, variously, a schools versus adult lifelong learning balancing act; or a 16–19 versus adult lifelong learning trade-off; or even a universities versus lifelong learning tug o' war. In these narrow visions, lifelong learning is either just the latest manifestation of the tradition of extramural/liberal arts/adult continuing education, stretching back into the nineteenth century. Or it is something vocational and somehow instrumental, done by the further education sector. Or – among older universities – something of greater interest to the further education colleges and 'post-1992 universities'.

There can be no hope of a real strategy until there is a realization at the highest levels that lifelong learning is the one integrating idea capable of drawing together the whole scene of learning. Unless this is grasped, meaningless discussions on the trade-off between lifelong learning and various bits of education will continue, while the lifelong learning concept should really be seen as the field where all the key choices of learning policy have to be made. Questions of the government's allocation of resources – between initial and post-initial learning, or between statutory education and the rest, for example – are all lifelong learning issues. The key question for every sector where the nation's learning activities take place is, 'What can this sector do for the lifelong learning agenda?' Anything which sets up a funding dichotomy between a particular sector and lifelong learning is a fundamental and costly mistake.

Departmental scope

Acknowledging the wider vision means structural changes. The labour market is becoming so flexible that people are likely to spend no more than about a third of their lives in organized employment. Conventional 'employment' is being replaced by a broader concept of 'work', as the RSA study, *The Future of Work*[1] has shown. Similarly the concept of 'education' is increasingly seen as just one corner of a much wider vision of learning (see Chapter 1). It does not help continually to squeeze that vision back into narrow institutional confinement. The task now is to nourish networks which facilitate learning in all manner of other contexts – the home, the community and the work place – in the wider sense of work.

The office of Secretary of State for Education and Employment therefore needs to be replaced by a 'Secretary of State for Lifelong Learning and Work', with the relevant government department renamed accordingly. Shifting the focus from 'education and employment' to 'learning and work' will signal the government's understanding of the fundamental changes taking place, and will encourage a focus on the lifelong learning agenda as the overarching concept.

The government can be seen moving hesitantly towards this in its launch of a National Grid for Learning (for teachers), and the Learning Direct[2] national helpline for information and advice. It is also reaching for something larger in its plans for a 'University for Industry', but the precise issues of what, how and who pays remain unclear.

This shift in concept should be accompanied by a restatement of the now famous New Labour priority – 'Education, Education, Education' – in terms of lifelong learning in the wider sense. As most construe it, the 'Education × 3' format signals formal education in the schools as virtually the whole of the government's ambition. The schools are certainly long overdue for reform, but this task falls a long way short of the full lifelong learning agenda.

Within the new Department of Learning and Work, the separate official fiefdoms which currently divide up the education scene will need to convert to the new agenda. They would continue to have large scope to manage the details of the individual learning sectors, but would be bound to an overall lifelong learning policy, overseen by a very senior official.

Advisory bodies also need to be rationalized. Temporary advisory groups and committees, whose standing and accountability are very unclear, have proliferated under New Labour. The criteria for selection of members is not clear, and some may find themselves appearing to give moral support to policies which they do not always commend, or even understand. In particular, the current National Advisory Group on Continuing Education and Lifelong Learning (NAGCELL) – whose portmanteau title strains to contain the relevant interests – will need to be replaced by a new independent body representing the full spread of opinion. This might be called the 'UK Lifelong Learning Advisory Group'.

Members of this Advisory Group would be chosen on the grounds of experience, some being carried over from NAGCELL. All would be people who are seen to be independent of government and able to speak freely. The Group would consult and draw on a wide range of ideas, and publish reports from time to time. It would also manage an associated Lifelong Learning Research and Policy Unit, which could be based in a university. This Unit would also be independent of government and its ministers.

Governance

There also needs to be a ministerial Cabinet Committee for Lifelong Learning which sits permanently and frequently, with a matching shadow committee of officials from a number of government departments. This would strengthen current *ad hoc* co-ordination facilities. The new remit would be to bring together the lifelong learning policies and activities of England, Wales, Scotland and Northern Ireland into a comprehensive long-term strategic approach for the whole of the United Kingdom.

The Department for Lifelong Learning and Work would lead these arrangements. The Department of Culture, Media and Sport, the Department of Trade and Industry, the Cabinet Office and the Treasury would also be represented. Each territorial department would need a high-level official – second permanent secretary standing, in the English case – to prepare and oversee the implementation of the agreed strategy.

The Committee and officials will have a large agenda to cover (see Box 9. 1).

A UK Lifelong Learning Partnership

The lifelong learning strategy will need to be owned and championed by an effective working partnership between government and all the other major stakeholders. A new 'UK Lifelong Learning Partnership' should be established to represent the independent power structures involved. Many bodies will vie energetically for an invitation to this table. It will be necessary to distinguish between members – that is, those who can deliver the strategy – and observers, who can assist. Among those in the latter camp would be a number of quangos whose ultimate existence – and sometimes principal policies – are set by the government. Bodies likely to be abolished under a lifelong learning strategy would not be included in the membership.

- Decentralization of government powers.
- Institutional framework.
- Stimulating demand.
- Information advice and guidance.
- Qualifications and credit.
- Curriculum.
- Teaching and teachers.
- Learner services.
- Customer protection and redress.
- Quality assurance.
- Lifelong learning research and development.
- Financing arrangements.
- Money.

Box 9.1 Strategic agenda for lifelong learning.

The Lifelong Learning Partnership would be a voluntary association, supported by its own officers. and acting under the chairmanship of the Secretary of State for Lifelong Learning and Work. The strategy would be developed and adopted by the Partnership as an association – it would not be a government strategy only. Partnership members would be expected to co-operate in implementing the agreed plan, using directly any influence they have, and any powers which they acquire under legislation or regulation. Members of the Partnership would appear before a new Select Committee on Lifelong Learning on a regular basis. The Partnership would have a number of special sub-committees, addressing particular themes such as marketing, quality and qualifications. These would meet regularly to consider proposed updates and to monitor progress.

INFRASTRUCTURE DESIGN AND DEVELOPMENT

The Partnership's plan would be an integrated and costed 'strategy and programme of activities' stretching ten years ahead, the first five years being set out in detail. It would be revised and rolled forward on an annual basis. The strategy document itself would be an overview. It would not aim to have all the myriad details of all the constituent activities within its covers. It would be accessible, contain clear definitions and success criteria, and give an account of reason and philosophy.

This strategy would overtake the activities of the National Advisory Council on the Education and Training Targets (NACETT), which would be abolished. This is because the strategy will need to go well beyond the logic of the current national targets. These are aspirational levels unsupported by specific implementation plans, and there is no calculation which connects the targets with what the UK needs specifically to deal with social exclusion, and with weaknesses in competitiveness.

Box 9.2 shows the main responsibilities of a government-funded Support Unit, dedicated to providing administrative and developmental support for the Partnership.

The Support Unit's main responsibilities would be to:

- provide secretariat services;
- propose and publish a technical rationale for the strategy, and to undertake projections and costings relating to the strategy as a whole;
- co-ordinate an overall monitoring of the strategy;
- operate a research and development strategy, in support of the strategy as a whole, making disbursements to partnership members and others to undertake key research and development work in support of the strategy. (This would complement the research and development work of the government and other individual partnership members, not replace it.);
- develop a UK website on lifelong learning issues covering the whole of the UK or any particular part within it. There would be hyperlinks through to all main members and observers in the Partnership, all of whom would have their own lifelong learning web sites.

Box 9.2 Partnership Support Unit.

STRATEGY MONITORING

The emerging lifelong learning strategy will need a wealth of up-to-date information, fit for a new century in the 'Information Age'. At present there is no comprehensive monitoring system which addresses the whole lifelong learning agenda. This partly reflects the size of the task; but it also bears the mark of the restrictive policies of the last Conservative Government, which prided itself on cutting back on the vital data actually needed to construct effective learning policies.

The Partnership would need to put in place and co-ordinate a proper process of monitoring for the strategy. This would involve monitoring the actions of the partners in discharging their agreed contribution to the overall strategy, all learning being undertaken in the United Kingdom, and relevant activity and developments elsewhere in Europe or further afield.

Monitoring the partners' contributions

It would be a condition of partnership that each member or observer should undertake to monitor its agreed contribution to the strategy, and to make available its regular assessments of progress. It would be for the Support Unit to publish these in collated form on its Internet site. Monitoring would be quarterly, done to a common timetable allowing a full report to be made available for the regular Partnership meetings. The Partnership, being a non-executive body, would not take its own executive action on the progress reports but would make representations and give its advice to the relevant partner.

Monitoring lifelong learning itself

The task of monitoring the learning being undertaken is a major enterprise for the government. It amounts to a revamp of statistical policies covering the whole of the UK learning scene. (Elements of this are currently under way, following the merger of the former Department of Education and the Employment Department.)

- *Initial learning system:* a basic requirement is to gather together the whole body of statistics for all stages of initial education, ensuring a compatible presentation of statistics. This indicates the need for a universal individual student record, of the kind now found in the further education sector. Such a record would unify the statistical worlds of education and training. It would mean adopting a universal individual identifying code, which could – with appropriate data protection safeguards – be used over time for cohort analysis, for individual lifelong learning accounts (ILLAs – described in Chapter 10) and for achievement profiles. Data would be passed electronically through the Internet to the relevant department of state. The usual programme statistics would be covered by these means.
- *Guidance, and learning plans:* in addition there would be sound information about the use made of guidance in the counselling sense, and the holding of learning plans. This would address an embarrassing gap in the statistical record.
- *Post-initial learning:* there would be full collection of data for formal, taught courses in further and higher education. But it would not be feasible to apply this to short- course learning outside the ambit of state funding system, nor would it be possible to apply it to the private sector or to community-based learning organized by the local authorities. For the last of these a more straightforward enumeration system would be all that could reliably be collected – with information on learning episode starts and completions, and some basic age, gender, socio-economic, and purpose information.
- *A national sample household survey of learning activity:* this would be undertaken in each of the territorial countries in the United Kingdom. The surveys would use wide definitions and would be undertaken at two-year intervals, not three years as at present. The sample would be generous enough to permit a fine breakdown of data by ethnic or religious categories, or important categories like 'unemployed' and 'retired'. There have been several major surveys of this kind in recent years, conducted by NIACE/The Campaign for Learning, and the DfEE. NALS'97 is the most recent and most authoritative of these. Any further efforts will need to be co-ordinated by the Partnership.
- A national survey of the kind envisaged here will require some particular changes to be made: to cover learning in retirement, beyond the 69-year limit currently used; to provide much better coverage for information, advice and guidance; to give closer attention to the concept of lifelong learning in the questionnaire; and to

construct sampling of young people in the initial education system (including pre-school), and of their parents.

- *An over-time cohort study of lifelong learning:* this might be composed of a sample of learners starting at different key ages, reflecting the key stages of initial education, and stages in adult life. This cohort study would be used to build good, over-time data on learning and on the interactions with economic and domestic conditions. There would have to be a firm commitment to keep this going for the long term.
- *Specialist surveys:* these general surveys would need to be supplemented by specialist surveys conducted on an occasional basis as necessary. Specialized marketing surveys will undoubtedly be needed, as would surveys of providers and employers (along the lines of those conducted for the *Training in Britain* survey 1987, and the Employment Department surveys of 1994).
- *Overview diagram:* each year an overview diagram should be published showing the flow of funds into and out of all learning sectors. This would be a large-scale undertaking in social accounting, which has implications for national accounts.
- *Annual expenditure:* in this specialized area, there would need to be regular annual surveys of expenditure by all stakeholders on learning and training as distributed over all kinds of supply, including learning support services as well as the basic fees. There would have to be capital account data to show how far the cash demand was met by loans and the stock of savings, as opposed to current spending.

This thoroughgoing approach would replace the present reliance on simple statistics of funding, derived mainly from the operations of funding councils. A national strategy cannot be properly monitored without data of the kind suggested here.

EVALUATION AND FEEDBACK

The Lifelong Learning Partnership would commission an independent professional evaluation of its strategy once a year, drawing on the performance reports and other evidence. In addition, the government could commission a small number of expert assessments from overseas (such as the influential OECD Lifelong Learning team, under Albert Tuijmann).

All these assessments, together with the government's own assessment, would be published in paper-based form and on the Internet. They would be based on *ad hoc* studies, and also on the evaluation work done by each of the stakeholders on its contribution to the overall strategy. It would be a basic policy of the Partnership that these stakeholder contributions should be professionally and independently evaluated, if necessary with a government contribution and with advice from the Partnership Support Unit. The assessments, and public comments on them, would be taken by the Partnership at a key meeting each year, timed to influence the government's three-yearly public expenditure review.

A number of feedback processes need to be brought together to close the design loop. A major speech by the Prime Minister once a year would share his or her understanding of the strategy with the general public. He or she would lead the strategy, supported by the relevant Secretaries of State. The Select Committee on Lifelong Learning would also hold hearings and take evidence. It would publish its own views annually, and in good time for the Partnership and the Government to consider them in the three-yearly public expenditure round. The Partnership should have an annual programme of properly designed focus groups, to test out popular reactions to the strategy overall and to particular ideas within it. It should publicize its strategy widely and in accessible form, with leaflets, videos and other materials.

NOTES AND REFERENCES

1. Bayliss (1998).
2. Described in: DfEE (1998: 2).

Chapter 10

Financial Infrastructure

A new financial infrastructure is needed to carry the flexible operations of the lifelong learning market, meeting the specification set out in Chapter 8. The change in culture will not happen without it. This chapter outlines what the infrastructure would look like.

FUNDAMENTAL IDEAS

Two matters need to be clarified at the outset: *state involvement* and the notion of an *infrastructure.*

State involvement

The state will have to address two tendencies in its moves towards a lifelong learning society: firstly, that British society in general inclines toward underinvestment in learning; secondly, that the learning tends to be unevenly distributed. A *laissez-faire* approach, ignoring these two factors, could pick up the theme of personal and organizational commitment to learning – but it would be inefficient overall. This is because the externalities of learning and of new patterns in its spread are large, and benefit society as a whole rather than individuals or organizations. They would therefore not influence choices about learning made by individuals or organizations. The state cannot ignore this situation.

In the broadest terms, there are three ways in which a government can take a grip on these issues: through compulsion, through 'buying and giving', and through incentives. If the state compels, personal commitment will suffer, and the incipient culture of lifelong learning will be damaged. If the state 'buys and gives', there will be a deficiency of consumer sovereignty (the 'customer-in-charge' principle), and experience shows that learning opportunities will be unevenly spread. Both outcomes are inconsistent with the new culture. If, however, the state uses special incentives within a market framework, it will be able to foster consumer sovereignty and be redistributive – but only if it has the right framework to work with.

Of the three approaches, only the last is fully consistent with all the key features of the lifelong learning culture. It therefore forms the basis for the proposals brought forward here. In practice the other modes of state influence may continue to operate in parts of the learning market – particularly for compulsory schooling up to the age of 16, for reasons recognized in Chapter 8. The market-incentives system can however co-exist with these other approaches, for as long as politicians want.

From evidence of other markets (notably the housing market) consistent subsidy incentives over long periods can be relied on to shift the volume and pattern of expenditure. Normally this would still mean that the (larger) expenditure would face diminishing returns at the margin. It gets progressively harder to find good buys. In the case of learning it could well be different. The big prize from use of incentives is to turn the individuals and organizations which make up the national scene into self-motivated lifelong learners, whose combined efforts can drive up society's marginal rates of return to learning, rather than drive them down.

This is like pushing at an open door. It can happen if Britain can break out of the so-called 'low skill equilibrium'. This is a depressed state, where everyone acts as if the knowledge and skill constraints on economic performance will never be remedied, and plans accordingly. The labour market and product market then fail to signal the worth of learning correctly. For most people and organizations, the apparent returns on individual learning will seem relatively low. But in fact the nation's prosperity and cohesion are on the line as never before, and avoiding the economic slippery slope would be a huge benefit compared with the alternatives. Put more positively: a more aggressive approach to winning business in world markets, on the basis of a vigorous lifelong learning culture, has the potential at one remove to open up new returns on learning which are currently hardly visible.

Chapter 3 argued that the best chance of breaking out of the low skill equilibrium is to invest in the lifelong learning culture through the incentives route. Options which involve the state in taking on a predominant providing role for learning, or which attempt to conscript learners or their employers, cannot produce the necessary energy. The plane may trundle along the runway, but it will never fly.

Financial infrastructure

The idea of a financial infrastructure is fundamental to the incentives approach. We need a new national financial framework which can support a lifelong learning culture in all its forms and varieties. In such a culture there will always be a diversity and flux of learning policy and its financing. Having a financial infrastructure means that the financial framework should be able to express the changing priorities and the diverse actions of the stakeholders, without itself having to be radically adjusted every time someone has a bright idea.

This is like a motorway system, which enables all sorts of people and organizations to travel in different directions, for their own very different purposes, using the same system and covered by the same basic rules of the road. No stakeholder in a lifelong learning society should be left trying to hitch a lift on the slip road, or be stranded on the hard shoulder. A permanent infrastructure is needed which everyone can use openly for a wide variety of purposes.

INDIVIDUAL LIFELONG LEARNING ACCOUNTS IN OUTLINE

In 1997 the authors published outline proposals for a new national infrastructure of individual lifelong learning accounts (ILLAs).[1] These proposals were expressly built on the idea of incentives in a market framework, using the concept of a general infrastructure. They expanded the somewhat narrow ideas of learning accounts outlined in the New Labour manifesto of 1997, which focused on industrial upskilling. ILLAs are designed to provide an infrastructure supporting change to a widespread lifelong learning culture.

The government, persisting with its short-term approach, subsequently announced the introduction of a scheme of Individual Learning Accounts (ILAs) related to the world of work, and due to start in 1999. The fate of this ill-starred and under-researched scheme will need its own discussion in due course. This chapter explores the more fundamental ILLA concept, geared to the aim of culture change for learning, cradle to grave.

The ILLA account

We envisage the ILLA as a three-part financial account – not unlike an ordinary bank account – which people of any age can take out for the purpose of funding their lifelong learning activities. It would be an individual account, over which only the account-holder has control. It would have saving, borrowing, and credit functions dedicated only to learning-related expenditure. The saving and borrowing would be cash functions; the credit function would be in 'near-money' (conditional purchasing power).

An ordinary bank account can normally be used to save, and also to borrow on overdraft up to set limits. The ILLA's cash functions would be much the same. It would be possible to save and borrow cash for learning using the account. The single account could be said to bring together the two cash functions: the 'save-to-learn' function, and the 'borrow-to-learn' function.

A third function would be the 'credit-to-learn' function. This would work like any loyalty card account: the learner collects 'points' in the account which can be spent (redeemed for) only on approved items of learning.

The 'learning points' would work in the following way:

- The potential learner would use the ILLA to store the points collected from an issuer. Collection could be via a mandate, rather like a direct debit mandate. But it could also be via a plastic card, or similar device.
- The learner could spend the particular points stored in the ILLA on items from an approved list of learning goods and services drawn up by the issuer. The points would be passed to the learning provider as part of the learning transaction.
- The provider would then credit the learner with their redemption value, and subsequently redeem the points by presenting them to the issuer for reimbursement.

The usual term for 'learning points' is credit, but this is not the same as the idea of an 'academic credit' – where some previous learning is recognized as counting towards a qualification. Nor is it the sort of credit which account holders can get on a credit card – that is, a small loan from the credit card company. As used here, credit is conditional purchasing power, given to a learner for learning purposes. It can be turned into cash if and when it is used in a transaction which qualifies under the rules laid down. Supermarkets and retail stores have made such a system very familiar in recent years.

The ILLA account therefore would have three components: save-to-learn; borrow-to-learn; and credit-to-learn. People can build up purchasing power for learning by using their accounts to save and to borrow; and they can also use them to pick up learning credits from whoever may be giving them away. This could be the government, a local authority, an employer, a charity, a retailer, or even a relative or friend.

The account would support multi-sourced financing. Individuals would be able to mix their own resources, and it would also be possible to bring in other stakeholders to share the task. If, for example, a large learning purchase has to be made, the learner may want to put all money saved for learning on the table – but still be short of what is wanted. She may want to borrow more money to top up the cash amount, and – if the learning qualifies for learning credits – she may put some credits into the transaction as well. The government and/or her employer may, for example, give her learning credits for a basic skills course; or she may have a relative or friend who is willing to donate a modest sum into the savings part of the ILLA. All these sources of funds can be brought together, using the ILLA account and its attached mechanisms to co-ordinate the three basic functions within the account.

This means that a single transaction for learning can be paid for by bringing all three functions in the ILLA into play at the same time. Clearly it is not absolutely straightforward to put savings and borrowing – both of which are straight money concepts – together with credits, which are near-money. But banking software can put the 'credits redeeming process' together with the money procedures of the ILLA account in one seamless operation. The basic idea of the ILLA is summarized in Box 10.1.

- Everyone who wants an ILLA could take one out from any bank, building society or any other financial services institution.

- ILLAs are called Individual Lifelong Learning Accounts because each account would be owned by the individual, who alone would have control of the use of the account.

- ILLAs are called lifelong learning accounts because they would be available cradle-to-grave, and would last a lifetime. There would be no age limit, and they support the principle of the continuity of learning.

- ILLAs support personal and social commitment to learning individuals by providing a convenient way for to individuals to combine all kinds of funding for the learning which they do at any time in their lives.

Box 10.1 Key features of Individual Lifelong Learning Accounts.

Everyone would be free to take out an ILLA, using an individual identifier number. At any one time, some accounts might be dormant, but others would be heavily used.

Individual use would tend to vary over the lifespan. In some periods there may be little saving, but a reliance on borrowing. At other times it may be the reverse. At some ages there may be relevant state entitlements, expressed as credits, but not at other ages.

This spread of accounts across the population and the different stages of life would form an infrastructure to fund all kinds of planned learning. If the state, for example. should want a scheme to improve basic skills, it could cause credits to be placed in the ILLAs of people who show up as needing help when tested. Or the employer in a particular firm might make a bonus payment into the ILLA of a deserving worker, to be spent on learning. Or a grandparent might guarantee a learning loan for her grandson's ILLA, so that the bank keeping the ILLA would advance money for the required learning course. Or the local TEC might use the ILLA to place a youth credit, which could be used to fund a Modern Apprenticeship. Or a supermarket chain might want to allow customers to use their loyalty points on learning. Customers might also arrange for some of those loyalty points to be transferred into other people's ILLAs just as some people already donate their supermarket loyalty points to others.

These possibilities illustrate how the infrastructure can be used by all sorts of people in all sorts of ways – just like the motorway. Figure 10.1 shows how the ILLA would sit at the centre of the learning scene. It contrasts sharply with Figure 7.1 (p. 112). Operated to its full potential, the account would collect resources provided by individuals, family members, and employers; it would act as a channel for borrowing; and it would attract public sector purchasing power away from the funding councils and the whole 'back door' institutional funding route. This diversion would be effected largely through the credit function within the ILLA, although donations to the savings function could be used in special circumstances.

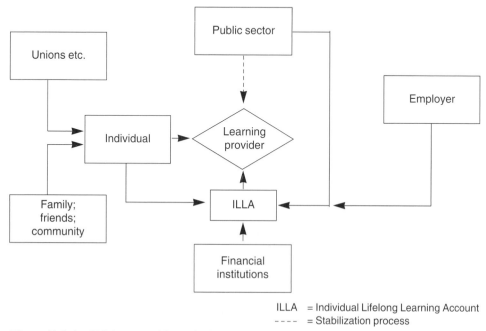

ILLA　= Individual Lifelong Learning Account
---- = Stabilization process

Figure 10.1 An ILLA-centred financial infrastructure.

Incentives

There are two good reasons for the government to create a general incentive to go with the ILLA account. Firstly, and fundamentally, the case for a general subsidy derives from the tendency of the market system to underinvest in learning. As we have noted, this is due mainly to the poor signalling of learning returns in the markets, and in particular to the several kinds of market failure which make up the 'low skills equilibrium'. But it is also a reflection of the problems people have in perceiving the benefit of learning – through lack of good information and guidance, or because they take an excessively short-term view – and importantly, because individuals and organizations largely ignore the external benefits to society in their individual learning decisions.

Secondly, there is the very practical reason that there might be little point in holding an ILLA without a general incentive. It is possible now to save and (with difficulty) to borrow for learning using quite normal banking services, without any restrictive framework. It is also possible to use loyalty cards to pick up credits, and to devote those credits to learning, if that is what the issuers want people to do. The ILLA would have to have a clear edge over these other possibilities.

To introduce the general incentive the government could create a tax-based instrument rather like the existing vocational training relief. This is a relief already available to learners buying certain forms of vocational training. It takes the form of a discount when the individual purchases an episode of qualifying learning from a registered provider. The discount is a relief against income tax, and so it is valued at standard tax rate for most taxpayers. The discount is available also to non-taxpayers who are below the tax threshold. A system like this, with the eligibility extended to a wide definition of learning and learning services, could be attached to all learning spending made out of ILLA accounts. In this way the incentive to buy learning through the ILLA comprises the sizeable discount that it would pick up when the account is drawn down for learning.

There are other ways of adding incentive. One alternative is for the government to encourage savings and borrowings for learning by giving an income tax relief on interest – on retained interest earnings in the case of ILLA savings, or on interest paid as an element in ILLA loan charges, or both. Another is where the government defrays the administrative charges which would otherwise bear upon the accounts. Finally, the government could use the ILLA system to create a general linked credit, using the matched funding principle. If somebody uses their ILLA for spending on specified learning out of savings or borrowings, the government would pay a matching subsidy at, say, 20 pence in the pound. It would pay this in the form of conditional credits placed in the ILLA – almost as if the learner were scoring 'points' in buying groceries at the supermarket.

We have adopted all but the linked credit, and built them into the design. This is not because we believe the three selected elements are necessarily the best, or only ways to proceed – much more analysis is required to establish that. It is however a reasonable starting point in considering the ILLA design. Tax relief is likely to be regarded as more permanent than other forms of incentive. Similar relief applies in the areas of personal pensions and housing, both supported as merit goods by government. Familiarity will signal long-run stability. Also the cost of the tax relief does not appear in the public expenditure accounts, since it is revenue forgone, whereas direct subsidies would certainly be included, and would have to vie with all other items inside the public budget. Administrative cost support is likely to help the financial services industry to participate more readily in offering the accounts.

Specific incentives will be needed to act against the background of the general incentives. This is required to take account of local conditions and particular externalities. The ILLA system can handle this very neatly, principally through credits – a conditional gift from the issuer. The expectation is that the ILLA system would become the standard method for launching any sort of learning credits, whether from the state, from the individual employer, or from any other source.

These incentives would encourage everyone interested in learning to open an account. Funds and purchasing power held in any of the three functions of the account would be dedicated to learning, and when spent on learning would attract a supporting general subsidy from the state. The accounts could support personal commitment to learning on a lifelong continuing basis. They could express and develop social commitment to learning by fostering mutual funding and donations between people. Moreover they can be used by the state to target particular individuals and groups for support, opening up a rich vein of redistributive possibilities.

All this is a staightforward, but very big idea. As a concept, it satisfies the design criteria of Chapter 7, and – unlike the present threadbare arrangements – it fits a general culture of lifelong learning like the proverbial glove.

BASIC DESIGN FEATURES OF THE ILLA SYSTEM

The basic design of an ILLA system reflects the need for it to be simple for learners to understand and to use.

Choosing an ILLA from competing financial institutions

Everyone would be able to open at least one account. The accounts would be on offer throughout the financial services industry, including the high street banks, the building societies, the new retail banks, and other responsible bodies, ranging from the Post Office to credit unions. Even providers of learning – acting individually or in consortia – could offer accounts. Common protocols (rules of procedure) of system operation would be binding on all providers of accounts.

This broad-based approach has a great advantage over the idea of setting up a single new Learning Bank, as urged by the National Commission on Education;[2] or the idea of using just one or two financial institutions to cover the UK. The danger with the former is that it takes too long to set up, and there would be difficulties in national coverage; it is not necessarily proof against hard competitive pressure from other banks. The difficulty with the latter is that the government may become trapped in a relationship with a small number of finance houses, which impedes the widening or developing of the scheme at a later stage, as happened to the Career Development Loan scheme.

The broad approach, on the other hand, guarantees national coverage, and it would swing behind the new structure all the formidable marketing talents of the assembled financial services sector. A competitive implementation by many institutions would create strong forward momentum. The precise terms of the ILLA franchise would be flexible within limits, allowing the institutions to compete on differences in the marketplace. But all institutions would have to abide by the basic design requirements and the common terms of operation.

The competitive activity reflects the main benefit which the accounts would bring to financial institutions. There is very little direct profit for institutions in holding personal accounts. The main benefit comes from the lifelong loyalty effects which a financial institution can build up with clients who are learners. There would be heavy competition on this basis.

Each account opened would have its own account code. There would also be a unique personal identifier code, which could be the same code as that proposed by ministers for use in the schools, and by the Universities and Colleges Admissions Service (UCAS) for use in university entry arrangements. Every genuine applicant would be guaranteed the chance to have an ILLA, if they wanted one. The government would have a 'last resort' arrangement with a single institution, to create an account if no other institution was prepared to make an offer to a particular person.

Three functions of the ILLA

Save-to-learn: in the savings function of the account, any savings would earn interest much as they would do in any savings account with a bank or building society. This interest would be ploughed back into the account, tax-free. When in due course the account has been drawn down to pay for an episode of personal eligible learning, the expenditure would also attract learning tax relief at standard tax rate. Learning tax relief would be a new wider form of vocational training relief, only available through the ILLA.

Borrow-to-learn: in the borrowing function, there would be two kinds of borrowing: small overdraft borrowings up to a limit; and medium-term loans on individually negotiated terms. The first are rather like small overdraft or credit card transactions within a limit of, say, £500 or £1,000 for a client with good credit standing. These borrowings would be available automatically, without detailed scrutiny of the learning expenditure. The second is more like a personal loan. The terms would be determined according to each person's creditworthiness. The sums might be up to several thousands of pounds, and the payback period would typically be several years.

Within the latter category, there would be three different loan 'products': *a simple commercial loan:* a replacement for the Career Development Loan, where the government would pay the interest on the loan during the period of learning and during any period of agreed delay in repayment, and guarantee the finance house against default; and *a general student loan scheme*, available to all students in initial higher education, irrespective of age or of full-time or part-time status. The latter would complete the process of privatizing the student loan scheme already begun by the government, by drawing in capital from the financial sector instead of from the public purse. The public purse would compensate the finance house for supplying the loan on the standard 'soft' terms for student loans.

For the small borrowings and the simple commercial loan, the interest element would gather tax relief through a system akin to the system which operates to give relief at source for mortgage interest. In this way the tax relief on savings and the tax relief on straightforward borrowings would be symmetrical. The two more complicated loan schemes would carry their own subsidy systems.

Credit-to-learn: the credit function is more complicated. It is however central to the redistribution of learning opportunities – a key feature of the new culture. The government would have to set up a credit agency, operating rather like a direct banking service or call centre, which would receive mandates to set up credits; place the mandates in the ILLA accounts of the individuals concerned; and in due course arrange for the credits to be redeemed when learning providers present the credits for payment.

The mandates would have to pinpoint the recipient, using the personal identifier; and specify the account itself, using the account code. The mandates would have to stipulate the amount of the credit in money terms, and the conditions attaching to redemption: for example that it should be a learning expenditure of a certain kind, or undertaken at a given place, or in given circumstances. Mandates would be taken by the credit agency in any form convenient to the learner: by phone, as in telephone banking; or by Internet link; or on paper over the counter or through the post. The conditions would be taken from a standard menu, enabling the conditions to be reduced to a small number of computer codes. The process would be like placing a direct debit mandate. The credit agency would charge a small percentage on redemptions for its services.

The ILLA account, as held by the issuing finance house, would carry a record of the mandates held by the account holder, obtained automatically down the cable from the agency. The agency would write mandates down or off when redemption takes place, reflecting learning expenditures made by the individual. The credit mandates would not be transferable between people but they could be cancelled by the issuer, using a simple order form. For the individual the credit is like a gift, although normally conditional. There is no call therefore for an incentive through tax relief towards the spending of the credits. The state could, if it chose, support the placing of a particular credit by an employer or other party, by giving a matching credit from the public purse. This would only be triggered if the initiating credit were triggered. This joint-credit is important. It can be a key feature in multi-sourced financing.

Regular reports to the learner

ILLA-holders would be able to check regularly with their finance house on the state of the whole three-part ILLA, and be able to take stock of their personal learning plans in the light of that information. At regular intervals every person holding an ILLA would receive an 'ILLA statement' – like any other kind of account statement – and be charged a proportion of administrative costs.

The statement would contain a summary 'consolidated' cash statement. This would show the cash position for spending on learning, after allowing for any savings put in, donations received, transfers to and from other ILLAs, interest and capital repayments, in the case where loans are outstanding, and, of course, payments made for qualifying learning. The credit account, on the other hand, being a list of conditional items, could not be simply added up to show a total spendable amount. It would remain a list of redeemable credits, as updated for recent redemptions.

Smart cards and the 'one-stop shop'

Any learner wishing to make a learning purchase would approach the provider with an ILLA smart card and personal identifier number (PIN), issued by the ILLA finance house. The card would bear secure personal identifiers, establishing that individual as the ILLA holder with a right to access that particular ILLA, and to enter protected databases. The learning provider would have a personal computer with appropriate software, a modem or ISDN link, and a smart card reader/writer machine (an inexpensive device, no more costly than a modem).

Reading the smart card would enable the learner, assisted by the provider, to check whether he or she could afford a course suggested by the provider. It would also show whether the course would be eligible for any financial credits. The provider would be connected to the credit agency via modem or ISDN, and would then be asked by the software to vouch for certain characteristics of the course or of the person's circumstances. On this basis the agency would decide, more or less on the spot, whether or not to give authority for a redemption to be made.

If the learner can afford the proposed learning – after putting together all the three functions of the ILLA – the transaction would be concluded. The smart card would give authority for the transaction to be committed, and for the learning tax relief to be claimed. In effect, this is a 'one-stop shop' allowing the learner, in one transaction, to bring to bear all the resources at his or her command – including credits – in a mixed funding package, if that is what is needed; to commit those resources; and to claim tax relief on the purchase in a painless way.

Once the transaction is authorized, the provider can use the software to claim money in a phased way from the ILLA account, and to summon the credit agency to redeem the credits on a similar timetable.

For the learner, the whole experience would be rather like booking a holiday with a travel agent. The provider would proceed in stages, according to the software, to address the questions raised. The transaction would be recorded for audit. The settlement would go through immediately, for small transactions; but there might be a 'cooling off' period for larger transactions.

Raising a negotiated loan

If a learner could not afford the proposed transaction, even with a small borrowing within the overdraft limit, he or she might need to consider negotiating an ILLA loan. If this business is not done electronically, the smart card could be used to convey the key details to the finance house, and then to register the finance house's approval of the loan. In this case the learner would have to contact the provider again, to clinch the deal.

Complexity and order

These brief indications of the ILLA system reveal something of the degree of complexity in the arrangements which are needed backstage to make a simple idea work out-front. On the other hand, the outline proposals are within the range of modern technology, and would produce a general system of financing which matches the design criteria closely. A thorough development project is needed to explore the mechanics further.

The complexity should also be seen in context. Financing arrangements in the current system have great complexity, but they are not orderly. Their transaction cost is very high, and is off-putting for many would-be learners. The proposed ILLA arrangements are complex (but computable) below the surface, and cheap, transparent and orderly above it. Just as with a good watch, using the ILLA would be simple, and the user would not need to be concerned with the detail of its workings.

FURTHER DESIGN FEATURES

There are several possibilities for enhancement of the basic idea.

Information, advice and guidance

The provision of guidance could be treated like any other learning possibility funded under the basic specification. The proposed system also offers a possibility for raising guidance funding for people who have no finance of their own in their ILLAs. A small percentage charge could be openly made on all transactions flowing through the system, to fund an entitlement for guidance. This would enable credits for approved guidance to be issued to targeted groups of people. The same approach could be used to create a resource for funding the free supply of information at the 'front end' of the learning system, and for defraying some of the basic costs of the 'University for Industry'.

A qualifications database and an achievement profile

The smart card could enable the learner to have access to personal qualifications data, and an outline profile of achievement lodged on a secure national database. This would be particularly helpful in guidance interviews. It could also have significant uses for employers who – at one remove, and only with the permission of the user – might verify employees' qualifications with the database. These arrangements would facilitate new policies directly addressing the depreciation of knowledge and skill over time. That would be a significant prize.

Marketing

The idea of taking a 'precept' from the flow of transactions in the national ILLA system could also be applied to marketing and promoting the new culture of lifelong learning itself. The Campaign for Learning, for example, could be set up as a board of trustees to receive and disperse money for these purposes quite independently from the government of the day. The separation of the promotion task from short-term political pressures would make for much-needed long-term promotional strategies, with a high degree of stability.

Closing the 'poaching' gap

In principle the credit function can be used to address the 'poaching' question. Employers tend to underinvest in learning because they fear that workers who have been educated and trained at their expense will be tempted to leave before the learning fully pays off for the employer. Employers could use the credit mechanism to insure against these risks. This could be done in all cases where the original learning is bought through the credit arrangements of the ILLA. It would work by creating an inverse credit in favour of the employer related to the original redemption (see Figure 10.2). This credit would be issued against a special insurance fund set up as part of the ILLA system.

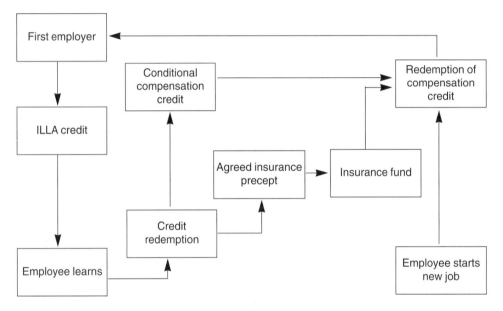

Figure 10.2 Compensation for lost learning outlay on job change.

Guarantees for loans

The system would allow transfers of cash between ILLAs as part of the basic specification. But the system should also enable people to support each other's spending through a guarantee scheme, allowing individuals and organizations to pledge guarantees in support of loans taken out by others. The guarantee would be made by a special credit mechanism, entitling the financial institution to call in the guarantee in the event of a default. This approach addresses the task of risk reduction in a way not seen in current arrangements.

Group accounts

The system could also handle group accounts which families, households, credit unions, clubs and any other organization might hold in common (in addition to any personal ILLAs held by any of the members). This would enable whole groups to enjoy similar advantages to those of individuals.

Funding the learner: a programme for reform

Development of the ILLA system in these ways shows how it can serve as the basis for the rationalization over time of the whole of the financing scene for learning. Not only would it pick up the themes of personal and social commitment, it could readily support learning on a cradle-to-grave basis, fostering continuity and progression through loyalty schemes and other devices.

Prominent amongst the prospects for reform is the idea of a large-scale decentralization of government funding, in favour of regional and local bodies. This would be done by giving them a devolved budget for distribution through the credit function. This would bypass the funding councils and the revenue support grant, both very blunt instruments for reshaping the pattern of learning.

We would expect the main funding of statutory education to be left essentially unchanged, but with reform to ensure that the local education authorities spend amounts at least equivalent to the money allocated by central government. The proposals (see Chapter 12) for individual development plans for pupils – covering learning outside statutory education – could be a fruitful use of ILLAs, helping to familiarize pupils and their parents with the operation of the system. There could also be uses in the area of guidance, and in other matters such as free school meals.

The main reform would come in further and higher education. Over time, the ILLA credit functions should be used to switch to the individual the bulk of funding from funding councils and the revenue support grant. This would apply to 16–19 learning and initial higher education, as well as to all publicly supported post-initial learning. This switch would enable a much more precise targeting of funding on the non-learning sections of the community, and on areas where social problems have high priority. These possibilities are explored in Chapter 11.

ISSUES

This use of ILLAs highlights particular issues as follows.

Social exclusion

Some commentators have said that the ILLA system would not be effective for poor and socially excluded people. The reasons suggested are various: some people might be too feckless; some might prefer moneylenders to banks; some might hold an account, but then forget how to apply it through lack of use; and some would not be attractive customers to the financial system because of past financial failings. There are real issues here, which are often skirted in discussion because of the risk of patronizing poor people. But, as Box 10.2 shows, there is no shortage of answers.

Compulsion

The ILLA system can be readily adapted to a policy of compelling employers to support learning, by the enforced issue of credits. Many would see this as an advantage for the ILLA system. But introducing compulsion poses considerable dangers for the intended cultural change, and it is not an option we would recommend. The government of the day should consider a range of carrots before resorting to the stick. They can, for example, improve accounting arrangements. There is a good case for obliging employers to declare their record in supporting learning. They can use linked credits to lever small firms into support for learning, as part of a general employee development programme – such as the 'Return to Learn' model already used effectively in Kent.[3] If that fails they can consider legislation to create a duty on employers to assess training needs jointly with each worker on a regular basis, and to consider appropriate solutions.

Above all, they should reflect on the virtues of securing culture change. The whole point is to stop flogging the dead horse, and to go for something which moves under its own steam.

- Poor people could receive targeted state credits for learning into their accounts, which they could not access any other way. This redistribution would be a powerful argument for people to hold and use an ILLA account.

- Everyone wanting an ILLA would get one somewhere, under special guarantees operated by government.

- Poor people are used to credit-based schemes. They use loyalty accounts and the National Lottery without any difficulty.

- The accounts are voluntary. No one will be forced into debt.

- ILLAs would be marketed as something for everybody, not as executive toys.

- Cards will cost £1–2 at most to produce, so lost or damaged cards can be replaced easily.

- The smart card could serve all kinds of other uses, such as a loyalty points card, a 'campus/school card', a personal identity card, or a welfare card.

- The ILLA would be entirely separate from any ordinary bank account; and the government could arrange for funds in an ILLA to be exempt from welfare claw-back.

- People could recover their savings in an emergency.

- Credit unions would have an important role.

- There seems to be nothing that would work better, for excluded groups in the population, than the smart card.

Box 10.2 ILLAs and social inclusion.

Displacement among stakeholders

A stakeholder in this context is anyone who pays for, or shares in, the cost of learning. Displacement might happen when a stakeholder, such as an employer, takes advantage of the new ILLA system to withdraw support which would otherwise have been expected, and tries to push the obligation to pay for learning onto the individual or any other party. This buck-passing is gamesmanship between stakeholders, and goes on all the time, whatever the funding arrangements for learning. There is no reason at all to think that the ILLA system would worsen the problem.

On the contrary, there is a reasonable prospect that the ILLA would make for a significant improvement. The new ILLA system provides an opportunity for the unions and staff associations to pay much more attention to the contributions of employers. It could capitalize on a growing interest in this area. Moreover the joint credit concept can help to offset any tendency to displacement. This would be done by leveraged deals, where the public body – perhaps a TEC – would promise to lay credits into the ILLA system, on condition they were matched by linked credits issued by others. ILLAs would, in short, make for greater transparency, and those seeking an unfair advantage are more likely, rather than less, to be exposed.

Emergency access to savings

An effective save-to-learn function in the ILLA depends on the account holder being able to recover funds to pay for emergency needs of a more general nature. The way to secure this is for the government to use the same principle which it is adopting for the ISA – the new individual savings acccount, which took over from the TESSA in 1999. This will not make interest relief conditional on tying up savings for five years. It will be possible to withdraw ISA deposits on demand without making any tax readjustments. The same approach can readily apply to ILLAs. In fact, the ILLA can be an ISA, in respect of any net cash holdings in the account.

Concerns about technology and security

The ILLA, as presented here, works through a smart card. It is however entirely possible that the system could run on the Internet; or be partly smart card and partly Internet-based in its operation. These options need to be explored as part of a thorough technical study.

Whatever the technology, there are bound to be worries over security and fraud in a system of ILLAs – just as there are concerns about the current very different funding structures. The answer for smart cards is that they can be designed as secure from the bottom up. This accords with the principle that nothing happens, and nothing moves, without the free and direct consent of the individual ILLA-holder. This is entirely feasible.

Breadth of definition for learning

The definition of eligible learning expenditure within the ILLA system must be clear. This may be partly a question of specific authorization, and partly a question of the scope of tax relief, when it applies.

- In the credit function, the conditions for each credit would specify the nature of the learning expenditure which would be supported. Tax relief definitions will not be relevant in the case of state credits.
- On the negotiated loan front, the lender would determine what learning they are prepared to lend for. But here the tax relief on purchase would introduce restrictions, if tax relief is to be claimed.

- On the cash parts of the ILLA – mainly the short borrowings and the expenditures out of savings – tax relief will commonly require eligibility conditions to be laid down.

In the case of ILLAs, therefore, the general subsidies proposed through the tax system and learning tax relief would need definitional boundaries, if only to prevent people drawing on subsidy to buy items which have a tenuous – or entirely nominal – connection with real learning.

The lifelong learning culture requires a wide definition, extending well beyond the traditional formal courses, and including the purchase of books, equipment and other services, such as child care. It would certainly be necessary to avoid limiting the subsidy to taught courses aimed at qualifications.

NOTES AND REFERENCES

1. Full details of the proposals can be found in Smith and Spurling, (1997).
2. National Commission on Education (1993).
3. This involves a 50/50% funding partnership between employer and the public sector (which is the TEC in the Kent case).

Chapter 11

Learning Infrastructure

Strategy and finance are not enough in themselves. The new culture will need a new, vastly improved learning infrastructure (see Figure 11.1) to support the learning market. The changes must be conducive to personal commitment by putting the onus on individuals, and by developing their motivation; they should foster social commitment, notably by giving people in their local communities a key role in the control of the learning system; and they must aid the forward planning of learning.

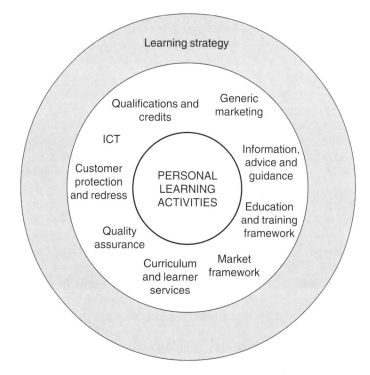

Figure 11.1 Marketplace infrastructure.

Such changes will not be achieved overnight. The agenda presented here might take twenty years to accomplish in full.

INSTITUTIONS AND MARKETS

Providing an efficient marketplace, and regulating the conduct of clients and providers in it, are essential infrastructural tasks. Problems of competition, pricing, planning and co-ordination, and brokerage all have to be considered. Yet the force of nostalgic resistance to the whole idea of learning as a 'traded good' is such that issues in these areas have not been adequately debated. When initial education was predominant, and training was not regarded as real education, it was possible to regard the learning world as a kind of self-contained national health service: taxpayers' money was used by the state and local government to dispense free educational entitlements through a bureaucratic apparatus. But that is the non-market perspective of a past age.

The post-initial marketplace

A vigorous market is already active in post-initial learning. Much is a normal free market, with little or no subsidy. This is set to grow hugely in a new general culture of lifelong learning.

Where the state is involved in post-initial learning however, the arrangements have features of quasi-markets – that is, on our definition, they have some of the main features of a free market, but not all. An important case is where the learner makes a cash payment, but in signing on for learning also attracts a partial state subsidy to a particular provider. In further education for example, a large proportion of post-initial learning is subsidized by the FEFC to around 75%, using the same complex subsidy formulae as apply to the 16–19 age group. Some particular groups – principally those on state benefits – attract full fee remission at the state's expense. Among these are unemployed people and other benefit recipients who are – according to current regulations – attending for less than sixteen hours of supervised learning a week. A similar form of market arrangement is commonly found in community education provided directly by the local education authority. Here the learner will typically pay some fees; but the local authority, drawing from a pool of central government grant and local council tax resources, will apply subsidy towards the costs of its provision.

In these kinds of quasi-market, the subsidies make an uneven playing field between different providers. It is odd to limit the subsidy to a single provider if the intention is to produce a general subsidy to learning for social and wider economic reasons. But this situation is seen every day in the adult learning market. It represents a denial of choice and useful competition between the public and private providers. If the argument is that public sector learning providers have some inherent advantage in providing the learning, it should be clearly demonstrated what that advantage is, and that a preferential subsidy arrangement is the only way to achieve it. This is not easily argued.

It would be far better if the local education authority – acting under its statutory duties to make adequate provision for adult learning – should cease subsidizing its own provision exclusively, and move to a system where it subsidizes equivalent learning irrespective of provider. Not only will this level the field – with useful consequences for choice, efficiency and innovation – but it will also free communities to provide for themselves directly rather than 'through the town hall', if that seems best. Instead of politicians deciding through their own provision what courses to lay on and where local authorities would use their duty to subsidize the sort of learning and groups of learners needed by local economies and communities.

Further education colleges' activities in post-initial education should also cease to be subsidized from the centre on a preferential basis. They should compete for post-initial business, including some of the community business opened up by the local authority, in an open market with other providers. The subsidy should come through the local authority, and should be attached to the learning or to the person, not to a particular approved provider.

Likewise, all the money which currently goes through the DfEE to fund full-time training fees for registered unemployed people or their dependants should be diverted to the local authority, to be fed through to the relevant groups – leaving the benefit payments to be paid through the usual Giro system.

Figure 11.2 shows how these three proposals would be integrated by the creation of an ILLA system, introducing for the first time an overall budget for post-initial learning.

All central public money for post-initial learning would be fed down to local

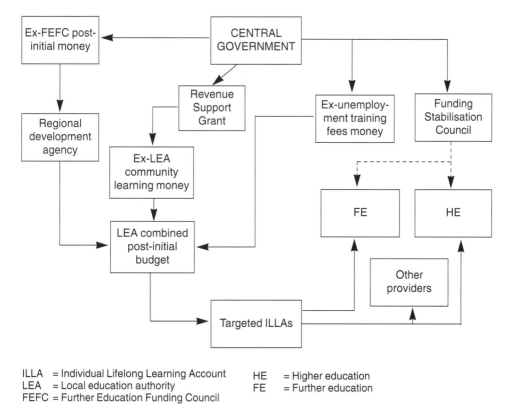

ILLA = Individual Lifelong Learning Account   HE = Higher education
LEA = Local education authority   FE = Further education
FEFC = Further Education Funding Council

Figure 11.2 Proposed funding for post-initial learning.

education authorities, for dispersal through targeted learning accounts. The local authority's own contribution, when taken together with its spending on initial education, would *at least* have to match the assumed total contribution in the revenue support grant. The local authority money currently going to post-initial day and evening classes would be put into the new budget, together with the money made available for post-initial learners under the currently ailing discretionary grants provision. The local council taxpayers could add on extra resources if they chose.

The authority would then distribute purchasing power against this composite budget by placing conditional credits into targeted ILLA accounts. The targeting would be based on priorities for lifelong learning set up in the local authority's published funding plans. The credits would be used by individuals to obtain learning from locally approved providers in an open learning market satisfying individual choice. Figure 11.2 also shows how a revenue stabilization process in the background can iron out any undue initial swings in the institutional income for further education and higher education, as the switch to ILLAs takes place.

This new arrangement brings a new unity of purpose about the targeting and priorities for subsidization, which would be set democratically by the local political process. It would put an end to the half-centralized/half-localized mess which currently prevails. This decentralizing solution should be strongly conducive to personal and social commitment. It has potential to press learning into the corners of the population where national policy might fail. Within this unified solution, policy for training and educating unemployed people would itself come together. A whole range of disparate policies – where central government, further education and local authorities are all promoting learning for unemployed people on quite different bases – would be rationalized. The proposed regime would permit all manner of flexible and imaginative responses, while still leaving the government to determine benefit eligibility.

Left to themselves, people often want to learn for quite pedestrian, instrumental reasons. There is nothing wrong with that. But the function of the public sector, and notably of the local authorities working through ILLAs, would be to see that there is an incentive for the learning to have wider social purposes in mind, including the critical learning which is so necessary if the new culture is to improve itself further.

The role envisaged for the localities would be an act of faith and a major institutional change, reversing decades of mistrust and vilification of local democracy. If the local authority can be trusted with the schools, it can certainly be trusted with the rest. Thus empowered, new, more effective local authorities will emerge as part of the new culture, acting as practising lifelong learning institutions, with a mission to lead the local expression of social commitment to learning. No other bodies can do the job. The best local authorities, Birmingham for example, already do it.

This open subsidized market would still have to be locally regulated. There might still be instances of predatory pricing; or the emergence of a few large corporate suppliers, driving out the smaller providers with discounted offers; or providers colluding to divide up the map amongst themselves. These risks need to be addressed. Local education authorities, acting with the support of local partners, should have the responsibility and powers to carry out democratic regulation of the local learning market in the public interest.

Action could take several forms. The local authority would, for example, be obliged to issue licences to all local providers operating in its area who meet national lifelong learning criteria, and who do not already have a licence issued by the government. This would give freedom of entry to appropriate providers. If the prices and cost diverge too much the local authority would have power to refuse or withdraw a licence for the ILLA scheme, on grounds of uncompetitive practice. Through its control of credit redemption, the authority can tackle excessive market dominance.

The local authority would also be expected to convene local provider networks, and to encourage them to analyze supply and demand, against the backcloth of public subsidy policy. They would look for a judicious balance between collaboration and the competitive decisions which providers make about the prospectuses which they offer the public.

Finally there is the prospect of local authority playing a role in brokerage within the local post-initial learning market. This is where there are other players to contend with. Free associations of providers are already emerging in many areas to smooth the operation of the local market for potential clients, working together on information, guidance, promotion, recruitment and shared facilities. In addition the government intends its 'University for Industry' (UfI) to act as a broker in the marketplace. There has been very little hard research on the justification for this supervention. In particular, it is not clear how this concept will fit in with the local efforts, or with the duties proposed here for elected local authorities to have a role in regulating and developing the local learning market in the name of lifelong learning.

Central ideas for the UfI are: to take potential clients, see that they are appropriately informed, advised and guided, and then find them links to suitable providers; to note gaps in provision, and promote a remedy, either by commissioning materials on its own account for use by providers, or by arranging for new offerings by providers; and to supply computerized local learning centres for access to distance learning materials and the Internet.

The case for these activities has yet to be fully articulated.

One-stop booking

A 'one-stop' booking-in service can prevent would-be learners slipping away. There is however no call for this to be national and standardized. Under our proposals, associations of local providers, brought together by the local authority, can operate good local booking-in arrangements, as part of the operation of the ILLA system. They can be linked easily by modern technologies.

Information and advice

It is difficult for an organization with learning recruitment objectives to maintain full independence in information, advice and guidance. The natural seat for these services is the local education authority, given the roles already set down for it in the proposals above; a new organization – with a national, rather then local, remit – would tend to duplicate information, advice and guidance facilities available to adults at local level, which should improve considerably as ILLAs come in (see below).

Remedying gaps in provision

This will overlap with the duties of the local education authorities. in planning and regulating the local marketplace in the public interest and under democratic control.

Supplying computerized local learning centres
There is a lack of evidence of a looming market failure in this area, which might justify a privileged use of public money to subsidize cyber-connections to learning. Access to computers and Internet services for the general population, including many of the socially excluded, will grow very rapidly. In this scenario the UfI learning centres, like the mass of launderettes, are likely to have a short life. By the time the network of UfI centres is mature it will probably be cheaper to give socially excluded learners direct access to computers and to the Internet.

The 'University for Industry' therefore does not figure prominently in this book. It looks too much like yet another patch on the old culture, rather than a new concept fully in keeping with a lifelong learning scenario.

Initial learning market

Under 16
If post-initial adult provision can be rationalized and unified, the question is whether the same can be done for the initial learning system (see Figure 11.3 for the current position). We shall see how the ILLA system offers a great deal of scope for this, although it cannot be taken quite so far. For pre-school, primary and secondary education under 16, we envisage no major reforms in institutional structure or finance, over and above those emerging from the legislative process. ILLAs would be used in statutory provision for certain ancillary purposes, but not for mainstream funding. For other parts of the initial education system however, there is much to be said for a switch to ILLAs, to give more scope for personal commitment and competition.

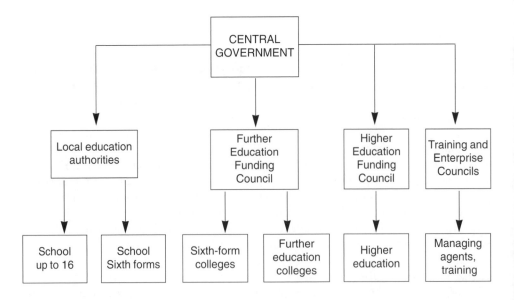

Figure 11.3 Initial learning – current institutional framework.

The key reason for treating pre-school and under-16 education differently from the rest is that more is lost by intensifying social polarization through uninhibited market choices, than might be gained by market choice and the economic advantages of competition on costs and innovation. It seems, in any case, beyond practical politics to shift school education out of the bureaucratic vice into which it is now locked. We therefore expect the quasi-market approach to continue. The state will continue to provide free places for all children by funding local authorities through the back door; but there will remain some degree of choice for parents as to where those places are taken up. And – more fundamentally – parents will have some power to influence the local authority towards setting up non-exclusive specialized schools reflecting different cultural, religious or ethnic backgrounds.

Under the lifelong learning culture, just as now, parental choices would be informed by the regular publication of performance data on schools, reflecting added value against the essential lifelong learning skills. No lifelong learning parents would be happy to accept a school or college place purely as handed down by some bureaucratic process, without wishing to express a preference. Such exercise of preferences serves both to allow free rein to personal and social commitment, and also to allow different ethnic, religious and social groups to enjoy state-funded education in terms which express aspects of their own culture and heritage.

There is however a darker side. Choices which are exercised well by lifelong learners may be abused by others. A lifelong learning society will abhor a situation where parents favour selected state-funded institutions because they are exclusive on grounds of ability, income, religion or race, and not for their general performance in lifelong learning. The reputation of the establishment in such a case would not be a reflection of the lifelong learning pursued there, but of *who else is selected to go there*.

Once selection establishes a school's reputation in this sense it stimulates the processes of stratification in the population. Institutions with links to the dominant culture tend toward high 'esteem', and those with links to minority cultures tend to the opposite. This is the polarization that leads large numbers of people to abandon learning. It particularly affects secondary schools. Neither pupils nor teachers find it easy to raise motivation for learning if their school is held in contempt.

Grant Maintained schools have played a large role in sustaining the polarization process, through their selective recruitment.[1] The present government is bringing them nearer to the mainstream to reduce this effect. Steps are also being taken to improve the administration of policies for parental choice of school at local level. But much more needs to be done to improve the ways in which the principles of choice and balanced intakes for secondary school entry are reconciled at local level. The present rules impose unacceptable uncertainties and tensions on children, as illustrated in Box 2.2 (page 37).

There is therefore a quandary over school choice. We propose that local education authorities should undertake a new computerized procedure, which specifically reconciles the legitimate preferences of parents with the need to avoid polarization in the choice of secondary school. The resulting pattern would be an openly balanced and weighted compromise between the preferences of the parents for particular features of the school (such as ethnic or religious curriculum), and the evenness of the mixture of each school's suggested recruitment. Although the computer procedure would be complex, the trade-offs would be clear, following value judgements made democratically by the local education authority. The allocation would conform as closely as possible to parental preferences, giving high weight to the cultural preferences or to any specialisms sought. But this would be within the constraints of overall capacity, and only as far as the local authority is prepared to tolerate divergence in recruitment composition from average profiles.

A system of this sort is a heavy intervention in the market, and can only work if all local state schools are in the system. Cross-boundary recruitment would be an issue, forcing many adjacent authorities into running specially created joint arrangements. The current legal rule which allows parents in one area to choose a school or schools in another, would require some amendment. On the other hand it would be far better than the present chaos. The proposed arrangements would support lifelong learning. They would help the local authority take strong action to avoid sink schools – which can demotivate people for life. At the same time they would express legitimate cultural or functional specialisms, which work with the grain of multicultural society.

16–19 learning

Learning for the 16–19 age group offers scope for major institutional and financial changes. These would serve to unify a divided scene, to make it more conducive to lifelong learning. Social class polarization and sifting by ability remain strong factors in further education post-16, as Joan Payne has shown.[2] This largely works through the existence of sixth forms and sixth-form colleges, which separate out an academic strand, with damaging effects on other providers' status and balance of intakes. Figure 11.4 shows proposals for progressive institutional reform. Figure 11.5 illustrates the funding mechanism which would unfold alongside the institutional changes.

The fundamental idea is a progressive merging of school sixth forms and sixth-form colleges into general further education colleges, so terminating all local authority schools at age 16. This means ending the separate existence of sixth forms, which are generally uneconomic, and which will be too small to provide the new, integrated curriculum proposed in Chapter 8. Initially this would mean link-ups between the various institutions. In the longer run, the emerging lifelong learning model would be the all-in further education college, an independent corporate body offering wide opportunities for 16–19 and post-initial learning, and working to comprehensive principles. The local authority would be able to agree the creation of more colleges, some of which might be 'licensed' providers in the private sector.

Financially, the local education authority will be set up as a budget holder to finance the whole of publicly-supported 16–19 learning in its area as 'initial further learning'. The local authority will receive a fees budget from central government – which it can add to, but not subtract from. Both the FEFC and the TECs will withdraw from the scene, the latter moving to other functions. The unified budget would represent a merging of the money formerly going to further education, with the money which the LEA would have spent from its own resources on the school sixth-form element, and the money which would formerly have gone to the local TEC for initial training. The TECs would cease to contract with government for initial training. Higher education – with its large institutions and wide recruiting patterns – would stand apart from the arrangement.

The local authority would then place the purchasing power into ILLA accounts for

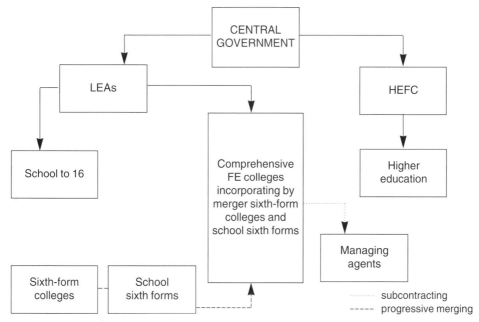

Figure 11.4 Initial learning – proposed longer-term institutional framework.

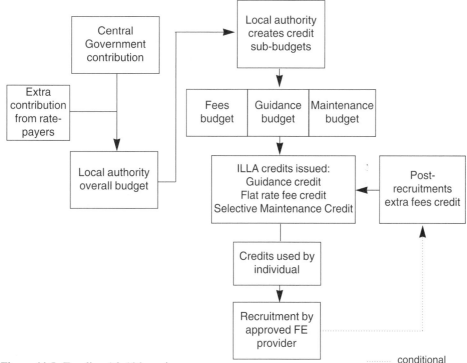

Figure 11.5 Funding 16–19 learning.

HEFC Higher Education Funding Council
FE   Further education

ILLA   Individual Lifelong Learning Account
LEA   Local education authority

all young people in the relevant age group. This would be in the form of flat rate, time-shiftable, conditional credits, covering the fees for a full-time or part-time Level 3 course with an approved further education provider in accordance with the new unitized curriculum. Entitlements carrying over from pre-16 would also be placed as conditional credits into ILLAs, on a similar time-shift arrangement. A basic rule would prevent any student being charged more than the value of the flat rate credit issued, and each student would be guaranteed a place somewhere in the system.

The approved further education provider would act as head contractor for the vocational training options within the curriculum – bringing in employers and managing agents much as the TEC would have done, while being able to organize the integration of the training route into the curriculum framework. It is likely that the general further education college will become the key provider for this purpose, as the institutional changes take effect.

The ILLA cash would flow into approved institutions 'across the counter', through redemption of credits reflecting individual learners' choices. Purchasing a place would be a real process of choice for the young people concerned, and there would be an ILLA credit for guidance to support them in making their choices. Credits for fees would be at a flat rate, but there would be linked credits for extra redemption to cover the extra cost of expensive courses, or for young people needing special support. As with the post-initial arrangements, institutions would have access to stabilization funds to even out the cash flow in the early phase of implementation. Fears of 'instability' should not be overdone. The current system is not as stable as institutional interests often make out; and transitional arrangements can readily be applied, and have a long history of effectiveness, in both education and training.

The national ILLA system would carry all the transactions. The credits themselves would be portable and time-shiftable. Flat-rate fee credits would vary across the country, reflecting local priorities and budgets. But a simple arrangement would allow anyone to replace an unused or partially used flat-rate credit from one authority, with another from the authority where they currently reside.

An important element within the unified budget would be ring-fenced money newly supplied by central government for 16–19 student maintenance. The government already intends to pilot grants in this area. The money would come from a removal of Child Benefit payments to parents of 16–18-year-olds in education, and a transfer from the government's block funding for local authorities. This would be distributed in a targeted way as an ILLA maintenance credit, conditional on the redemption of credits for fees, and payable through the provider to the individual learner's personal bank account.

These institutional and financial policies would be conducive to lifelong learning in a number of ways. Institutions' efficiency savings would be ploughed back into learning; education and training would be unified, offering greater comparability of institutional reputation; and the emergence of the general further education college as the cornerstone of the system would effectively extend the comprehensive principle to the whole of the 16–19 sector.

The proposals have important advantages. They bring the notion of personal commitment into 16–19 learning. At 16, young people ought to be learning how to handle their own learning choices, and the ILLA approach would be ideal to encourage that. They would end the present split of funding between sixth forms and other institutions; and they would enable the local authority to address local priorities directly, through the contributions which it makes to the various kinds of credits.

The TECs would be liberated from the bread-and-butter training role, to concentrate on their preferred activities as catalysts for the local economy. Their finances would need to be reconstituted. They would no longer need to fund their objectives through profits wrung from hard-pressed training programmes by output-related funding or by contracting pressure, at the expense of quality in learning.

Higher education

Three ways to stimulate lifelong learning in higher education are considered here: the use of ILLAs to support student learning; research funding; and quality competition.

Firstly, learners will find it natural to use ILLAs at higher-education level, once they have become used to the system at further-education level (see Figure 11.6). ILLAs would be used to carry flat-rate and additional fees credits in a similar way to the proposals for 16–19. They would also replace the current loan facilities with ILLA loans on similar terms, sourced from financial services institutions rather than from the public purse. As part of this approach the withdrawal of means-tested maintenance

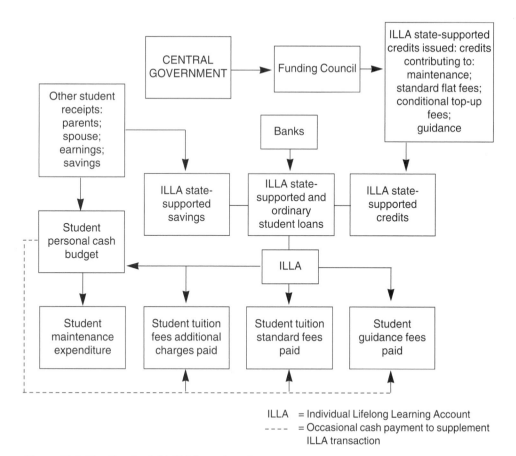

Figure 11.6 Funding for initial higher education.

grants, introduced by the New Labour Government, would be reversed. Maintenance credits would be issued in a way similar to that proposed for 16–19 students. During the run-in period for the ILLAs, a stabilization fund (not shown here) would be managed by the HEFC to smooth institutional income.

These measures would make a strong impact on the personal commitment agenda, and reinforce efforts to strengthen teaching functions in higher education. They would also help students to grasp the size of the investments which they are making. This system has the great merit of flexibility, enabling students to make the most of the unitized, time-flexible courses of the future.

Secondly, all vestiges of the research assessment exercise should be removed – lock, stock and barrel. This process and its structures distribute a major part of public funding for university research through peer group assessment of the publication records of university departments. The exercise elevates publication to a position where it dominates all the learning functions of institutions, debasing scholarship as much as it spawns journals packed with half-baked material. Worst of all, it weakens the central teaching functions on which the whole lifelong learning agenda depends, through its effect on staff turnover and a bias towards research. All this raises issues which go well beyond the scope of this book. Nevertheless, better ways to fund research simply have to be found. What we have now is less than clever.

Thirdly, universities should, if they wish, be able to charge fees above the standard level (covered by the credit for flat-rate fees – plus the individual contribution, and the added linked credits for extra fees) in exchange for a high quality, upmarket product. The non-state loan facilities and other services in the ILLA would be available to make up the difference, if other personal and family resources were not immediately at hand. The consequence of this is to open up quality competition, something which can be more safely implemented for older learners than it can be for the 16–19 age group.

This suggested move, which is not uncontroversial, is based on two arguments. The first is that the deleterious effects on motivation for lifelong learning – through social polarization (adverse selection) in learning institutions – are significantly weakened by the time young people are qualified for university entry. The second is that it is both efficient and necessary to give people more choice over the kind of higher education they want, and how much they have to pay for it – given the large element of personal investment now involved in higher education. Nobody would dream of standardizing the housing market or the purchase of cars, so why standardize higher education, which is also now bought in the market place?

This new approach would free less affluent learners from the tyranny of having to pay a high price for a 'finishing school' product, and leave them able to choose a more local, part-time option which would be easier to run in parallel with employment. It would be left to the universities facing excess demand in the short term to ration places on the basis of assessed ability, or on price, or both. Universities which are very popular would be able to draw in expansion funds from the market, as some students would be willing to incur greater debt to obtain more highly valued, longer-term benefits.

Merging further and higher education
Over 10% of higher education is now delivered under licence through further education colleges; there is some, but much less overlap in the other direction. Against this background, interest (outside government) has been growing rapidly in a greater

institutional blending of further and higher education. Much of the interest is undoubtedly fuelled by financial hardship, as institutions in both further and higher education feel the squeeze on public resources. But a lifelong learning perspective prompts a wider critique. The sharp stratification between further and higher has serious drawbacks. It fosters the fable that critical thinking and research are the preserves of the universities; it helps to position vocational studies down the hierarchy; and, at the level of the individual learner, it creates a break in continuity which too easily becomes a barrier to progression and participation. A sense of exclusive spaces denies lifelong learning.

Despite all this the merger theme is *not* on our agenda. The best way to proceed is by removing the barriers through the use of ILLAs and reform of the funding flows, unitized curricula, and credit accumulation and transfer arrangements properly integrated across the sectors and stages. This does not need grand institutional mergers – which might in any case pose huge administrative problems, and create vertical channels within single institutions which deny the learner variety and choice.

PARTICULAR INFRASTRUCTURAL SERVICES

A number of major infrastructural issues, bearing mainly on the learner, arise from the institutional and financial framework set out above. They have an important and direct effect on motivation and culture building.

Generic marketing for lifelong learning

Generic marketing for lifelong learning is marketing which aims to develop the new general culture of lifelong learning, without being slanted towards any particular scheme or provider. Marketing of this kind can cover a wide range of activity. Its design problems, and its implications for the lifelong learning concept, have never been adequately debated in public.

There have been many pitfalls. Politicians – as the main paymasters – have been notorious for wanting to portray learning as a rags-to-riches, one-way route to career success. The 'Learning Pays' dictum is almost invariably put positively ('this is the ladder of opportunity to climb'), seldom in precautionary terms ('that is the trap you need to avoid'). The remorseless portrayal of success, saturated with the values of the dominant learning culture, is viewed with widespread scepticism. At the same time, governments have shrunk from using the most effective medium – television – on grounds of cost. This mistake is not made by business, in advertising things which compete with learning for the money in people's pockets.

Indecision about the precise aims and the target groups has also blurred the focus of the generic marketing that has been tried. Should there be emphasis on the near-lifelong learners – those who need least persuasion? Or should there be an all-out effort to get the most excluded people into range? Should it be about adults returning to learn? Or basic skills? Or family learning? There has been a failure to see that any overall campaign needs to be multi-layered and multifaceted, with a high degree of co-ordination across the whole learning scene.

An unfolding national marketing strategy is needed to resolve these problems – led by learning providers, and based on substantial research. To cover this ground, the UK Lifelong Learning Partnership (see Chapter 9) should set up a permanent sub-committee, mainly representing and led by provider interests. Its brief should be to prepare and run a well-researched continuing campaign towards these objectives, building on and incorporating the work of the Campaign for Learning. The expenditure could be met by a mandatory precept from all public funds made available to providers; or, alternatively by an equivalent precept on the expenditure passing through ILLAs (see Chapter 10).

Information, advice and guidance

A new, comprehensive two-stage model for information, advice and guidance, is needed to support the new culture (see Figure 11.7). This would be a general infrastructure, *which applies to the whole of the guidance industry and to clients of any age*. The local education authority would be responsible for managing a composite budget, providing disbursements to support the model. The use of protocols would enable local services to be co-ordinated into an effective national network.

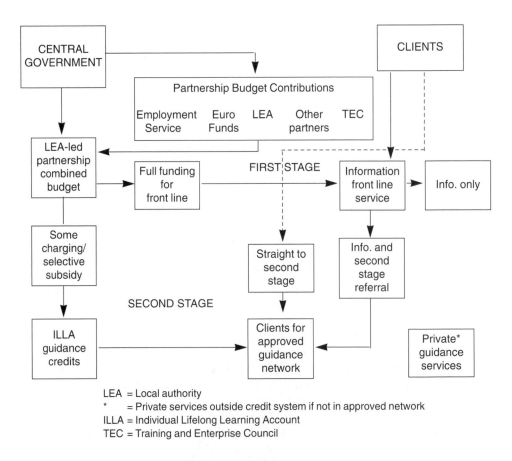

LEA = Local authority
*   = Private services outside credit system if not in approved network
ILLA = Individual Lifelong Learning Account
TEC = Training and Enterprise Council

Figure 11.7 Two-stage funding model for lifelong guidance.

Figure 11.7 shows an informational first stage, which would deal with a good many of the problems that people wish to address, leading to a speedy diagnosis and direct referral to opportunities for learning or work. This service would be independent, and free to the user. People are unwilling to pay for such information, so information services would be supported at full cost by LEAs, with supporting contributions from government, Employment Service and others. Among these would be the body gathering a precept from transactions on ILLAs to subsidize local information and guidance. These local services would be linked to Learning Direct – the national information helpline due to become part of the 'University for Industry'.

A minority of clients would be referred to members of a network of independent 'kite marked' professional guidance providers for face-to-face counselling at a second stage. The service would extend from counselling and the assessment of prior learning right through to helping people to book themselves into chosen learning opportunities. It is not necessarily free: some clients would pay the full price for what is in any case a private good; others would attract varying degrees of public subsidy.

At the second stage, guidance providers would have to meet the Guidance Council's service quality standards individually. They would also need to meet network standards, yet to be developed. The providers would be licensed for ILLA purposes by the local authority, on the basis of being quality assured in these terms and prepared to participate in the local authority's arrangements covering, for example, cross referral and the use of common data sets. They would be able to do cash business; but they would also be linked to the ILLA system, and would conduct a large part of their business through ILLA transactions, including the redemption of credits. Some private providers of guidance would remain outside the ambit of the redemption arrangements and of the local licensing system.

The budget underlying the second stage would be supported on a more long-term and stable basis by earmarked funds from government; from a precept on ILLA transactions; from transfers from the budget for post-initial lifelong learning; from the rate fund; and from other sources.

It will be particularly important in the new culture for children under 16 and their parents to have access to the independent lifelong guidance that they need. The ILLA system can offer this access, and there is no reason to keep the present careers service companies operating, as they do at present, on a backdoor-funded, quasi-market basis. Direct government funding to contracted careers service companies would therefore cease, leaving them to compete in a regulated open market. The government would put guidance credits into the credit-to-learn function of young people's ILLAs at key stages under 16, to be spent within a competitive guidance industry. Individuals' funding could be supplemented through the wider resources of the ILLA system, for people whose special needs demand an expensive level of service. Schools would be empowered to act *in loco parentis*, in cases where parents do not support the use of the guidance credits.

Students aged 16–19, and those in initial higher education, would also receive free guidance credits to spend in the same competitive industry. The funding could be supplemented, just as in the case of younger learners. The provision of free guidance by colleges and universities – funded by funding councils and other institutional income – would come to an end, to be replaced by ILLA credits, issued either by the local authority or by the universities. The existing institutional careers guidance services could find their place as independent specialists in the new open industry.

In post-initial learning, anybody would be able to use an ILLA for guidance as well as for learning expenditures. The ILLA would enable loans, credits and savings to be brought together to fund guidance. This reflects the principle that guidance is a form of learning.

An important part of the post-initial arrangements is to accept that the guidance functions of the Employment Service are inescapably compromised by the so-called 'requiring agenda' – that is, the government's declared wish to get people off benefit payments and into jobs as quickly as possible, to save on the benefit bill. The functions of the Employment Service would therefore have to be split: one part would be devoted to giving *truly independent advice* to unemployed clients; the other part would work with individuals, to help them in their job search. On this basis the Employment Service could transfer funds to the local authority to enable unemployed people to have credits for independent guidance, and these credits would be spent through the ILLA system using the LEA's guidance network.

Behind the two-stage model there would have to be reliable, standardized and integrated data on learning opportunities covering providers of all kinds and levels across the whole country, accessible by computer network. Learning providers need to improve their supply of information if this is to be achieved. The public sector will also have to insist – by regulation and other means – that public providers adhere to the technical *standards* for collecting, recording and supplying information on a timely basis. The problems of data reliability and effective information service are set to grow with the increasing complexity involved in the unitization of courses and the growth in credit accumulation and transfer facilities.

Most important of all, behind the two-stage model there should be an over-time concept for the guidance function itself. At any moment in the lifespan, a person may seek advice – and possibly guidance – in response to their immediate situation. This is like going to the doctor in the case of illness, and being referred on to a specialist consultant: the GP is like the adviser, and the hospital consultant like the guidance worker. But advice and guidance can be sought on a recurrent basis, not just at times of stress and decision. This is where the lifelong learner would look for help in reassessing a learning plan and career/life development path. The medical analogy is the routine screening consultation, where the client's intention is to prevent and pre-empt trouble, rather than seek a cure for a problem that already exists. Calling this pre-emptive model *lifelong advice and guidance* distinguishes it from the one-off, reactive kind.

A session of lifelong guidance has a very different context and content from a session of the other sort: it is premised on an ongoing relationship over time; it draws on records of consultations carried over from previous occasions; it monitors and adjusts an unfolding strategy for personal development. Some guidance experts say that these perspectives are already part of the content of good guidance; but that is to confuse professional aspiration with the reality. The perspective of true lifelong advice and guidance is relatively rare in application, except in the private executive market.

There is a strong case for a general incentive to encourage people to use the ILLA system to build up a habit of lifelong guidance. A background incentive in the whole of the ILLA system will have *some* benefits for guidance – since guidance is just a form of learning experience. But a more focused incentive is also needed, particularly for

---

- Guidance is a very strong motivator.

- A means-related credit would support the wider spread of learning strongly.

- It would help to improve the image of the guidance market.

- Access would help people to avoid mistakes in their learning.

- Helping people to find jobs which best suit their skills and meet the employer's specification would make the job market work better and more quickly.

Box 11.1 Reasons for an entitlement to lifelong guidance.

adults, who are not learning about guidance in initial education. There are good lifelong learning arguments for a periodic, means-related credit which the government will finance through the local authority (see Box 11.1).

All this would mean radical changes in the guidance world. The fault line which exists at present between the free careers services for schools and colleges and the freer market for adults would disappear. The latter would be able more readily to charge a proper price for its services, because clients would not expect guidance to be a free handout service. The problem of bias in reputation between the high status careers services for young people – with their guaranteed income – and the Cinderella adult guidance services struggling to survive, would also dissolve away.

The changes would be a golden opportunity for the guidance community to throw off the image of an impoverished public sector service, whose ambitions are hobbled by self-doubt and the tightness of the public sector's budgetary strings. Instead, it would be able to move to a freer market role, with the market supported through ILLA credits for chosen groups in the community.

Mentoring

Mentoring is becoming a more generally familiar concept. Being a mentor means acting as a constructive but critically challenging friend. We use it to refer to voluntary, unpaid support for a learner, provided by a person of independent view and with experience and some status relevant to the learner's fields of interest. A mentor acts as a sounding board for the learner to test out personal decisions about learning and lifespan development. This support needs to be available before, during and after any programme of learning. Crucially, mentoring should not be confused with independent and professional information and guidance functions. It only takes place at the instigation of the learner.

In a general lifelong learning culture mentoring will be held in high esteem, and will be widely practised. It provides a means for people to express social commitment, and is a popular informal role among older members of families and communities. It is a way for individuals to offer wisdom, and for society to value it.

Local authorities, learning institutions and business could all very appropriately make the support of monitoring schemes a strong element in their lifelong learning policies. These would aim to capture the spirit of local voluntary involvement and professional ethos, which has been so well developed by the Samaritans and the Relate marriage guidance organization. These show that very careful preparation is needed. It is no use, for example, employers simply declaring that line managers will henceforth be mentors. And a rigid centralized state scheme would threaten the sense of spontaneity and personal choice which makes for successful mentoring. Serious questions of security and training are involved in any such scheme.

Support for mentoring can be given in a number of ways. Government funding can be channelled by local authorities through the ILLA system, into short courses in mentoring. Mentoring should also be included more directly in the Investors in People standard; in a new personal equivalent standard, 'Investor in Lifelong Learning' (see below); in lifelong learning modules in higher education; and in good-practice principles for learning in a variety of contexts.

Quality standards

Many industries have customer protection guaranteed by independent quality assurance and regulatory frameworks. As retail customers, individuals have the general protection of the local authority under the customer protection legislation. The former nationalized utilities have facilities such as Ofwat for water, and Oftel for telecommunications. The current learning market has Ofsted and the DfEE Standards and Effectiveness Unit – and a possible new DfEE division monitoring LEAs' school management and standards; an inspectorate for further education and the TECs; and the Quality Assurance Agency for higher education.

These are comprehensive facilities, but despite their size they are not altogether appropriate to a lifelong learning scenario. There is a marked antithesis about the current arrangements. The emphasis in initial education is on whether the taxpayer and society are getting value for money: it is not strongly on learner protection. The value-for-money questions are pressed with great insistence, and almost all the state's efforts are consumed in this area. There is no concern for the separate private market at all. Post-initial learning shows the same neglect of the private provider, but this time hardly any consideration of social targets. If there is any emphasis, it is on customer satisfaction, and that is deemed to be something for customers to attend to for themselves. The dominant philosophy is 'Let the buyer beware'.

This immediately points up two senses of the quality concept. First, the quality of the experience to the learner; and second, the value of the experience to the state in return for the money expended. Both are important and need to be pursued. There is, however, a prior question: 'Does the learning experience help to develop a culture of lifelong learning?' This has to be the starting point for new policy.

On this dimension, lifelong learning standards should be laid down for all kinds of providers of learning – whether in the initial education system or elsewhere – and quality must be assured to those standards. The standards would conform to the principles of lifelong learning, and would set minimum levels of practice, behaviour and understanding with respect to building the new culture. They would relate to all learning providers, and to providers of information, advice and guidance. 'Lifelong Learning Investor' standards should also be developed for much the same purpose, which would be available to individuals, families, employing organizations and communities.

These measures would enable anybody – individuals or organizations – to achieve formal certificates recording their success in meeting the quality standards for lifelong learning, on the basis of an independent assessment. In due course it would be compulsory for formal learning and guidance providers to meet these standards as a condition of being able to receive public money. For the rest, the standards will be voluntary, much as the Investors in People (IiP) standard is now.

Customer protection: a Lifelong Learner's Charter

A universal Lifelong Learner's Charter is also needed, for clients' rights and responsibilities. This would be a key element in the providers' lifelong learning standard. Arrangements for implementing it would be reviewed as part of the quality assurance process for providers. The Charter would also have full legal standing in all contracts for learning between provider and learner, and for every pupil in initial state-funded education.

The Lifelong Learner's Charter would set down, for the first time, the core principles of proper treatment for lifelong learning customers (see Box 11.2). This list brings together the best in existing charters, similar provisions made for training through the contracts between the government and TECs, and elements of good institutional practice.

- A personal learning plan, suitable to assessed learning needs and with clear objectives;

- the right to have the planned programme delivered;

- the right to have the plan amended only by agreement;

- rights of redress;

- insurance arrangements if hazards (illness, accident, etc.) disrupt the learning;

- money-back guarantees;

- equal opportunities in every aspect of provision.

Box 11.2 Elements of the Lifelong Learner's Charter.

Two other proposals sit alongside the Charter. A full 'learning ombudsman' service should be created to cover the complete learning system, not just the schools. It would be equipped with powers to fine providers and settle costs for breach of the Charter. There should also be a new scheme for access funds (small budgets used to help selected students in temporary distress). An ILLA-based system would replace current arrangements. This would charge a small fee – perhaps 1% of fees paid through the ILLA – for a student relief fund.

Achievement profiles

People in a lifelong learning society will need an appropriate achievement profile, to help them to reflect on their progress. Such a record can also serve as evidence of lifelong learner activity, which employers may ask for as an aspect of recruitment.

A new, voluntary system of records of achievement should be available, to run with every individual from 'cradle to grave'.

A summary profile of achievement for every learner should be held in a secure computer file on a national database to which only the learner – or somebody with the learner's authority – has access. This facility can be linked to the ILLA smart card system (see Chapter 10). The existence and controlled availability of these computer records could save millions of pounds each year in administrative costs, particularly in recruitment and personnel management.

To support this, the Lifelong Learner's Charter would give a guarantee that the provider would ensure the accurate recording of main details of the learning plan on the learner's file, at the start of a course of learning. On completion of the course (or on the learner leaving, if earlier), the provider would be required to update the record of achievement with (verified) information on qualifications obtained. This guarantee would be binding on all providers, whether publicly supported or not.

The individual learner, *and no one else,* would control the use made of this material. The learning data would be used in aggregate and anonymously to study the learning records of the population, in total or in key groups or localities. This is vital for monitoring the relationship between lifelong learning and the needs of the economy, or the issues of social exclusion. It could also be used, at the instigation of learners, to remind them of the dwindling shelf-life of any parts of their qualifications. This would, for the first time, open up the prospect of effective national policy addressing the obsolescence of skills and knowledge. Technological developments now make such a system to record achievement very much easier than it formerly was. The set-up costs would have to be borne by the state.

Information and communications technology (ICT)

There is very wide agreement that Britain cannot afford to hold back from computer-based learning and learning communications, if it is not to drop back irrevocably in the global learning league. The cost savings of new technology are rapidly becoming very significant, and 'the knowledge media' offer a flexibility in learning which can circumvent some of the complex constraints of modern lives. But reflection of this general agreement – in effective policies on availability, content and regulation – is very slow. The state must therefore find ways to ensure that rising generations have access to computers for learning across the population.

In the initial learning system, the government is currently offering pump-priming funding for the shift of technology which will help to make savings in the future. In the post-initial system, ministers are showing a keenness to see that there are no market impediments to the maximum use of computers which can be sustained by the market.

But ICT is not just a change in technology. It is much more fundamental than swapping slates for exercise books, or biros for pen and ink, and it has many implications for the criteria of excellence and achievement. The computer has opened up new modes and standards of communication. In a world divided by language, the current cultural value placed on literacy and literature – compared with other forms of symbolic communication – may already be changing in response. Sophisticated graphics are available to help explain complex concepts, and the technology itself stimulates new intellectual skills. The level of technical support that computers provide – through spreadsheets and graphics, for example – may help to turn attention in assessment away from performance and towards understanding.

The computer's capacity to overcome physical limitations is also of first importance. It is a powerful learning tool, whether a learner's limitations are due to inexperience, physical weakness or disability, or to aspects of place or distance. It allows learning processes to be separated, timed and delivered according to the learner's needs, rather than according to the convenience of others. The development of robust and relatively inexpensive hardware offers the possibilities of work for isolated or unsocialized learners, whatever the source of their problems.

The government's proposals on a 'University for Industry' show the temptation for politicians to set about creating arrays of local on-line learning centres for distance learning, for the post-initial learning market. It is probably better to avoid grandiose schemes, and to look to support home-based facilities instead. The government should fund LEAs to operate a selective means-tested bursary scheme for course-related hardware, using credits placed in ILLAs. The learning provider would have to vouch for the need for the computer to do the course in each case.

In addition, the government should ensure the widest possible awareness and familiarity with computer-based learning across the whole population. It will need to put credits into ILLAs to subsidize courses addressing this need on a large scale.

Every adult who can satisfy the local authority that they need basic awareness training should be able to apply for a partially subsidized state credit. There should also be research in depth into the issues of pedagogy and andragogy; quality control; client care; modes of assessment; 'kite marking' and intellectual property rights for the new learning media. Any learner should be able to establish easily and clearly the identity and commercial interests of authors of learning materials. New policies are also needed to deal with uncompetitive practices in the supply of learning media. UK policies on these matters may be difficult because of the global, offshore character of the Internet.

These are the things which really matter in the technology field, rather than high specification grids. Investing directly in grid facilities looks as if it will be overtaken by commercial and technological developments. Box 11.3 shows a scheme using standard electrical cable linking substation to home, for example. This may suffice to meet all reasonable needs for Internet communication capacity, except in very poor areas.

In initial learning, the emerging demand from pupils is unstoppable. The aim must be to ensure that *every pupil and every student* has ready access (without queuing) to a networked computer work station; full access to the National Grid for Learning; and a personal identifier and e-mail address. This would mean major installation costs in educational institutions, and a continuing training programme for teachers and lecturers, with new mandatory competences as a condition of licence to teach. It would also require substantial support costs, for systems support and development within each school and throughout each local education authority area.

These are large challenges. But one concern dwarfs them all: it is the thought that any government might choose to oblige teachers to download state-provided materials from the Internet, just because it will be impossible financially to do anything else. A new authority is needed to deal with the threat to liberty that this could impose. It should be a body controlled by the teaching profession and funded by a charge on

Electricity power lines may eventually replace modems and telephone lines, as a way of gaining access to the Internet. NORWEB, which supplies electricity to Seymour Park in Manchester, is running a three-year development project to see if the spare capacity in electricity cables can be used for Internet access. The time taken to download data is about 20 times faster than conventional speeds. This is an advantage in ICT work with impatient young learners in schools, as well as for business users.

Street lamps pose a challenge for developers of NORWEB's system. Trials showed that, 'If you set out to design radio aerials to fit with this system, they would look like streetlamps . . . They are just the right vertical length of conductor.' This means that data being downloaded by people using the system are broadcast as radio waves between 2 and 10 megahertz. These frequencies are used by the BBC, the Civil Aviation Authority and GCHQ, among others.

The trials show that the technology will need to be modified to avoid interference, and appropriate regulations will have to be developed. But NORWEB is confident that the problem can be solved.

Box 11.3 Internet through the electricity supply. Source: adapted from Ward (1998) and Coughlan (1998).

schools; and it should take over all responsibility for 'kite marking' the supply of materials to schools through the National Learning Grid. The private market, including educational establishments, would supply the materials through the standard licensing system. No government should supply materials of its own.

NOTES AND REFERENCES

1. Benn and Chitty (1996).
2. Payne, Cheng and Witherspoon (1996).

Chapter 12

Policies for Flexibility

This chapter presents suggestions and proposals for greater flexibility of supply to meet demand in the marketplace, within the context of strategy and new ideas for infrastructure already explored. Much of what is identified here already takes place as good practice in the form of 'extracurricular activities', or 'supporting facilities'. But the cultural agenda for lifelong learning promotes them from their current subsidiary role into defining themes and key responsibilities.

INDIVIDUALS

There are some things that a lifelong learning society would aim to give all individuals access to through life, according to their wishes and capabilities. These are set out in Box 12.1.

Pre-school provision

Pre-school provision should encourage collaboration between parents, child-minders, staff and assistants in play-groups and nurseries. At this age the closely related issues of health and learning are a particular focus. Parents and other home-based carers should have opportunities for basic education in child development, in learning support and in children's socialization. This would offer support for families before problems become an obstacle to learning. It would also help parents to avoid forming premature and excessive expectations for pre-school children.

Parents would also be encouraged to help staff in pre-school groups, and this would be supported by awareness training in such areas as active encouragement for learning, and the countering of stereotyping attitudes. Such training would also be a way of drawing parents towards other learning opportunities on their own account. An extensive programme of pre-school staff training would provide every pre-school group with a core of professionally-trained staff. The state would not be prescriptive regarding the pre-school curriculum, but would lay down a set of objectives, against which quality can be defined.

- Parenting skills to support children's early start in lifelong learning;
- pre-school learning from the age of 3, conducive to lifelong learning;
- opportunity at school pre-16 to acquire essential foundation skills as lifelong learners;
- opportunities in initial further education and training 16–19 to
  - continue exploring and developing talent;
  - develop specialized skills and knowledge for work, life in the community, and higher education;
  - improve lifelong learning skills up to advanced standard;
- opportunities in initial higher education for all who achieve the entry standard to learn skills of analysis, synthesis and research in chosen fields, and to develop leadership potential in lifelong learning;
- ways for those who are beyond the initial education system to sustain learning at times of conflict between family development and career development;
- ways for workers to keep knowledge and skills up-to-date;
- ways to continue learning in the later years of life, and to pass on experience and knowledge to the rising generation.

Box 12.1   Lifespan learning opportunities for individuals.

On transfer to primary school, around the age of 5, every child would be given a unique learner identifier number; a personal development plan; a record of achievement profile; and an opportunity to have an ILLA. No child should receive baseline assessment before this point.

School up to age 16

A radical change is needed in schools if pupils are to be prepared for lifelong learning. School experience pre-16 would still involve opportunities for subject learning, but the dominant focus would be on providing the foundation skills for lifelong learning, combining good learning skills, self-confidence, a degree of self-knowledge, and some experience of the adult world. This preparation would be a sound basis for a more subject-based curriculum post-16. It would allow more people to handle subject learning more competently than the current culture could ever achieve.

To achieve this, every pupil should have a personal development plan, agreed between the teacher acting for the school, and the parent(s). In cases where there is no co-operative parent, the school could offer the services of a mentor to parent and to pupil, at no cost. Pupils would be assessed for progress against their plans on a six-monthly basis. There would be discussions between parents and teaching staff to review progress and new objectives.

The personal development plan would organize the child's learning using three kinds of learning time:

School *core time* would be organized by the school. It would be defined by law as a given proportion of the school day, equivalent to mornings (60%), but it might be spread over part of the morning and part of the afternoon. Core time would focus on the essential skills required by the lifelong learning curriculum, developed up to Foundation level (Level 2) competence.

Non-core time would be organized by the school in the remaining time for statutory attendance. This would be used for individual and small group activity, on subject work, and on personal activities including sport, visits, community and work experience.

Personal development time would be a parental responsibility, agreed according to the pupil's development plan. It would draw appropriately on available time not in the first two categories. It would engage the pupil's wider family, household, friends etc. in his or her developmental activities. These would include hobbies, sports, music, drama, community activity, careers guidance etc. Costs would be covered by agreed entitlements according to parental means. In many cases the expenditure would be introduced by the school into the pupil's ILLA (see Chapter 10).

The personal development plan would include careers education, and careers information and advice, to be provided through the school. Professional guidance would come under the new ILLA arrangements.

The *National Curriculum* would be redefined as a core entitlement (see Chapter 8) for foundation level essential lifelong learning skills (Box 12.2). This would be related to a public assessment, normally at age 16, for the Foundation Certificate of Essential Lifelong Learning. Key stages, with required average levels of attainment in the essential lifelong learning skills, would continue to apply.

Essential skills of lifelong learning:

* ability to communicate and calculate at basic level;
* ability to operate computers at basic level;
* self-awareness and self-development skills;
* financial and consumer rights awareness;
* understanding the values of lifelong learning and the courage to apply them;
* ability to think inductively and deductively;
* ability and confidence to find things out, and to take a critical view;
* ability to learn with others, in mixed groups;
* realization of aptitudes and intelligences;
* ability to apply learning creatively and to socially responsible ends;
* basic knowledge of planning a learning career, and basic awareness of the systems for learning and guidance.

The new curriculum is effective content chosen to prepare pupils for the new Foundation Certificate of Essential Lifelong Learning Skills, usually at or before 16.

Box 12.2   A new curriculum.

The testing of all young people against the entitlement would continue – but only at key stages, not in the intervening years. Parents would be able to see the particular test results for their children, and members of the public would see the general results of tests for the schools in question, which would inevitably be league-tabled. The results would be prepared on a value-added basis, using the prior key stage or (better still) school entry standard as a base. The results would be adjusted on the basis of socio-economic status of the household, reflected in free school meals. This information is needed by school managers for efficiency purposes, and by parents collecting information as a background for school choice.

This whole approach for schoolchildren under 16 organizes the learning around the priority objectives of lifelong learning. It liberates learning from exclusive use of the school environment, and it enables young people to experience learning in the home, the local community, the workplace and other contexts. It finds priority time for young learners to develop Level 2 lifelong learning skills, develop interests and enthusiasms, and to cultivate personal talent. The National Curriculum would no longer smother the central task of developing lifelong learning. In this model, parents would retain their role as major players in their children's learning, sharing their responsibility with professionals and the local community, but not being usurped by them.

This approach allows greater flexibility of time for learners with special learning needs. The firm links between age and learning stage would be softened. In particular, learners with exceptional talents would be able to join more advanced learning groups according to their need. They would be allowed to take the lifelong learning skills assessment and to move into initial further education *when ready,* moving beyond the scope of statutory attendance. Pupils who are slow learners for any reason would also benefit from the greater flexibility; and pupils who are disaffected would be allowed to attend special learning centres or further education, as appropriate. Some could be funded by ILLA credit.

Local education authorities and schools would need very large increases in resources for these high priority objectives to work. They would need to develop appropriate pedagogy oriented to lifelong learning culture and practice; to increase the numbers and remuneration of teachers significantly, and improve their initial and in-service training; to increase the range and training of support staff for administration, supervision and transport; to maintain professional assessment of learning performance against the personal development plan of each pupil; to make stimulating use of the school and its grounds as a learning environment; to provide access to computer work stations for every pupil; and to provide access to independent advice and guidance available to each pupil – both on learning and on career options – at key stages and as need arises. This service, funded through the ILLA, would enable parents to seek advice and psychological assessment apart from the school.

Initial further education and training: 16–19

There is a serious need to extend the full advantages of comprehensive education to initial learners over the age of 16. Reducing the likelihood of drop-out at age 16 must be a paramount lifelong learning objective. Those who continue as students at age 16 are much more likely to become lifelong learners than those who do not.

To meet these aims, we envisage the introduction of an integrated, unitized and modularized assessment structure, with linked curriculum, covering three domains of specialized learning at advanced level, and also preparation for an advanced level certificate in lifelong learning skills (see Chapter 8). The new structure would bring together into a common framework the three largely separate tracks of traditional workplace training, general vocational education, and academic A-levels. Anything less than this would be futile and fainthearted.

The intention is to prevent young people from being irretrievably filtered into separate selective streams of unequal esteem. Although many would choose to follow a specialized path, it would be open to all to experiment across the whole field of choice, and to mix options freely, without losing any of the options at age 19. They would be able to work for an advanced level Lifelong Learning Skills Certificate, once they had reached the Foundation standard. This, alongside sufficient specialized units, would enable young people to achieve a Baccalaureate, permitting entry into higher education around age 18 or 19, or later. At the same time, young people would benefit from a time-shifted entitlement for Foundation level lifelong learning skills, if they did not meet the standard pre-16.

Some people believe that attendance in further education before the age of 18 should be mandatory. But there is a categorical contradiction between helping students to mature as lifelong learners, and aiming to keep them in education by the force of truancy laws. Those laws become difficult to reconcile with some aspects of the lifelong learning concept, even in pre-16 education. Culture change is best achieved by voluntary means, by advocacy and by example – not by force. A better approach is to create time flexibility. Individuals, who choose not to enter further education or to leave it prematurely, would retain their entitlement to free education for learning up to Level 3. In effect, if they duck it or blow their chances the first time around, they can try again at any time, without charge.

Carrying through the new curriculum on lifelong learning terms has serious implications. Teachers would be expected to apply effective andragogy ('pedagogy' for adults), according to the best principles. This would involve a large training task, and would mean raising the status, pay and working conditions of professionals at this level. Learner support would also count for more. Every student would need personal access to computer facilities without having to wait or queue. Each would need a personal development plan with regular running assessment, and an achievement profile. As with schools, some learning organized as part of the plan would take place off college premises. This would include work experience, residential visits (in the UK and abroad) and community activities. Secure arrangements would be important for under-18s.

Learners aged 16–19 in further education need to be treated as young adults from the start of the process. Even so, they would need a considerable amount of support in sorting out their intentions and choices for later learning or work. In the lifelong learning process, initial further education is where young adults should taste various options, and learn how to take and sustain independent decisions about more specialized learning, supported by good guidance.

To facilitate all this, colleges would need good quality, well-equipped premises properly organized for adults' self-directed learning and for the support of groups of learners, both socially and in activities of learning collaboration. This would typically entail an increase in learning work stations, social space, and a reduction in the number of classrooms.

Some young people are very concerned that their families simply cannot afford them to continue in further education. This indicates the need for two major reforms.

First, it has to be accepted that there would be proportionately larger numbers of part-time learners in 16–19 education. The curriculum therefore has to be unitized to allow affordable build-up of units towards full qualifications. Second, financial support must be provided in the form of means-tested maintenance grants. These would be grants and not loans, because at this phase of education most young people would still be experimenting with options – not committing to particular remunerative investments in learning. Pilots for such grants are already planned by the government. They could be made available through ILLAs.

Vocational training, long separated off, would be bound closely into the new 16–19 structure. There has been a deep prejudice against state-supported vocational training for young people in the current learning culture. Training schemes have been open to accusations of exploitation by employers, and to doubts about the training programmes and the qualifications used – normally national vocational qualifications. In particular, government training programmes have been criticized for lack of clear andragogical principles; lack of properly organized training processes; lack of rigour in defining competences; lack of clarity about the knowledge required of trainees, to underpin more practical skills. The problems have been compounded by lack of independence in assessment, and lack of a grading structure in assessment results. Many of these criticisms are grossly unfair, and have become accepted as 'truths' only through constant assertion. Nevertheless, the low esteem of a work-based learning option – which would otherwise suit many learners – is a tragic failure from a lifelong learning perspective. It results in many young people taking wholly inappropriate academic or general vocational options, with low achievement and high dropout as the inevitable outcome. In a lifelong learning culture, it would be recognized that the workplace provides a very challenging environment for learning.

There is no reason why a good 16–19 curriculum for learning should not be set up to exploit this opportunity, given appropriate training of staff as trainers and assessors. It would link closely with wider processes of learning for adults. The lifelong learning solution would involve learners choosing training units firmly based in the further education college, as far as the co-ordination and oversight of their learning is concerned; and for these learners to have personal learning plans created in three-way discussion with the employer, tutor and learner; college staff would need better training for this new role, and relevant work experience.

These possibilities have been addressed in some of the schemes of training devised by the National Training Organizations, in the context of Modern Apprenticeships, and in the methodology for workplace–college links developed by Derek Portwood at Middlesex University.

Higher education

Despite many changes in higher education in recent years, the persistent image of initial university learning for young people is the three-year finishing school, at a distance from home. This has passed its use-by date as a typical model for the purposes of designing a higher education process. For most students, the new financial realities (a substantial personal contribution to fees, and heavy debt obligations) leave their mark. In many cases, university students who are officially 'full-time' are part-timers in practice. They are following full-time courses in institutions designed with full-time students in mind. But these learners cannot use the full opportunities of the university for broader development – for them it is a struggle to get through the basic course. Without extensive reform in the 'finishing school' paradigm, it will be difficult to raise the proportion of the population having university experience much above the present levels. This is where the flexibilities of time and space explored in Chapters 5 and 6 come into their own.

We envisage much greater time flexibility in higher education. Universities, like colleges, should enable learners of all kinds to use the credit accumulation and transfer mechanism (see Chapter 8) to build up their studies incrementally, and with intermissions if needed. Students should then have a free choice between part-time and full-time status, with *pro rata* financial support for the part-timers; and mature students would be able apply for state-supported initial university education without any age bar. Many more older adults would be encouraged to take the Access route to university learning.

Learners would be able to take time out between units or courses identified in their personal learning programme, according to their needs and circumstances. In that event, universities should identify 'time out' projects, to help students to keep in practice, and in touch. A period of work experience or travel between the end of full-time college education and entry to higher education would become commonplace .

Timing of the academic year, or within the course, would also be more flexible. The rigid academic year, with all courses starting at more or less the same time, would fade. The admission pattern would be on a 'roll-on/roll-off' basis – adult learners should not have to wait anything up to a year to start a course if it suits their personal learning plan to start sooner. Modularization of course, going hand-in-hand with unitization, helps this process.

Moreover, learners in higher education need time to explore their subjects; to be involved in informal group discussion; to develop their critical skills – in other communities, as well as in a university setting; and, quite simply, to think. Such time should be a recognized part of the personal learning plan, and needs to be properly resourced.

Distance learning is likely to become established as the predominant learning process, supported by occasional short-term residential sessions (see Chapter 6). This means that the use of space in university estates will need to change. Many students (and their families) will still want residential, full-time courses. But many more are likely to be studying at a distance as members of small groups or of 'cells' within larger groups. Fewer purpose-built lecture theatres would then be needed; and lectures would be given in spaces equipped for other kinds of learning activity, such as drama, film, music and dance. The number and size of seminar rooms could also change. As the student body changes to include more older learners, paying a higher proportion of the costs themselves, they will demand a learning environment which is more than minimally comfortable.

It should therefore pay universities to convert large sums of capital tied up in real estate – lecture theatres, halls and old student accommodation – into money, or into assets of greater utility, such as web sites, networks, video computer links, efficient computerized library access, improved short-stay accommodation and car parking space. Some campus universities could convert totally to non-campus accommodation. Universities will rent and hire more publicly or privately owned buildings, accommodation and car parks on short- and long-term basis, and spend much more on communications facilities.

The learning itself will also need to be structured differently. Learners in a lifelong learning culture will demand greater clarity about the precise purpose(s) of the degree. There is a key choice here between keeping or abandoning the current honours system. A broader degree, differently structured, might well suit many lifelong learners, whose ambitions are not to be top-flight researchers. The government should consult with representative bodies and individuals on this, and lay down acceptable purposes for the degree as a condition of state support for higher-education students. Such prescription of purpose is not in itself a challenge to academic freedom. Without it the nature of the andragogical task cannot be understood.

The purpose of a degree should be to produce learners with good lifelong learning skills who can simultaneously: demonstrate their ability to learn continuously; be creative and to live as effective and critical beings; apply learning of a high degree of difficulty usefully in a range of contexts; *and* show subject mastery in selected area(s) of knowledge or skill.

This definition of 'graduateness' reveals a duality in degree-level learning between personal qualities (the first two elements) and specialist knowledge (the third). This mirrors a similar duality in initial further education. Lifelong learning requires a balance to be established and maintained between these two – subject mastery is not enough. It is culturally very important that there are people who are masters of their subject. But curriculum approaches which are designed specifically for academics to replicate themselves over the generations are far too narrow for general use, and suit 10% of the student intake at most.

The implications of this dual-aspect curriculum for the training of teaching, technical and administrative staff, and for the organized development of students are considerable. At present it is commonly assumed that subject mastery subsumes most of the 'personal development' curriculum. This approach will have to be replaced with specific personal developmental activity – and its monitoring – in ways very similar to the processes we have outlined for schools and further education colleges. Similar strands have to run through all the stages.

The student's standing as a lifelong learner, as reflected in the profile of achievement, will therefore be at the heart of the andragogical process in universities, as elsewhere. Higher education teachers – most of whom are currently hard-pressed and distracted by the malign effects of the Research Assessment Exercise – will be expected to be professionally involved in the personal development of their students. Some of this already happens in higher education, but the efforts made are variable in quality, often small in effect, and lacking in professional recognition. Academic staff would need support and substantial training.

As part of the new structure for the degree, there would be a new higher certificate in lifelong learning skills, building on the foundation lifelong learning skills in schools, and on the advanced lifelong learning skills in initial further education. The certificate would bring together the 'personal qualities' part of the higher qualification. It would focus on developing critical thinking and action; skills of analysis and synthesis; creativity; the ability to seek out and carry through applications of learning; and the ability to lead and mentor lifelong learning in the community and at work. Portfolio methods of assessment would be needed to cover a range of this kind at higher education level.

This duality in the curriculum also means that advice and guidance functions will have to be built into the undergraduate course on a scale never before seen. Guidance concerning current course options would be covered by tuition fees; guidance concerned with future career and learning possibilities would be funded through ILLA credits. Mentoring within the university context would also have an important role.

Adult learners with young families

Chapter 5 highlighted the way that family preoccupations and the care of young children typically cause a marked hiatus in lifelong learning. The longer this break goes on, the more difficult the return to learning can be. Indeed, for some, the subsequent arrival of responsibility to care for older relatives can block such a return for good. Family learning schemes have the potential to address these difficulties, while at the same time benefiting the children. They build on parenthood and prompt reluctant adult learners to become lifelong learners in their own right.

Many parents, for example, have re-entered education as the result of being involved in pre-school playgroups. Where children are at school, family learning schemes can provide a route leading tentative adult learners back to learning, building on a greater expectation of parental involvement in childrens' learning. Yet they are also very effective in encouraging the children. Learning parents can be more closely associated with the personal development plans of pupils in schools, and more open to learning how to give effective support. Box 12.3 shows major lifelong learning measures which can assist this group.

- Pre-school arrangements and school–parent links to provide an opportunity for parental learning, both in child development and supported learning, and in adult learning itself;

- the use of time-shift to help people to return to learn free in further education, if their qualifications are below Level 3 standard;

- the use of time-shift and part-time arrangements in universities;

- non -academic postgraduate learning to be fostered by universities, through distance learning links with former students;

- help with information, advice and guidance;

- support for computer facilities in the home;

- wide definition of eligible support expenditures for tax incentives within the proposed ILLA system.

Box 12.3 Measures to support adult learners with young families.

Adult learners in mid-life

These learners fall into three main categories. The first group needs to keep up-to-date in the labour market. Their motivation is primarily economic. The second will increasingly see learning in terms of consumption or as an end in itself, rather than in highly instrumental terms. (They may also be 'updaters'.) The third want to re-enter learning after a long 'time-out', during which their skills and confidence may well have waned. They are likely to see themselves as uncompetitive in labour market terms. The consequences for them of returning to learn may well be to redefine long-standing family and social presumptions. Providers of learning need to have *very different* and *very flexible* responses to all three of these groups (which, for convenience, we shall refer to here as 'updaters', 'self-developers' and 'returners').

Updaters further divide into two groups: *crisis learners* who are reacting to a life-crisis – they may have lost the means of financial support, and may need to address their employability urgently, for example; and *pre-emptors* who are trying to avoid a crisis.

Crisis learners are likely to need fully impartial, professional guidance offering a full range of facilities. Beyond that, they need an appropriate qualification and curriculum response: neither General National Vocational Qualifications (GNVQ) nor National Vocational Qualifications (NVQ) are really suitable for these people. The first will take too long and is occupationally too indistinct. The second is not really a curriculum and is no good for critical job change situations unless the new job or a full-time training place in a workshop context has already been obtained.

This is where the approach of the 16–19 curriculum proposed in this book and its potential for tasting and experiment can point the way for these older clients. The material will need to be more strongly focused than for the post-16 students. But the modular and unit assessment structure, integration of education with training, and the close links with employers provide a good basis for a constructive response. They amount to a true adult version of the GNVQ route, within the array of available units. Such a model can link learning for occupational change to the needs of the local economy, and to particular employers undertaking new developments. The employer can, in effect, commission the learning places, and the college can recruit learners to take up those places.

Pre-emptors have more time. Some may be seeking promotion; or be expecting the employer to raise performance standards at work; others might be hoping to change occupations at some time in the future. The first group can make use of highly focused occupational educational material, much of it distance learning. Collaboration between the employer and the educational provider can provide effective training modules within the context of everyday work. Learners in the second category would be able to follow a similar path to those in crisis, but at a slower pace and with less emphasis on guidance and mentoring.

Self-developers include people wanting to upgrade their working skills to improve the quality of their work experience, and people wanting to learn quite apart from the working context, as a rewarding activity in itself, or for some domestic or social purpose. Some of these learners would wish to learn on their own; others would want the take part in groups of people, usually with shared interests. Providers need to unravel the various strands of motivation among these learners, and to provide suitably tailored opportunities to match. Box 12.4 sets out some possibilities.

Returners typically require a wide range of responses from the learning provider for confidence-building; group career- and self-development seminars; outreach into the community; taster sessions; personal advice and guidance; updating of learning skills; ICT initiation and training. This is, above all, the group of clients which is

- Groups set up to address selected local issues constructively, in the tradition of community education and development;

- self-developmental groups, possibly centred on a particular curriculum and with relatively low interest in assessment;

- worker development schemes in the workplace, where a wide variety of non-work-related developmental and leisure courses are organized, to take place at convenient times and locations, often at the workplace itself. These schemes, of which the earliest, and still most notable, is the Ford EDAP scheme, have been very successful in producing business as well as personal benefits;

- group-based arts, crafts, sports and other leisure activities;

- learning targeted on job enrichment in the workplace.

Box 12.4 Possibilities for self-developers.

particularly sensitive to the cultural body-language of the learning provider's own organization. Overtly male-oriented, highly competitive academicism will win few adherents in this marketplace. The andragogy must give great attention to the sense of security and comfort for the learner.

There is a large potential here for the accreditation of prior learning (APL), which can motivate the learners, and help them understand that they have valued implicit and explicit knowledge which counts for a great deal in the job market and the community. APL facilities should be widely available. Access courses should continue to be used widely to avoid lengthy procedures for university entry, whether on a full- or part-time basis .

For all these groups the key lifelong learning objectives are to ensure good information, advice and guidance; continuity of learning, with providers following up learning completers keenly; effective and successful learning outcomes: and far wider participation by disadvantaged and excluded people.

It is for these groups that the flexible ILLA mechanism, and the local targeting and co-ordinating work of the education authority, should make a crucial difference. We can also envisage ILLA credits from the state in the form of continuity bonuses, and credits for time management and learning skills training. Here too the concept of negotiating space and time parameters on a customized basis would have particular force. Chapters 5 and 6 cover this in some detail.

Third-age learners

'Third-age learners' here includes people who have relatively limited time-horizons still left in work, or who have formally retired from the labour force. They may be moving into part-time or informal work, or into unpaid work for voluntary organizations. They may still need to develop work-related skills and knowledge, such as ICT skills. But increasingly their learning aspirations will be for interest or recreation; or for reflection on life experiences; or for transmitting what they have learnt to others. Some (perhaps the minority) will be looking for the challenge and recognition of learning through qualifications, others not. 'Social commitment' can be a literally vital force in this category of learners – giving new meaning and structure to life.

The Older and Bolder Campaign established by NIACE has articulated the need for a major response from providers in this area of the learning market. A large void in the learning record of many older people remains to be filled (see Chapter 2). Providers need to ensure that older learners have the learning opportunities and the convenient, socially-oriented facilities which they need, and do not face access problems.

Most important of all, older learners should not be patronized. They are not just customers. They represent a potential asset for learning – a resource for institutions, through involvement in mentorship schemes; and through the contribution of their enthusiasm, first-hand knowledge and memories to social history projects and a wide range of other studies. This is why learning providers need mechanisms to hold onto and to keep in touch with learners as they move beyond employment.

Resources will be a problem for many third-agers. Here the ILLA mechanism, which allows the local education authority to target credits, can be the way forward. These can be used for guidance as well as for learning in the more conventional sense. In a lifelong learning society it will be quite routine for older people to seek guidance for learning; and third-agers are perfectly capable of using credits.

Fourth-age learners

Involvement in learning can be a very useful therapy and morale raiser for people in the so-called fourth age, whenever it sets in. Activities may take the form of reflection and recall, or of interaction with young people. Specially trained staff are needed to facilitate learning activities in day centres and residential homes, and also in the private home. This is where the social services budget and the local authority adult-learning budgets could become intertwined.

Important social learning can happen where old people interact with supervised school pupils – this is an area with real potential for the school non-core curriculum. Many children never have the opportunity to get to know very old people in their families or neighbourhood. This is a serious gap in their social education.

Overview of individuals' learning

Drawing together all these perspectives of individuals' learning at the operational level, two general points stand out. The first is that the ILLA system should be used to pump-prime the flexible operation of the learning market, by helping providers and individuals to negotiate flexible arrangements which bend time, space and content to suit the needs of the lifelong learner. The second is that there is room for large numbers of individuals to take up the voluntary standards for lifelong learning discussed in Chapter 11. Flexibility is not just a matter for the provider. It has to be *demanded* by lifelong learners, and the new standard is a good way to promote that insistence. The state should support the spread of the standards through the ILLA system, just as it has supported the adoption of the Investors in People standards for employers. The 'University for Industry' could also help – indeed, the club of holders of the lifelong learning standard could be the real UfI.

FAMILIES AND HOUSEHOLDS

The discussion on individuals above looked at ways of promoting learning in the family context. But learning providers would be ill-advised to leave it at that. The family or household can be approached as a *unit* in the marketplace, and packaged offers can be made to that unit. Insurance companies provide a parallel example in another field: an individual can use the relationship with the insurer to cover the needs of other members of the family or household – identifying them as 'named driver' on the car policy, for example. So it should be with learning.

The current general practice in state-supported education is to take each learner as a discrete unit, and not to use the market contact with one person to open up avenues to their partners and close relatives. Learning providers pay relatively little attention to packages of learning offered to the whole domestic group. Private education is better motivated in this respect, but still does little.

There is therefore considerable scope for taking the family as an additional frame of reference for suppliers in any general culture of lifelong learning. Box 12.5 sets out a number of good practice possibilities. These ideas are so important to culture building that the state should use the ILLA system to issue credits to support parent and family learning developments. The idea of a group ILLA, as seen in Chapter 10, is also worth considering for application to the family or household, just as it is to charities, clubs and other social groupings.

- Worker development schemes can be extended from workers to their families – this already happens in some cases;

- schools and colleges can offer outline learning plans to other family members, alongside and in harmony with the plans for children;

- providers can offer jointly-timed facilities – infants in the creche, while the parent is in class; publicity for fourth-age learning groups targeted on mid-life learners, and groups timed to coincide at the same location;

- there is already a growing market in family activity/learning holidays, in the tourist industry, independent schools, and some universities. Residential learning is a market ripe for major development into the family dimension, alongside the established market for the lone hobbyist or for Open University students. These opportunities can extend to information, advice and guidance sessions on an individual or group basis.

Box 12.5 Good practice possibilities for families and households.

LEARNING ORGANIZATIONS

Chapter 3 showed how learning organizations are in effect 'corporate persons' who can learn, and have knowledge management policies of their own. Organizations can enhance their ability to pick up skills and knowledge from others, to create new skills and knowledge, to store them or preserve them in use, and to draw on them readily when needed.

Learning providers which are lifelong learning organizations themselves should be familiar with the thinking that needs to be encouraged, to develop this important part of the market. But comparatively little is currently done. Consultants and TECs have been active to a degree, and in recent years have helped many firms to become Investors in People, making assessments against established standards. But these relationships still fall far short of the creative possibilities which exist to 're-engineer' the knowledge arrangements of whole organizations.

This is a major market opportunity. It will not be realized without more well-focused research into the technologies and diagnostic tests needed to conduct the necessary knowledge re-engineering. Consultants may swoop in with a 'skill needs audit', and for them the 'job' is soon done. But the ramifications of a proper learning policy run far wider than that. They touch on questions of recruitment; of line managers' responsibilities; of libraries and databases; of redundancy; of custom and practice; of qualifications; of staff records; and of information, advice and guidance. Above all, they are deep issues of organizational culture.

Many of these questions would be articulated in the additional standard for Investors in People, proposed in Chapter 11. Those standards should be supported for an initial period by the government, using the ILLA system. Also important for lifelong learning would be credits, available on a significant scale nationally, to promote broad-based worker development schemes, run jointly by employers and unions, or by unions or employers alone. These will need to cater for workers of any employment status, not just for full-time employees. Properly set up they can have a marked cultural effect in an organization.

Beyond that, learning providers have a large job to do in supporting the new standards, by developing the all-round diagnostic skills to make this approach a reality. More important still, they should themselves adopt the status of learning organization. If they are slow to apply the discipline to themselves they cannot be effective in getting the lifelong learning message across to learners. They need to ensure that *all* staff – not just teachers – are lifelong learners, and fully skilled at the jobs they have to do. They should be high on the list of organizations receiving state pump-priming support for the new standards.

The emphasis placed here on culture change is not uncontested. There are always those who will reach for a rule book when motivation is lacking. So it is that UK governments periodically come under pressure to require employers to support the learning of their workers by mandatory time off for learning. This draws on evidence that time constraints associated with work are a major factor in restricting access to learning. Tempting as it is to solve this problem by a law requiring employers to give learning time-off with pay, this route is seriously flawed.

The element of compulsion would be hostile to the culture change which is needed. Beyond that lie a host of more practical difficulties. The time allowance would be difficult to enforce at a time when many workers are happy to have any job, and are wracked with anxiety about losing it. There is a high risk of deadweight, implying that some kind of statutory 'Blunkett days' would be offset against days which the employer would have made available for learning anyway. Any attempt to define the purpose of the days as *general education* rather than *job-specific learning* would give rise to serious problems of definition. And there is a considerable danger that granted time off would not be at a time convenient for learning, and might deteriorate (in learning terms) into time merely not at work.

Surely what is crucial is that the employer and worker collaborate to ensure that the typical learning opportunity is used to real learning purpose, both for the individual and for the organization. In this context it is better to concentrate on growing the workplace culture which would allow these arrangements to flourish, rather than to rely on compulsion destined to be resented or abused.

LIFELONG LEARNING COMMUNITIES

'Lifelong learning community' refers here to areas or, more generally, spaces at a variety of scales, where people and organizations collaborate deliberately to develop lifelong learning. The relevant 'community' might be defined by geographical, administrative or social boundaries. 'Lifelong learning cities' are currently the most familiar of such communities, building on the existing urban infrastructure. But any area where residents and others have a sense of area identity has the potential to be a lifelong learning community. Whether it realizes the potential depends upon the existence of well-motivated groups from the public, private and voluntary sectors which can work together. A general lifelong learning culture can be seen as a linked network of lifelong learning estates, lifelong learning villages, lifelong learning valleys, and so on, all working to lifelong learning criteria.

There is a question about the exact purpose of such organizations, prompting – in its turn – a question about how flexible providers of lifelong learning would relate to them. Learning communities have the potential to work in a number of ways. A selection of these is set out in Box 12.5. In many parts of the UK there are already

---

- Support generic marketing of learning, dovetailing efforts into national promotional strategy;
- give community recognition and reward to particular learners, providers and learning organizations;
- benchmark lifelong learning activity of their area in comparison with other areas;
- cross-fertilize ideas between areas;
- apply local targets for participation in lifelong learning, and establish monitoring arrangements;
- make alliances between the supply side of the learning market and the local processes of economic and community development;
- establish good communications and networks between providers to ensure that any competitive imbalances and gaps in local learning provision are quickly identified and addressed;
- organized learning 'landscapes' in negotiation with learning providers and learners.
- make collaborative investments in infrastructure;
- apply local forms of quality assurance procedures against lifelong learning criteria;
- promote high standards of client care, and provide a means of redress against proven abuse;
- broker particular provision in the community, acting as a front for providers.

Box 12.6 Different functions for lifelong learning communities.

organizations heavily engaged in a number of these tasks, and some organizations may have legal or official remits to discharge them. But it is generally a kaleidoscope of possibilities, with little overall rationale. Two clues from previous chapters may throw light on the rationale.

The first may be found in the 'learning organization' concept of Chapter 3. The learning organization is, after all, just a special kind of learning community, often having very well-focused economic aims. It would therefore be strange if the learning community were not pressing the same sort of questions as those which a learning organization should be addressing:

- What stock of knowledge and skill does the community have?
- How is that stock kept available?
- What arrangements are there for extending the stock, and for keeping the stock fresh?
- What deficiencies and strengths does the local stock have?
- How can the community galvanize its knowledge and skill to address problems in the economy and the community?
- Who are the knowledge leaders?

The learning community will normally have more complex aims than learning companies and the like, covering social, spiritual and economic well-being. But there is much to be said for any lifelong learning community addressing the *same* list of questions, and setting up lifelong learning policies in the light of the answers, working with organizations at the next levels up and down.

In Britain, the LEA is the only local body which can exercise proper local democratic accountability over policies of this kind – many of which would relate to the statutory duties of the LEA anyway. In our vision of a lifelong learning society, the powers of the LEA as local catalyst for lifelong learning would be clarified, and its leadership of local partnership activities enhanced. Other possible leaders for this role can be discounted on various grounds. The TECs, despite the significant role they have played in opening up the theme of personal commitment to learning, are private bodies in contract to central government, with limited local democratic accountability. Learning providers, separately or in associations, have a strong incentive simply to regulate the overall market for their own convenience. They are not normally in a position to carry through unambiguous community policies, because they have different financial interests among themselves.

The second clue to a rationale for the learning community is set out in Chapter 6, which develops the idea of a community negotiating broadly defined learning environments with learning providers. This is to view the learning community as responsible for the externalities and environments for lifelong learning culture. Such an approach mirrors the duties which communities often have to plan and develop the physical environment. It is a powerful organizing concept. We look forward therefore to the first advertisements for local authority planners who would lead the search for better learning spaces.

NOTES AND REFERENCES

1. Ford, G. (1997).

Chapter 13

Riding the Tiger

At the beginning of Chapter 1 we identified those things that motivated us to write this book, and which have directed its path. An analysis of the current learning scene has helped to identify features of a general lifelong learning culture which would, in our view, establish an equitable spread of learning across the population, release the economy from the trap of low skills and poor application of knowledge, and promote a more humane and civilized society in the process. We argue that – given the necessary political will – the cultural change discussed here is attainable over the span of a generation, and that many of the suggestions made in the course of the book have an inevitability about them. We are not alone in believing that policies which have a different sense of direction, or quite different routes to similar objectives, would fail.

At the top of the agenda is the need for all sections of society to debate and learn about the implications of a true lifelong learning approach. They need to be set against other ideals and agenda; principles have to be debated; and costs and benefits should be identified and compared. This work has only just begun.

THE ARGUMENT

The current learning scene is stark. Too little learning of any kind is being done; a large section of society is doing none at all; and a large proportion of those have no intention of doing any in the future. The profile of learning falls off far too sharply with increasing poverty and increasing age. The population is under-qualified by international comparison, particularly at the craft and technician level.

A major culture shift is required to change all this. It means getting it across to people that the old model – where *learning is for the young, and the prizes are for the academic strand* – has to give way to a new approach where *all people learn habitually and continuously throughout their lives.* This will keep the nation 'learning fit'. This is the best defence against the perils of global competition, fast growing social exclusion, and the loss of social cohesion which afflicts large parts of society.

THE APPROACH

The discussion in this book has followed a particular path, with ethical as well as economic directions. Starting from a cradle-to-grave definition of lifelong learning, it reviewed the current learning culture in terms of specific *principles* rather than *volumes*. The current culture was shown to be antagonistic to these principles at virtually every point. Moreover, it was replicating itself and showed no sign of being able to unfold into a lifelong learning model of its own accord. This replication meant that learning would remain unevenly spread in terms of social class and age, and the discontinuity and lack of direction in contemporary learning would remain unchallenged. The technicians of learning policy were trying to squeeze more blood out of the stone. But, however worthy the intention, their efforts were fatally flawed because they were taking insufficient account of the cultural processes underpinning current arrangements. Too many people talk 'culture change' while doing everything to avoid it.

The conclusion was that there had to be a fresh start: that a major shift in learning culture, involving systems changes to induce the necessary cultural shift, should now take centre stage. Chapter 3 reviewed what this shift would entail, and the reasons which made it essential. Economic prosperity, and social coherence and inclusion were seen to be at the heart of the matter, although they were by no means the only factors. The essential aim was to democratize learning – getting it out of the special spaces and particular groups in which it was corralled, into the wider spaces of society at large, to create a 'skills owning democracy'.

Action would be needed at three levels to achieve this goal: an effective overall strategy (something still palpably lacking); radical changes in infrastructure; and new, more flexible approaches by suppliers in the learning marketplace. If this degree of change was to be contemplated, it was essential to develop a much clearer picture of what needed to be done in cultural and economic terms. The middle part of the book examined ways of thinking about learning processes, the time frames used for learning, spaces and communications, and financial structures.

The final chapters developed suggestions at all three levels of action, including a new financial system based on the idea of the individual lifelong learning account (ILLA). Such a system would not only support greater volumes of learning, but essentially would help to spread the learning into the right places, and work to build up the culture. On this basis, further suggestions were made to develop the infrastructure and to improve supply at the 'sharp end', drawing on the approaches developed in the middle chapters.

The suggestions and proposals in Chapters 9 to 12 were deliberately expressed as if there were no resource constraints and political resistance. Seen in this way they amount, perhaps, to the biggest challenge to UK policy-makers in peace time. It is easy to be intimidated by their implications. But to shrink from listing the key requirements would be to fall at the first fence. Without this degree of clarification it would be quite impossible to set a clear sense of direction for the lifelong learning project, with its many interlocking strands. The whole conception needs to be on the table before the question, 'Can the UK afford this?' can be examined. Our final questions are therefore, 'Can we get the resources to make this work?' 'Is there sufficient political will?' Our conclusions tend towards optimism, not least because we believe that once the goal is clear and the policies indicated here begin to succeed, the 'affordability' constraint will itself begin to lift.

THE AGENDA FOR CHANGE

The issue of culture change therefore resolves into a number of important themes for action.

Cradle-to-grave strategy
The segregation of government policy for schools from policy for adults, cuts lifelong learning off at the knees. A well-developed, *through-designed* lifelong learning strategy can provide the unifying concept for the entire national learning project. It needs forward planning and commitment over decades. We propose that such a strategy should be developed by a UK Lifelong Learning Partnership, involving government and other major stakeholders. It must have clear long-term targets and success criteria, and be backed by a 'psychological contract' between the government and the other parties.

Replacing chaotic financing
The failure of the present financing system is critical. The system is difficult to use. It supports inadequate volume, and it sustains a selective and exclusive learning culture. After years of patch-and-mend attention, it needs to be redesigned from scratch. All sections of the community – not just central government – need a funding infra-structure they can use to put together all available resources for learning. In 1997 we published proposals for a system of individual lifelong learning accounts (ILLAs) to support the essential features of lifelong learning: personal and social commitment to learning; continuity and planning of learning; and the wish to spread larger quantities of all kinds of learning much more evenly across the population.

The sovereign consumer
Personal commitment to learning has to be a central pillar of the new culture. In addition to the ILLAs with their built-in incentive, we have outlined a Lifelong Learners' Charter and other consumer protection measures, which will ensure that learners have much stronger rights. There is a close affinity between personal commitment and the keen exercise of customer power in seeing that learners' needs are met, provision is efficient, and that wrongs are brought to redress. Warrantee rights should be available to all learners – in initial education as well as elsewhere.

Social commitment to lifelong learning
This book has stressed the need to balance personal commitment with the notion of social commitment – that is, the learners' commitment to learn with others, to share their learning with others, and to promote others' learning. This is how to begin the exploitation of learning's external benefits – the so-called 'benevolent virus'; and to make an impact on problems of social exclusion, social cohesion, and on the threat of cultural invasion. Problem-solving community learning – which has been practised to

good effect in war-torn Northern Ireland – points the way forward. The state could use the ILLA system to support such learning.

Structuring progression from initial to post-initial learning
All research shows that adults' motivation to learn is fundamentally (but not solely) conditioned by learning experiences in childhood and youth. Despite the efforts of hardworking professionals, the end of the initial education process still sees a quarter of the population having abandoned their hopes of learning, and the aspirations of many more blighted. Measures outlined in this book would allow schools and colleges up to tertiary level to focus on developing lifelong learners. This will enable individuals to keep on learning, in ways which suit them best, when it suits them best.

General incentives for individuals
Incentives are needed to tempt more people – and different people – into continuing learning. Non-learning individuals often fail to see the full benefits of learning *for them*. They are even less aware of the considerable benefits of their learning for society at large, or how these benefits form much of the cement which holds society together. Individuals have to be addressed with systematic marketing, and by the creation of specific long-term incentives. The ILLA system is suitable for this purpose, working through tax relief and other measures.

General incentives for employers
Incentives are also needed to counter employers' unsupportive attitudes: the short-termism of much of industry; inflexible conventions about who pays for learning; the fear of letting the uppity worker out of Pandora's box; and the spectre of skill-poaching. Low-skill assumptions are prevalent among UK producers and are built into their product strategies. We have resisted the temptation of compulsory policies on grounds that it would damage the desirable culture. We suggest voluntary measures instead – such as stronger accounting standards; moral suasion backed up by a new duty of care; and state support through credits for worker development schemes.

Supporting the learning lifespan
The particularly weak periods in the learning lifespan are, currently: early years, child-rearing, and third age onwards. The increased state funding to bring 3-year-olds into the pre-school system needs to go hand-in-hand with a delay in introducing formal instruction in letters and numbers, until the age of 6 or 7. A major expansion of family learning facilities is needed for families and households involved in child-rearing – more could be provided on the back of school provision. At the other end of the lifespan, roles need to be developed for older people in mentoring schemes and out-of-school activities. On a community basis, the government could make more money available for local authorities to use ILLA credits for subsidized learning. This would largely pay for itself through lower demands on health and welfare services.

Constructing continuity in learning
Learning providers need to focus on repeat business, and to develop the concept of client loyalty and long-term relationships with learners, either through their own services or with other providers. The learning industry is not generally geared up to do

this. This book identifies ways in which the continuity principle can be recognized: guidance; continuity credits in the ILLA system; marketing; records of achievement; and following up on skills obsolescence.

The curriculum and the skills of lifelong learning

Illiteracy and poor numeracy is a huge national problem – but the deficiency in core skills does not end there. The population at all levels is deficient in the skills needed for effective lifelong learning. A new definition of lifelong learning skills is needed which covers the needs of individuals and communities as well as the needs of employers. The definition we offer sweeps up the familiar shortlist of basic skills into something more extensive, supporting the full vision of lifelong learning.

A three-level qualification and curriculum structure flows from this, incorporating lifelong learning skills.

- The *foundation level* becomes the bedrock of the revised school curriculum, displacing the discredited subject-based National Curriculum.
- The *advanced level* is a required part of the proposed new Baccalaureate at age 18 or 19. This new qualification will integrate training and educational options, and replace the 'A-level gold standard' which, in so many ways expresses and symbolizes the old culture.
- The *higher level* could be incorporated into university degrees, effectively qualifying people to lead the move to the lifelong learning culture. The certificates – at this and the other levels – would be equally suitable for use in post-initial learning.

Critical thinking

Critical thinking is a key lifelong learning skill which must be developed in all parts of the learning scene. It is not the prerogative of graduates. It enables people to challenge received wisdom, and to sniff out hypocrisy and double standards. It should be incorporated into lifelong learning skills qualifications, and should be specifically supported by central and local government through the ILLA credit system.

Promoting lifelong learning – year in, year out

Learning needs long-term marketing and promotion. The reality of the national economic and social plight has still not dawned for many people. A subtle but persistent campaign is needed, over a run of years, if the penny is eventually to drop. It could be funded through precept on the transactions in the ILLA system. Failing that, the government must make the resources available.

Information, advice and lifelong guidance for all

Uncertainty and complexity of learning choices are set to continue in the home and the workplace. People need the skills and knowledge to be able to steer their own development, and the learning agenda must be backed up with much better information and guidance. For anyone outside the initial learning system, the present facilities are scrappy at best, and severely hampered by a poor image. This is based on false, but perfectly understandable, associations with oppressive welfare regimes, and state paternalism. New provision needs to be pump-primed by government, since the *current* demand for guidance lags behind the need. Our proposed ILLA system could be used to support a wide availability of credits for guidance, covering the whole of initial and post-initial learning. This would unify guidance services into a coherent industry.

State entitlements in the time warp

Policy which pegs most state entitlements to particular ages and stages needs to be scrapped. Rights to initial education should be time-flexible – that is time-shiftable, time-stretchable, pre-emptable, and postponable. To deny such rights rides roughshod over the time trade-offs that life perpetually demands. Greater flexibility allows people to see ways of fitting learning in without the impossible sacrifice of other goals; and it is important for those who 'screw up' first time around to be able to try again. A key advantage of the ILLA system is that it allows entitlements to be carried over time on a highly flexible basis.

Learning from life

There is widespread claustrophobia in the UK learning system, where learning is so often confined to special spaces. It is sharply segregated from learning opportunities in the everyday environments of home, work and community. We have suggested measures to encourage institutions to extend networks of learning beyond their walls, reaching into local communities as well as across the globe. This should be done both for initial learners, and also for adult learners in or out of work – many of whom will not be able to learn at all, if they do not learn directly in the domestic or work environment. This book contains a number of suggestions to this end, including the development of out-of-school learning plans for each child, and the systematic pump-priming of general learning in the workplace, through credits in the ILLA system.

Comprehensive education for the 16–19 age group.

Comprehensive principles have produced major benefits in participation and achievement for children from less privileged backgrounds. It shows the importance of avoiding an early sifting and grading of the population by 'ability'. For under-16s the gains made are under threat from adverse recruitment practises. For the 16–19 age group, selection by ability is built into the institutional separations between school sixth forms and sixth-form colleges on the one hand, and general further education colleges on the other; and also between education in all these forms and the world of vocational training. At these formative ages, such divisions make a huge impact on young people's motivation to learn. We urge reform on schools admissions in the secondary sector, and major curriculum and institutional changes for age 16–19, combined with a switch to ILLAs for funding.

Backing the teaching profession

A long-running crisis of self-esteem and motivation spreads across the whole teaching profession at every level of the state system. New contracts with proper career incentives for teachers are needed, and a major rise in pay for the whole profession, expressed as a ratio to average earnings. Teachers also need to be supported by teams of assistants, involved parents, and lifelong learners, helping to support their efforts. These helpers should be tied in, and have a critical role in the spreading of learning out from the classroom into more open learning environments.

Commercialism in the schools, colleges and universities
It is possible now for schools and other learning institutions to be penetrated for advertising purposes often bundled with privately subsidised educational services. This runs diametrically opposite to the principles of lifelong learning. Instead of yielding to the temptation to flirt with these interests for the sake of sponsorship contributions, the government must act swiftly to shut off the dangers, and to lay down the appropriate principles of conduct.

Encouraging decentralization
Local government should be a partner in the development of national lifelong learning strategy. This would be an act of empowerment without precedent in recent times, but without it there is no chance of developing the vital social commitment to learning. Our ideal envisages local education authorities, with their democratic mandate, being trusted to serve as the central focus of much of the allocation process for central funding. The ILLA system will allow them to direct resources into those parts of the population which are crying out for learning, but which cannot be reached effectively by government or funding councils.

Unitized learning throughout
Learning courses must be flexible and divisible into portions which learners can grasp. This means having unitized qualifications whose elements can be taken one by one, in bite-sized chunks. It also means being able to construct pick-and-mix combinations to suit individual need. A single integrated credit accumulation and transfer system is needed which extends across the whole field of post-statutory learning.

Honouring the lifelong learners
To recognize and encourage lifelong learning, a full set of voluntary standards needs to be developed for lifelong learners, families, organizations and communities, after the fashion of an enriched Investors in People standard. The implementation of these standards would be supported by the state, using the ILLA system. For employers, this would be akin to the RSA's *Tomorrow's Company* concept – pursuing policies to improve corporate access to implicit and explicit knowledge.

Computerization
Computers hold the key to the future, and learning has to help people to come to terms with a computer-led world. Computers have to be built into the curriculum at every level. They are a proven motivator, taking much of the pain out of the manipulation of data and information, and opening up new dimensions in lifelong learning itself. These potentialities cannot be bottled up. Every child at school, and every university and college student should have unrestricted access to a networked computer with Internet capability: and the government should ensure – in due course – that every household which cannot afford computer-based learning facilities for itself should have assistance through the state.

Reform of qualifications
Technological change has overtaken the old assumption that ongoing experience keeps skills up to date. If qualifications signify knowledge and skill, qualifications date

and decay very rapidly. If, on the other hand, qualifications are supposed to capture the maturing personal qualities of the learner, they are not very good at doing so. We have outlined new, more effective qualifications, which would give clearer signals *both* of personal attributes, and of specialized knowledge and skill, with its rate of obsolescence. Alongside these we envisage a database for learning achievements, which can help recruitment, and also be used by institutions to issue reminders and encouragement to individuals to keep up to date.

Redistribution is the key to lifelong learning
Finally, overarching all these points, it is necessary to confront the iron law that if the poor and excluded are to learn, resources have to be found that will enable them to do so. Lifelong learning needs funding systems which can deliver those resources, almost certainly at the expense of other groups in society. Some have hoped that funding councils could adjust their formulae to spread the support to where it is most needed. But the lesson of history runs against the optimists in such an exercise. The formulae are full of countervailing stresses, which are likely to offset the objective. Our ideal therefore envisages the ILLA system being used progressively to switch state funding to individuals through targeted ILLA credits, using the local authorities to find the best allocations to address the lifelong learning problems of their areas.

COSTS AND BENEFITS

Table 13.1 summarizes the main considerations of cost and benefit arising from the proposed culture change for the main stakeholders in lifelong learning. Although much in the table cannot be quantified, the main points are not invalid simply because they cannot be easily measured. This table concerns individuals – either in their own right, or in community; in work or in government. But lifelong learning is not an individualistic creed. At the heart of its definitions it recognizes the need for individuals not to shut themselves away in private boxes to do their learning, but to maintain all kinds of networks to share learning activities and their fruits with others. Many of the advantages of a shift to lifelong learning will depend on that social commitment.

The benefits should be considered in the light of 'what would otherwise be happening'. There is a (low) risk, for instance, that the lifelong learning culture might not be more prosperous than now, in absolute terms. In a global context where the storm clouds are gathering, it may be that many of the claimed advantages will just prevent things going from bad to much worse. We make two claims:

1. that lifelong learning is necessary if the bottom is not to fall out of the UK economy and society for large numbers of citizens with less favoured backgrounds and circumstances;
2. that without effective policies for lifelong learning, there is little chance of an effective challenge to the low-skill equilibrium.

Table 13.1 also depends on a wide, but not unbounded, definition of learning. This means that the exclusive doctrine of instrumental learning, long held in the Treasury

Table 13.1 Chart of costs and benefits.

	Benefits	*Costs*
Individual	More secure	More time needed
	Less alienated	More expenditure
	More prosperous	More effort
	Higher self-esteem	More career planning
	Better quality of life	
	Less cultural invasion	
Community	More connected	More time to discuss cross-community themes
	More harmonious	More expense to keep learning infrastructure
	Diverse cultures respected	Catering for more diverse needs sometimes contradictory
	Better services	
	Stronger economy	
	More democracy	
Employer	More connected	More expenditure on learning for all staff
	More competitive	More systematic approach to human resource development
	More loyalty	Longer-term view of human capital
	More secure	
	More innovative	
Government	More strategic role	More long-term commitment
	More decentralization	More resources to lead change
	More social cohesion	More power sharing
	Less social exclusion	Less compliance
	Stronger democracy	More diverse policies
	More prosperity	

and elsewhere, has to be abandoned for good. Those who wish to engineer a lifelong learning society must find a means to spread learning of all kinds – economic, artistic, spiritual, and critical. Only a broad definition can bring the benefits to bear. A learning system focused exclusively on training – with the providers 'stop-watched' on every detail of their activity – is a Fordist nightmare, doomed to fail. An effective economy cannot thrive in such an intellectual rubbish dump.

A ROBUST AGENDA

It is clear that the agenda identified here will need to be very robust, to gain ground for culture change in the face of the current, self-replicating culture.

Can the policies pay off in real life?

History teaches that transformations of the kind envisaged here are not unprecedented. The swings in attitudes on the status of women, the emergence of environmental consciousness, a more concerned attitude to healthy living, changes in habits on drinking and driving, are all examples where shifts have been made, affecting individual and social life at many levels. Experience in other countries, where learning has a more central role in living, also encourages the belief that progress can be made.

So if the proposed policies could be applied, how might they fail to bring the intended effects? They could fail because of internal *inconsistency of aims*; or through *behavioural/ intractability or contradiction*; or as a result of *political backlash*.

- The policy measures ought to be *consistent* in their aims, since they are all intended to implement the same set of lifelong learning principles. They are intended to reinforce each other, in a network of cross-linking influences.
- The main *behavioural risk* is that the proposals might involve swimming against the cultural tide. The proposed changes go with the cultural flow, however. They recognize that the networked society is now in place, that the age of the keen consumer has arrived, and that state paternalism is finished. At the same time they invoke a new principle of sharing learning in groups and communities. This provides the balance which pure market-driven policies lack.
- On the *political* aspect, there could be a backlash, if too many members of the middle classes feel squeezed by the effort to steer resources towards the more disadvantaged. Here the crucial point is that our agenda is not narrowly based – it offers substantial benefits to all. This is true, for instance, in areas such as financial reform, customers' rights, records of achievement, and guidance. The proposals are broadly based precisely because we oppose the view that the imperative is to focus on people in the very worst situation until the government makes the money flow. On the contrary, more affluent people have to be offered real improvements if they are to be less dependent upon public largesse. Given this wide appeal it seems possible to believe that the patterns of learning can indeed be shifted as the lifelong learning approach requires.

Can the agenda be afforded?

The arrangements set out in Chapter 9 need to be made first, before an operational strategy with clear time frames for expenditure and all principal costs can be fully specified. That work should be put in hand. For the time being the question of whether culture change policies can be afforded must be taken in a more intuitive sense, amounting to a test of credibility rather than of precise calculation. Precision is in any case elusive. This is because what we are proposing is essentially not a marginal project. The necessary transformation will entail a massive upheaval in economic and social arrangements. The economic implications for prices are such that the usual measuring rod of opportunity cost of resources will itself be severely distorted.

That said, we note that at the trend rate of growth (around 2.25% p.a.) gross domestic product (some £700 billion in 1995) could grow by well over half in the period

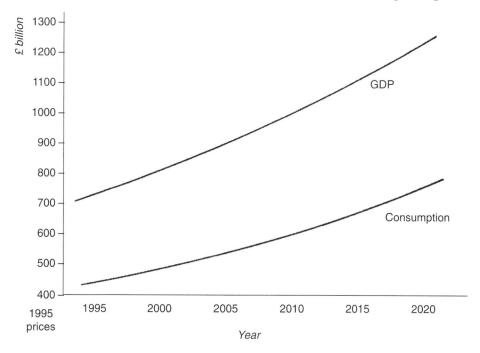

Figure 13.1 Financial futures. Source: calculated from the UK National Accounts Blue Book.

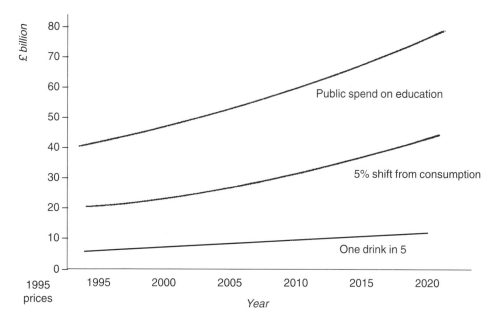

Figure 13.2 More financial futures. Source: calculated from the UK National Accounts Blue Book.

to year 2015, and by nearly double over the years to 2020. Figure 13.1 shows the progression. Final consumption would be likely to track that growth closely, at nearly two-thirds of gross domestic product (GDP). On a broad judgement, a diversion from consumption of the order of 5 percentage points could provide enough additional resources over a generation for this agenda to be credible, if that GDP growth rate can be sustained, and *if* learning remains top of the social agenda.

More specifically, Figure 13.2 shows what growth in *public* expenditure on education might look like if it keeps to the ratio of around 5.5% of GDP (OECD measure) which it fell to in the mid-1990s, assuming that GDP grows on trend. If, in addition to that, learning benefits from a 5% diversion from consumption (either taken from personal disposable incomes, or from wages and rentier incomes reflecting employers' expenditures), a sum of nearly £40 billion p.a. extra becomes available by the end of our period.

Figure 13.2 also offers a cultural perspective. It shows the resources (£10 billion) which would become available if the cost of, say, one alcoholic drink in five were dedicated to lifelong learning. That alone could almost double the throughput of higher education.

Against that background, a pile of closely worked pages of cost calculation are not needed to get to the central point: the agenda ought to be affordable if the economy stays on trend. This would be true even if the need to finance pensions and other rising claims on personal resources is recognized. Although there are no certainties, this is still a robust assumption because lifelong learning policies are the very best recipe for sustaining the output of GDP.

But it cannot be excluded that the UK's economic position may worsen relative to growth in economic activity world wide, at least over the period of international equalization of wage costs. This could put the UK trend rate of growth in doubt, despite all efforts, and prompt the thought – in some minds at least – that the policies of culture change explored in this book would be unaffordable, too voluntaristic, and too redistributive to defend living standards effectively.

Against such doctrines, the response would be clear. It beggars belief that playing back into the current elitist culture – the very one which has produced the low-skill equilibrium – could unleash more economic vital spirits than the lifelong learning agenda. Moreover attempts to travel the lifelong learning road by force rather than by conviction are likely to yield none of the externalities which are needed to raise economic performance above the mediocre. Resorting to handwringing, on the grounds that culture change cannot be afforded, would ignore the one clear political reality of the pessimistic scenario: namely, that the priority to be given to lifelong learning is likely to rise, not fall, in proportion to the perception of imminent economic decline. In a crisis, the motivation would be found.

The conclusion to be reached is not easy, but it is certainly comforting. If the economy holds its trend, the lifelong learning policies will pay for themselves and help to raise the trend still higher. If the economy falters, the lack of alternatives and the barefaced reality of the position will spur on the advocates of radical change. In these conditions no alternative policies look more feasible or likely to raise expected levels of GDP to a higher path than could be travelled by lifelong learners.

RIDING THE TIGER

So we come to the final question. It is the most important of all – *should we now commit to the lifelong learning project?* Taking a broad judgement, the project looks a sound investment. The issue is not however just one of the viability of a large national investment. We have argued that lifelong learning is right because it fulfils deep human needs. A humane and civilized society would consider it worth pursuing for that reason alone.

The lifelong learning project, in all its dimensions, energizes society as a whole to take responsibility for its learning. The alternative to that is a hopeless decline, or a statist solution where politicians try to turn all the wheels and fill all the coffers through tax-and-spend policies. It is evident that such policies are futile, and out of joint with the times.

There is no point therefore in pretending that the UK has many choices in the present social, economic and spiritual context. There is only one ride available: lifelong learning. When you feel the tiger's breath in your face, it is neither plausible nor prudent to stop and tie the laces of present learning arrangements. The best hope is to jump on, hang on tight, and steer towards something really worthwhile. Have we courage enough to take the ride?

Abbreviations and Acronyms

APL/APEL	accreditation of prior learning/accreditation of prior experiential learning
CATS	credit accumulation and transfer systems
CBI	Confederation of British Industry
DfEE	Department for Education and Employment (UK Government)
FEDA	Further Education Development Agency
FEFC	Further Education Funding Council. The term is used generically in the text to refer to the relevant funding bodies for each country in the UK.
GCSE	General Certificate in Secondary Education
GM	Grant Maintained (secondary schools)
HEFC	Higher Education Funding Council. The term is used generically in the text to refer to the relevant funding bodies for each country in the UK.
ICT	information and communications technology
IiP	Investors in People (training standard)
ILLA	Individual Lifelong Learning Account
ISA	Individual Savings Account
LEA	local education authority
NAGCELL	National Advisory Group for Continuing Education and Lifelong Learning
NALS'97	National Adult Learning Survey, 1997
NIACE	National Institute for Adult Continuing Education
NICEC	National Institute for Careers Education and Counselling
NVQ/SVQ	National/Scottish Vocational Qualifications
OECD	Organisation for Economic Co-operation and Development
Ofsted	Office for Standards in Education
RSA	Royal Society for the encouragement of Arts, Manufactures,Commerce
TEC/LEC	Training and Enterprise Council (in England and Wales) / Local Enterprise Company (in Scotland) – now often amalgamated with local Chambers of Commerce
TESSA	Tax Exempt Special Savings Account
UfI	University for Industry
UNESCO	United Nations Educational, Scientific and Cultural Organisation
VTR	vocational training relief

References and Selected Reading

Adam, B. and Stuart, A. (1995) *Theorizing Culture*. London: UCL Press.

Adam, B. (1990) *Time and Social Theory*. Cambridge: Polity Press.

Allen, G. and Martin, I. (1992) *Education and Community: The Politics of Practice.* London: Cassell.

Allred, J. (1990) *Open Learning and Public Libraries.* London: DfEE.

Anderson, M., Bechhofer, M. and Gershuny, J. (1994) *The Social and Political Economy of the Household.* London: Oxford University Press.

Andrews, M. (1991) *Lifetimes of Commitment: Ageing, Politics, Psychology.* Cambridge: Cambridge University Press.

Apple, M. (1996) *Culture, Politics and Education.* Buckingham: Open University Press.

Arnold, J. (1997) *Managing Careers into the 21st Century.* London: Paul Chapman.

Avis, J., Bloomer, M., Esland, G., Gleeson, D. and Hodkinson, P. (1996) *Knowledge and Nationhood: Education, Politics and Work.* London: Cassell.

Baird, I. (1997) 'Imprisoned bodies – free minds: incarcerated women and liberatory learning' in J. Holford, C. Griffin and P. Jarvis, *Lifelong Learning: Reality, Rhetoric and Public Policy.* Guildford: University of Surrey.

Baltes, P. and Graf, P. (1996) 'Psychological aspects of ageing: facts and frontiers' in D. Magnusson (ed.) *The Lifespan Development of Individuals.* Cambridge: Cambridge University Press.

Banks, S. (1998) 'Getting netted' in *Adults Learning*, Vol. 9, No. 9. Leicester: National Institute for Adult Continuing Education.

Barber, M. (1996) *The Learning Game.* London: Gollancz.

Barnett, R. (1997) *Higher Education: A Critical Business.* Buckingham: Society for Research in Higher Education and Open University.

Bayliss, V. (1998) *Redefining Work.* London: RSA.

Becher, T. (1994) *Governments and Professional Education.* Buckingham: Society for Research in Higher Education and Open University.

Becker, G. (1993) *Human Capital.* 3rd edition. London: University of Chicago Press.

Beinart, S. and Smith, P. (1997) *National Adult Learning Survey.* London: Department for Education and Employment.

Benn, C. and Chitty, C. (1996) *Thirty Years On: Is Comprehensive Education Alive and Well or Struggling to Survive?* London: David Fulton.

Booth, A. and Snower, D. (1996) *Acquiring Skills: Market Failures, Their Symptoms and Policy Responses.* Cambridge: University of Cambridge.

Bourne, J., Bridges, L. and Searle, C. (1994) *Outcast England: How Schools Exclude Black Children.* London: Institute of Race Relations.

Bourner, T. *et al.* (1991) *Part-time Students and their Experience of Higher Education.* Buckingham: Society for Research in Higher Education and Open University.

Bridges, D. and McLaughlin, T. (1994) *Education and the Market Place.* London: Falmer Press.

Brooks, G., Bridges, L. and Searle, C. (1996) *Family Literacy – the NFER Evaluation of the Basic Skills Agency's Demonstration Programmes.* London: Basic Skills Agency.

Brooks, R. (1997) *Special Educational Needs and Information Technology.* Slough: National Foundation for Educational Research.

Bruner, J. (1996) *The Culture of Education.* London: Harvard University Press.

Burt, G. (1997) *Face to Face with Distance Education.* London: Open and Distance Education Statistics.

Bynner, J. and Parsons, S. (1997) *It Doesn't Get Any Better.* London: Basic Skills Agency.

Caine, G. and Caine, R. (1997) *Education on the Edge of Possibility.* Alexandria, Virginia: ASCD.

Calder, J. (1993) *Disaffection and Diversity: Overcoming Barriers for Adult Learners.* London: The Falmer Press.

Carvel, J. (1998) *The Guardian.* 19 May. London: Guardian Newspapers.

Castells, M. (1996–98) *The Rise of the Network Society.* Volume 1: *The Information Age: Economy, Society and Culture;* Volume 2: *The Power of Identity;* Volume 3: *The End of Millennium.* Oxford: Blackwell.

Chapman, J. and Aspin, D. (1997) *The School, the Community and Lifelong Learning.* London: Cassell.

Chitty, C. (1992) *The Education System Transformed: A Guide to the School Reforms.* Manchester: Baseline Books.

Clark, D. (1996) *Schools as Learning Communities.* London: Cassell.

Claxton, G. (ed.) (1996) *Liberating the Learner: Lessons for Professional Development in Education.* London: Routledge.

Coffield, F. (1997: 1) *Can the UK Become a Learning Society?* London: Long's College London.

Coffield, F. (1997: 2) *A National Strategy for Lifelong Learning.* Newcastle upon Tyne: University of Newcastle Department of Education.

Coffield, F. (1998) 'Students need training to help them detect BSE'. *Times Educational Supplement.* London: Times Newspapers Ltd.

Coffield, F. and Vignoles, A. (1997) *Widening Participation in Higher Education by Ethnic Minorities, Women and Alternative Students – NCIHE, Report 5.* London: Her Majesty's Stationery Office.

Coffield, F. and Williamson, B. (1997) *Repositioning Higher Education.* Buckingham: Society for Research in Higher Education and Open University.

Confederation of British Industry (1994) *Flexible Labour Markets – Who Pays for Training?* London: CBI.

Confederation of British Industry (1998) *In Search of Employability: A Discussion Document.* London: CBI.

Coopers and Lybrand (1995) *National Evaluation of Skill Choice.* London: Employment Department.

Coughlan, S. (1998) 'Current account' in *TES Online Education.* 13 March. London: Times Newspapers.

Daniel, J. (1996) *Mega-Universities and Knowledge.* London: Kogan Page.

Day, J. (1995) *Access Technology: Making the Right Choice.* Coventry: National Council for Educational Technology.

Demos Quarterly (1995), Issue 5, 'The time squeeze'. London: Demos.

Demos Quarterly (1997), Issue 12. 'The wealth and poverty of networks: tackling social exclusion'. London: Demos.

Department for Education and Employment and the Cabinet Office (1996) *The Skills Audit.* London: Department for Education and Employment.

Department for Education and Employment [DfEE] (1996) *Education Statistics for the United Kingdom.* London: The Stationery Office.

Department for Education and Employment (1997: 1) *Excellence in Schools.* London: The Stationery Office.

Department for Education and Employment (1997: 2) *Connecting the Learning Society.* London: The Stationery Office.

Department for Education and Employment (1998: 1) *The Learning Age: A Renaissance for a New Britain.* London: The Stationery Office.

Department for Education and Employment (1998: 2) *University for Industry: Engaging People in Learning for Life – Pathfinder Prospectus.* London: The Stationery Office.

Department for Education and Employment (1998: 3) *Individual Learning Accounts Development Guide.* London: The Stationery Office.

Department for Education and Employment (1998: 4) *DfEE Skills and Enterprise Briefing* Issue 2/98. London: DfEE.

Douglas, M. (1997) 'Knowing the code' in *Demos Quarterly*, Issue 12. London: Demos.

Duke, C. (1992) *The Learning University: Towards a New Paradigm.* Buckingham: Society for Research in Higher Education and Open University.

Edwards, R. (1997) *Changes Places? Flexibility, Lifelong Learning and a Learning Society.* London: Routledge.

Edwards, R., Sieminski, S. and Zeldin, D. (1993) *Adult Learners, Education and Training.* London: Routledge.

Edwards, T. *et al.*(1997) *Separate but Equal? A Levels and GNVQs.* London: Routledge.

Evans, T. (1994) *Understanding Learners in Open and Distance Education.* London: Kogan Page.

Featherstone, M. (1995) *Undoing Culture: Globalization, Postmodernism and Identity.* London: Sage.

Ferrier, F. (1997) 'User choice: a "brillig" idea or just another policy nonsense?' in J. Holford, C. Griffin and P. Jarvis, *Lifelong Learning: Reality, Rhetoric and Public Policy.* Guildford: University of Surrey.

Field, J. (1997) *Electronic Pathways: Adult Learning and the New Communication Technologies.* Leicester: National Institute for Adult Continuing Education.

Ford, G. (1997) *Career Guidance in the Third Age: A Mapping Exercise.* Cambridge: CRAC/Hobsons Publishing.

Ford, R. (1996) *Childcare in the Balance.* London: Policy Studies Institute.

Fordham, P., Poulton, G. and Randle, L. (1979) *Learning Networks in Adult Education: Non-Formal Education on a Housing Estate.* London: Routledge.

Frank, F., Garrod, P., Hunter, L. and Percy, K. (1998) *Reaching the Non-Traditional Learner Through Employee Development Schemes: the Lancaster Employee Development Consortium.* Lancaster: Lancaster University.

Freire, P. (1993) *Pedagogy of the Oppressed.* 2nd edition. London: Penguin Books.

Friedland, R. and Boden, D. (1994) *Nowhere: Space, Time and Modernity.* Berkeley, CA: University of California Press.

Fryer, R. (1997) *Learning for the Twenty-First Century: First Report of the National Advisory Group for Continuing Education and Lifelong Learning.* London: NAGCELL.

Gallie, D. and White, M. (1993) *Employee Commitment and the Skills Revolution: First Findings from the Employment in Britain Survey.* London: Policy Studies Institute.

Gardner, H. (1993) *Frames of Mind: Multiple Intelligences.* New York: Harper Collins.

Gillborn, D. (1996) 'Exclusions from school' in *Viewpoint 5.* London: Institute of Education.

Goleman, D. (1996) *Emotional Intelligence: Why it Matters More than IQ.* London: Bloomsbury Books.

Goodall, P. (1995) *High Culture, Popular Culture.* St Leonards, NSW: Allen and Unwin.

Gray, D. (1997) 'The Internet in lifelong learning: liberation or alienation' in J. Holford, C. Griffin and P. Jarvis, *Lifelong Learning: Reality, Rhetoric, Public Policy.* Guildford: University of Surrey.

Gray, J. (1998) *False Dawn: the Delusions of Global Capitalism.* London: Granta Books.

Hall, P. (1997) 'Social capital: a fragile asset' in *Demos Quarterly,* Issue 12. London: Demos.

Halsey, A. H. *et al.* (1997) *Education: Culture, Economy, Society.* Oxford: Oxford University Press.

Hampden-Turner, C. and Trompenaars, F. (1994) *The Seven Cultures of Capitalism: Value Systems for Creating Wealth.* London: Piatkus.

Harrison, M. and Lang, T. (1997) 'Running on empty' in *Demos Quarterly,* Issue 12. London: Demos.

Harvey, L., Moon, S. and Geall, V. (1997) *Graduates' Work: Organisational Change and Students' Attributes.* Birmingham: University of Central England.

Hendrey, L. *et al.* (1993) *Young People's Leisure and Lifestyles.* London: Routledge.

Hewitt, P. (1993) *About Time: The Revolution in Work and Family Life.* London: Rivers Oram Press.

Hirst, P. and Thompson, G. (1996) *Globalisation in Question.* Cambridge: Polity Press.

Hodgson, A. and Spours, K. (1997) *Dearing and Beyond: 14–19 Qualifications, Frameworks and Systems.* London: Kogan Page.

Hogarth, T. *et al.* (1997) *The Participation of Non-Traditional Students in Higher Education: Full Report.* Warwick: Institute for Educational Research/Higher Education Funding Council for England.

Hogg, M. and Abrams, D. (1988) *Social Identifications: a Social Psychology of Intergroup Relations and Group Processes.* London: Routledge.

Hutton, W. (1995) *The State We're In.* London: Jonathan Cape.

IFF Research (1998) *Skill Needs in Britain Survey – 1997.* London: IFF Research.

Johnson, D. and Johnson, R. (1993) 'What we know about collaborative learning at the college level' in *Co-operative Learning,* Vol. 13, No. 3. New York: IASCE.

Jordan, B. (1996) *A Theory of Poverty and Social Exclusion.* Cambridge: Polity Press.

Julius, C. (1998) 'Trainers score in extra time' in *Times Educational Supplement.* 13 March. London: Times Newspapers.

Kaplan, J. (1996) *Smart Cards: the Global Information Passport.* New York: Thompson Computer Press.

Kennedy, H. (1997) *Learning Works: Widening Participation in Further Education.* Coventry: Further Education Funding Council.

Kolb, D. (1984) *Experiential Learning: Experience as the Source of Learning and Development.* Englewood Cliffs: Prentice Hall PTR.

Le Grand, J. and Battel, W. (1993) *Quasi-Markets and Social Policy.* London: Macmillan.

Library and Information Commission (1997) *New Library: The People's Network.* London: Library and Information Commission.

Longworth, N. and Davies, W. K. (1996) *Lifelong Learning.* London: Kogan Page.

Lord, M. (1998) 'The learning age' in *Adults Learning,* Vol. 9, No. 8. Leicester: National Institute for Adult Continuing Education.

Magnus, S. M. (1998) 'Smart kids eat greens' in *The Guardian – G2.* 15 April. London: Guardian Newspapers.

McGivney, V. (1996) *Staying or Leaving the Course: Non-Completion and Retention of Students in Further and Higher Education.* Leicester: National Institute for Adult Continuing Education.

McNair, S. (ed.) (1996) *Putting Learners at the Centre.* London: Department for Education and Employment.

McNair, S. (1998) 'Making the "learning market" work better', *Adults Learning,* Vol. 9, No. 9. Leicester: National Institute for Adult Continuing Education.

McTaggart, M. (1998) 'Beam me up sir' in *TES Online Education.* 9 January. London: Times Newpapers.

Metcalf, H. (1997) *Class and Higher Education: the Participation of Young People from Lower Social Classes.* London: Council for Industry and Higher Education.

Metcalf, H., Walling, A. and Fogarty, M. (1994) *Individual Commitment to Learning: Employers' Attitudes*, Research Series No. 40. London: Employment Department.

MORI (1996) *Attitudes to Learning: MORI State of the Nation Poll Summary Report.* London: Campaign for Learning.

MORI (1998) *Attitudes to Learning: Survey of Adults and Young People.* London: Campaign for Learning.

Mulgan, G. and Wilkinson, H. (1995) 'Well-being and time' in *Demos Quarterly,* Issue 5. London: Demos.

Naremore, J. and Bratlinger, P. (eds) (1991) *Modernity and Mass Culture.* Bloomington: Indiana University Press.

National Commission on Education (1993) *Learning to Succeed: a Radical Look at Education Today and a Strategy for the Future.* London: Heinemann.

Newell, A. and Booth, L. (1991) 'The use of lexical and spelling aids with dyslexics' in C. Singleton, *Computers and Literacy Skills.* Hull: British Dyslexia Association.

O'Connor, M. (1998) 'New testing policy could send results soaring' in *Times Educational Supplement.* 6 February. London: Times Newpapers.

OECD (1995) *Education at a Glance.* Paris: OECD.

Office for National Statistics (1996) *National Population Projections 1994-based – Series PP2 No. 20.* London: HMSO.

Office for National Statistics (1996) *United Kingdom National Accounts – The Blue Book.* London: HMSO.

Office for National Statistics (1998) *Social Trends 28.* London: HMSO.

Office for Standards in Education (Ofsted) (1998) *Annual Report of Her Majesty's Chief Inspector of Schools, 1996–97.* London: HMSO.

Olson, M. (1995) *The Logic of Collective Action: Public Goods and the Theory of Groups.* Harvard: Harvard College.

Park, A. (1994) *Individual Commitment to Learning: Individuals' Attitudes – Report on the Quantitative Survey.* Research Series – No. 32. London: Employment Department.

Payne, J., Cheng, Y. and Witherspoon, S. (1996) *Education and Training for 16–18 Year Olds.* London: Policy Studies Institute.

Pitcher, T. (1995) 'Building blocks to transform learning' in *Altered Images: Transforming College Estates for a Learning Revolution – Innovations in FE,* 2. Bristol: Further Education Development Agency.

Postman, N. (1985) *Amusing Ourselves to Death: Public Discourse in the Age of Showbusiness.* New York: Penguin.

Poulson, L. *et al.* (1997) *Family Literacy – Practice in Local Programmes.* London: Basic Skills Agency.

Pratt, A. (1997) 'The emerging shape and form of innovation networks and institutions' in J. Simmie, *Innovation, Networks and Learning Regions?* London: Jessica Kingsley.

Ranson, S. (1994) *Towards the Learning Society.* London: Cassell.

Rifkin, J. (1995) 'The end of work as we know it' in *Demos Quarterly,* Issue 5. London: Demos.

Ritzer, G. (1998) *The McDonaldization Theory.* London: Sage.

Robertson, D. (1994) *Choosing to Change: Report of the National CATS Development Project.* London: Higher Education Quality Council.

Robertson, D. and Hillman, J. (1997) *Widening Participation in Higher Education for Students from Lower Social Classes and Students with Disabilities: NCIHE, Report 6.* London: Her Majesty's Stationery Office.

Rogers, C. (1993) 'The interpersonal relationship in the facilitation of learning' in M. Thorpe, R. Edwards and A. Hanson, *Culture and Processes of Adult Learning.* London: Open University.

Rowlingson, K. (1994) *Moneylenders and their Customers.* London: Policy Studies Institute.

RSA (1995) *Report of the Tomorrow's Company Inquiry.* London: RSA.

Russell, C. (1993) *Academic Freedom.* London: Routledge.

Sargant, N. *et al.* (1997) *The Learning Divide.* Leicester: National Institute for Adult Continuing Education.

Schuller, T. (1992) 'Age, gender and learning in the lifespan' in A. Tuijnmann and M. van der Kamp, *Learning Across the Lifespan.* Oxford: Pergamon Press.

Senge, P. (1992) *The Fifth Discipline: The Art and Practice of the Learning Organisation.* London: Doubleday.

Simmie, J. (ed.) (1997) *Innovation, Networks and Learning Regions?* London: Jessica Kingsley.

Skidelsky, R. (1996) *A Question of Standards: Raising Standards Through Choice.* London: Politeia.

Smith, A. and Webster, F. (1997) *The Postmodern University?: Contested Visions of Higher Education in Society.* Buckingham: Society for Research in Higher Education and Open University.

Smith, J. and Spurling, A. (1997) *Individual Lifelong Learning Accounts: Towards a Learning Revolution.* Leicester: National Institute for Adult Continuing Education.

Social and Community Planning Research (1997) *British Social Attitudes, 14th Report: The End of Conservative values?* Aldershot: Ashgate.

Stanton, G. (1997) 'Unitization: developing a common language for describing achievement' in A. Hodgson and K. Spours, *Dearing and Beyond.* London: Kogan Page.

Starkey, K. (ed.) (1996) *How Organizations Learn.* London: International Thompson Business Press.

Tamir, Y. (1995) *Democratic Education in a Multicultural State.* Oxford: Blackwell.

Theodossin, E. (1995) 'The ugly duckling transformed' in *Altered Images: Transforming College Estates for a Learning Revolution – Innovations in FE, 2.* Bristol: Further Education Development Agency.

Thorpe, M., Edwards, R. and Hanson, A. (1993) *Culture and Processes of Adult Learning.* London: Routledge and Open University.

Tobin, D. (1998) *The Knowledge-Enabled Organization.* New York: AMACOM.

Tosey, P. (1997) 'Beyond the threshold: organisational learning at the edge' in J. Holford, C. Griffin, and P. Jarvis, *Lifelong Learning: Reality, Rhetoric and Public Policy.* Guildford: University of Surrey.

Tremlett, N., Thomas, A. and Taylor, S. (1995) *Individual Commitment to Learning: Providers' Attitudes.* Research Series No. 47. London: Employment Department.

Tremlett, N., Park, A. and Dundon-Smith, D. (1995) *Individual Commitment to Learning Further Findings from the Individuals' Survey. Research Series No. 54.* London: Employment Department.

TUC/Investors in People UK (1997) *Investors in People and Trade Unions.* London: TUC.

Tuijnmann, A. and van der Kamp, M. (1992) *Learning Across the Lifespan: Theories, Research, Policies.* Oxford: Pergamon Press.

Walden, G. (1996) *We Should Know Better: Solving the Education Crisis.* London: Fourth Estate.

Walker, A. (1996) *The New Generational Contract.* London: UCL Press.

Walker, A. and Walker, C. (1997) *Britain Divided: the Growth of Social Exclusion in the 1980s and 1990s.* London: Child Poverty Action Group.

Ward, M. (1998) 'The light programme' in *New Scientist* No. 2136. 30 May. London: New Science Publications.

Watts, A. G. (1998) 'The learning age' in *Adults Learning*. Vol. 9, No. 8. Leicester: National Institute for Adult Continuing Education.

Whitehead, M. (1998) 'Broken herts', *Times Educational Supplement*. 7 April. London: Times Newspapers.

Williams, J. (1997) *Negotiating Access to Higher Education: The Discourse of Selectivity and Equity*. Buckingham: Society for Research in Higher Education and Open University.

Williamson, M. and Wallis, M. (1997) 'Can Cinderella go to the ball?: the role of the public library in lifelong learning' in J. Holford, C. Griffin and P. Jarvis, *Lifelong Learning: Reality, Rhetoric and Public Policy*. Guildford: University of Surrey.

Woodhead, C. (1998) 'All aboard the literacy liferaft' in *Times Educational Supplement*. London: Times Newspapers.

Yeo, S. (1996) 'Learning Materialism' in *Adults Learning*. Vol. 7, No. 5. Leicester: National Institute for Adult Continuing Education.

Index